ELBE RIVER

NETHERLANDS

GERMANY

RHINE RIVER

Berleburg

Euskirchen
ège   Eupen   Remagen
Stavelot   Malmédy   Giessen
rbomont   Limburg   Frankfurt
          St. Vith
ant   Aschaffenburg   Kitzingen
astogne   Ettelbruck   Würzburg   Nürnberg

LUXEMBOURG   Regensburg

RHINE RIVER

C E   DANUBE RIVER   Landshut
                                                            VE Day

                                          MUNICH

                    LIECHTENSTEIN   AUSTRIA

          SWITZERLAND

0   25   50   75   100 miles

Dale W. Covington

Hello, Janice

211th Engrs Co "G"
July 19 1943

Hello Janice.

I t was nice of you to write to me.

I was glad to hear from you and will now try to answer, by first saying that I'm not much at writing letters. (Which you will soon find out.)

Was glad to hear you were fortunate enough to get a seat to El Paso. I was afraid you might have to stand all the way.

I left Dallas around 7:00 oclock. Had extra good luck and was in taylor by 1:30. I ate lunch, looked around some and at five oclock I went to bed and slept until Thursday morning.

I came to camp and still had until Friday midnite to report back (which I didn't know) so I went to Austin for a night. Well so much for what happened to me.

I know it would possibly be out of your way to come by Camp Swift, And some trouble to you but I'm asking you with a prayer in

Hello, Janice

The Wartime Letters
of
Henry Giles

Dianne Watkins
Editor

THE UNIVERSITY PRESS OF KENTUCKY

Scholarly publisher for the Commonwealth,
serving Bellarmine College, Berea College, Centre
College of Kentucky, Eastern Kentucky University,
The Filson Club, Georgetown College, Kentucky
Historical Society, Kentucky State University,
Morehead State University, Murray State University,
Northern Kentucky University, Transylvania University,
University of Kentucky, University of Louisville,
and Western Kentucky University.

Editorial and Sales Offices: Lexington, Kentucky 40508-4008

Library of Congress Cataloging-in-Publication Data

Giles, Henry, 1916–1986.
   Hello, Janice : the wartime letters of Henry Giles / Dianne
Watkins, editor.
     p.   cm.
   Includes index.
   ISBN 0-8131-1784-4
   1. Giles, Janice Holt—Correspondence. 2. Giles, Henry,
1916–1986—Correspondence. 3. Novelists, American—20th century
—Correspondence. 4. World War, 1939–1945—Personal narratives,
American.   I. Giles, Janice Holt. II. Watkins, Dianne, 1941–
III. Title.
PS3513.I4628Z487   1992
813'.5409—dc20
[B]   91-34747

Contents

To the memory of
Henry and Janice Holt Giles
whose story is told
and
to Elizabeth Hancock

Acknowledgments

A book requiring research cannot be produced without dedicated and time-consuming assistance. Heartfelt thanks go to many people for the completion of *Hello, Janice.* I am most appreciative of the warm words of encouragement, enthusiasm, offer and fulfillment of every assistance from Janice Holt Giles's daughter, Elizabeth Moore Hancock. Also to Henry Giles's brother, Robert, sister, Irene Scott, and her daughters, Kay Young and Shirley Skotzke.

Sincere thanks to my colleagues of The Kentucky Library and Museum, Western Kentucky University, for their cooperation and support: Dean Michael B. Binder, Dr. Sally Ann Strickler, Riley Handy, Larry Scott, Pat Hodges, Sue Lynn McGuire, Nancy Baird, and Jonathan Jeffery, with a very special thanks to Connie Mills and Penny Harrison. I appreciate the generous research grant provided by the Faculty Research Committee and the use of resources and equipment of Library Special Collections.

I am greatly indebted to many librarians for their time in researching and mailing information to me: Ernest M. White, Librarian Emeritus, the Ernest Miller White Library, Louisville Presbyterian Theological Seminary; Billie Bair, Fort Smith Public Library, Fort Smith, Arkansas; Lee Ann Jesse and Randy H. Flowers, Adair County Public Library, Columbia, Kentucky; Dwight Stranburg, Dwight D. Eisenhower Library, Abilene, Kansas; and Della Sandoval and Marina Traynham, the Ernie Pyle Memorial Library, Albuquerque, New Mexico. Kindest appreciation to Dale W. Covington, Marietta, Georgia, for his inspiration, resourcefulness, and research assistance.

For their special contribution to this book, I warmly thank Velma, William, and Anthony Spires, Knifley, Kentucky. Also in Knifley, Helen and Johnnie Lee Giles.

Much praise is due Dr. Duane Osborne for his skills and patience in copying the family photographs for *Hello, Janice* and to Tom Street, Athens, Georgia, for providing the wartime travel photographs. Karen Jaffre, Linda Sparks, Catherine Calovich, Matt Williams, and Ron Schildknecht were most helpful with negatives and prints.

Great admiration is expressed to my brother, Ret. Col. David M. Winkler, and the gallant veterans of World War II who answered many questions: Ray Cossey, Julian Durbin, and Ret. Col. Jack Keyser.

Especial thanks to family and friends: Elizabeth Merritt, Harlan Leininger, Justine and Frank Maher, Dr. Lynwood Montell, Ann Severance, Gary Luhr, Sidney Saylor Farr, Stephen Lee, Verna Mae Slone, Julia Neal, Dr. Lowell Harrison, Dr. Tim and Jamie Whitaker, Trannie Abboushi, Bonnie and John O'Brien, Dr. Robert Browning, Sis and Ben Plain, Joe Ben Tucker, Tommy Hines, and Sheila Bass.

Happiest thanks to Dr. Wade H. Hall, whose own interest in Janice Holt Giles and encouraging words in the final stretch, brought this book into being.

Deepest appreciation is due to those whose patience with me deserves the greatest praise: Brian, Brad, Daphne, Danette, Brent, and Lee Watkins.

Prologue

Summer, 1943. The United States was at war. Rumblings of a second world war had been heard since September 1939, when Germany invaded Poland. Although Americans were not directly involved on battlefields at that time, they were waiting, watching, and preparing. The bombing of Pearl Harbor on December 7, 1941, plunged the United States into immediate action. President Franklin D. Roosevelt called the day "a date which will live in infamy" and signed a declaration of war against Japan on the next day. Japan's Axis partners, Germany and Italy, declared war on the United States on December 11. Congress reciprocated, and America entered into a four-year battle for peace that history would record as the most devastating of all time. The whole world would feel its effects.

By 1943, men in uniform were on the pages of every publication, the subject of many broadcasts. The mobility of soldiers to bases and camps across the country could be seen in all forms of transportation. Few families were untouched as the armed forces expanded to include nearly every able-bodied man in defense of his country. Women also responded and volunteered their services to assist in the field or at home in factories, Red Cross Centers, or wherever needed. Radio broadcasts, newspaper reports, magazine features, and family member involvement kept the war foremost in the minds and hearts of every citizen. Daily life and activities continued as best they could but were often hampered by the emotional intrusions of war's demands.

When Henry Giles enlisted in the army in 1939, he had no idea he would serve his country in a second world war. The firstborn child of Thomas Franklin and Bessie Hazel Bottoms Giles, Henry knew a simple childhood, growing up in a rugged, rural region of

Kentucky—the spurs and hollows of northern Adair County
where his great-great grandfather had settled in 1803.

As a small boy, he walked the wooded path down the old
church road with his sister, Irene, to the Spout Springs school-
house where five generations of Gileses had attended before
them. Along the way, he twirled a twig snatched from a nearby
tree to knock the dew-laden cobwebs away from his sister's face. A
pensive and inquisitive child, he loved the out-of-doors; he was
fascinated by the beauty and wonderment of all nature in the
thickly forested regions of his homeland.

Classmates recall him as a serious student, one who wanted
to "learn everything he could" and who did not want to be
bothered with play and mischief while he was trying to study.
As with most young boys raised on the ridge in the 1920s, his
schooling ended with the eighth grade; further studies would
take him away from home, where he was needed to help raise
a garden patch, a little corn, and a tobacco crop and to tend
a few head of livestock. Ridge families prided themselves on
self-sufficiency.

Henry spent most of his youth in the house built by his grandfather, James Washington Giles. The simple structure had only
two rooms before a kitchen and bedroom were added. Growing
up, Henry saw smoke curl from a mud and stick chimney as
meals were cooked on an open hearth, and then wood was added
to the fire which was the only source of warmth. Electricity and
telephones would be a long time in reaching the ridge.

As a young man, Henry Giles led the singing at the Caldwell
Ridge Community Church. Built to serve all denominations, the
church welcomed visiting ministers of the Church of God, Baptist, and other faiths who would take their turns behind the pulpit
expounding the gospel. Following the fiery preaching, those at-
tending joined together to sing the songs of Zion from the shaped
note hymnbooks—usually to the tunes of a guitar, which Henry
often played.

Henry completed eighth grade in 1931, a time when a depression affected the world's economy. A growing family had more
needs than a thin-soiled farm of less than 100 acres could provide. As Henry was the oldest of then four children, the burden
of responsibility passed from the weaker shoulders of the father to the strong, youthful shoulders of the son. "Mr. Frank"
Giles had received a medical discharge from service in World

War I and seemed unable to do the bulk of the work needed to provide for his family.

Jobs were scarce, and life on the ridge offered little opportunity. As a youth, Henry worked for the Civilian Conservation Corps and earned a letter of commendation to his parents for his labor. Later, as he assumed full responsibility for his family, he worked on the county road projects with the Works Progress Administration, smoothing gravel on the narrow passageways that threaded the countryside. However, Roosevelt's New Deal, designed to ease poverty, did little to help the continually depressed area of Henry's origin.

When he learned that his mother, just past forty, was expecting yet another child (which meant increased responsibility for him), Henry Giles decided to enlist in the army. "I enlisted for a good many reasons," he wrote. "For one, the depression hadn't ended down our way & I was sick & tired of the scrabbling & the shame of the commodity lines & no jobs but the WPA. You couldn't find a day's work in a month of Sundays."

But his decision was more than that. "It was the way we'd always lived," he continued, "hand to mouth, scrabbling along. Nobody knows what the army meant to me—security & pride & something fine & good. The first step to becoming a soldier is putting on the uniform. In my case putting on that uniform not only meant that for the first time in my life I had clothes I wasn't ashamed of, but for the first time in my life I *was* somebody. That uniform stood for something to me— . . . something pretty grand and fine, for *I* chose it, *it* didn't choose me."

Henry Giles was a good soldier. Four times he was offered an opportunity to go to Officer Candidate School at Fort Belvoir, Virginia. Four times he turned it down because he wanted to stay with the men in his company. Seldom did officers return to command their own units after OCS.

Henry's unit was activated at Camp Swift, Texas, and became a part of the 291st Engineer Combat Battalion. They drilled extensively to become proficient soldiers. December 7, 1941, changed their concentration dramatically. They switched to becoming war soldiers.

The 291st was sent to Missouri and then to the Tennessee hills for maneuvers. There was also winter training in Wisconsin, more on the beaches in Texas, and maneuvers in Louisiana. The training was long and intense. Time came for a furlough. Henry Giles returned home to the ridge in July 1943, to visit his family. He knew when he boarded a bus to return to camp that he would soon be going to Europe—to war.

Janice Meredith Holt received her name from the title of a book. Her mother, Lucy McGraw Holt, had spent the days prior to giving birth engrossed in reading Paul Leicester Ford's popular romantic Revolutionary War novel, *Janice Meredith*, published in 1899. She was to have been named Mary Catherine after her two grandmothers, but the sound of the words and the beautifully scrolled letters on the book's cover so impressed young Lucy that John Albert Holt was told the baby's intended name had been changed. Born March 28, 1905, at the home of her maternal grandparents in Altus, Arkansas, the child would be called Janice Meredith Holt.

John Albert and Lucy McGraw Holt were schoolteachers. They taught first in eastern Oklahoma and then moved in 1917 to accept positions in Ft. Smith, Arkansas. From age twelve to age sixteen, Janice worked after school until 9 P.M., all day on Saturdays, and the three months during the summer in the Carnegie Library. She graduated from Ft. Smith High School in 1922 and registered to enter Park College in Parkville, Missouri, but she was unable to attend when she learned her father had a borderline case of tuberculosis.

Instead of entering college, Janice stayed at home and helped her mother support the family of five. She worked first as a cashier in a movie theater and then as a laboratory technician in a medical clinic. She also became engaged to marry the brother of one of her high school classmates.

In November of 1923, at age eighteen, Janice Meredith Holt married Otto Jackson Moore, who was born in Yardelle, Arkansas, on February 5, 1896. Their daughter, Elizabeth Ann, was born September 28, 1924.

Through encouragement from her minister, Dr. Joseph Hunter, Janice Moore began her professional career in 1933 as secretary and later director of religious education of the Pulaski Heights Christian Church in Little Rock, Arkansas. In 1936, she was appointed director of children's work for the Arkansas-Louisiana Board of Missions, three years before her marriage ended in divorce.

Janice Moore and her daughter moved in 1939 to Kentucky where Janice became director of religious education for the First

Christian Church of Frankfort. Following the death of her father, she returned to Ft. Smith in the spring of 1940 to assist her mother again. She worked for a year as secretary to Jennings Stein, a former schoolmate and president of the Stein Wholesale Dry Goods Company.

Through a friend in the ministry, Janice Moore discovered that Dr. Lewis J. Sherrill, dean of the Louisville Presbyterian Theological Seminary, was seeking a secretary and preferred someone with a background in religious education. Excited by an opportunity to return to work she loved, she arranged an interview. Her acceptance of the position brought a permanent move to Kentucky in August 1941.

She was fortunate to have a month's vacation during the summer of 1943. Janice made plans to visit a favorite aunt in El Paso, Texas, before returning to Arkansas to be with her mother and sister. In spite of mixed feelings concerning travel in the face of the war, she made train reservations early and looked forward to the trip. A shift in office personnel at the seminary delayed her departure and caused her to cancel her reservations. She considered not taking the trip, but friends and relatives were expecting her visit. She chose to go.

Unable to reschedule train reservations, Janice Moore boarded a Greyhound bus that departed Louisville around 2 P.M., Monday, July 12, 1943. She sat directly behind the driver as the bus traveled to its next destination, Bowling Green. She later wrote that, as the vehicle approached the dock, she noticed a "very neat, trim, nice-looking soldier" standing at the station.

It was raining in Columbia, Kentucky, when Henry Giles boarded a Southeastern Greyhound bus to begin his long journey back to Camp Swift, Texas. Frustrated with the rain on the hot, sticky day, he planned on riding buses only to Nashville, Tennessee. From there, he would continue the trip by hitchhiking to save the cost of the fare, as he had before.

It was still raining when Henry reached Bowling Green, where he had to change buses and wait for the arrival of the one from Louisville. He was standing near a corner of the station reading a newspaper when the bus pulled in for a short supper stop. Many of the passengers got off the vehicle. When they returned, Henry held back to see what seats remained.

Stepping up into the bus, he saw only two. There was an empty seat in the very back of the bus and one up front directly

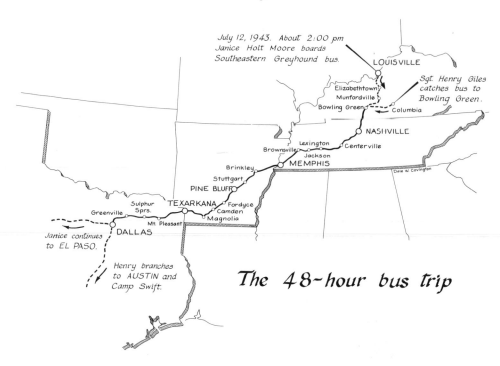

July 12, 1943. About 2:00 pm
Janice Holt Moore boards
Southeastern Greyhound bus.

LOUISVILLE

Sgt. Henry Giles
catches bus to
Bowling Green.

Elizabethtown
Munfordville
Bowling Green   Columbia

NASHVILLE

Lexington   Centerville
Brownsville
Jackson
Brinkley   MEMPHIS   Dale W. Covington

Stuttgart
PINE BLUFF

Sulphur   TEXARKANA Fordyce
Greenville   Sprs.   Camden
           Mt. Pleasant   Magnolia
Janice continues   DALLAS
to EL PASO.

Henry branches
to AUSTIN and
Camp Swift.

The 48-hour bus trip

behind the driver, beside a smartly dressed young woman. He chose the latter. Henry, in his crisp uniform, sat down beside the woman and soon learned that she, too, was traveling to Texas.

Conversation flowed effortlessly between the two and they began anticipating the two-hour layover in Nashville. They searched briefly for a place to savor a fried chicken dinner, settled for a steak house, and only then learned each other's names.

When Janice Moore and Henry Giles returned to the Nashville station following their dinner, they discovered a great number of people waiting to board the bus. An awareness of the priority of servicemen and their families and the now incessant call, "Servicemen first!" led Janice to believe she would have to return to Louisville. Henry encouraged her to remain and promised to obtain her a seat. He posed her as his wife.

Although the rain had now stopped, Henry chose to ride the bus rather than hitchhike. He had to purchase tickets about every 200 miles all the way to Dallas.

In the forty-eight hours of travel to Texas, the young couple were enchanted with their words of conversation and each other's affable presence. For two days and two nights, in the intimacy of a shared seat on a bus, they talked, laughed, enjoyed meals and stories, dozed and affectionately whiled away what could have been long, weary hours of solitude. By the time they reached Dallas, they felt, as Janice later expressed it, that they "knew each other pretty well."

Janice learned, in her own words, "what he liked to eat, and didn't." He found out in return that she "loved Chopin, asparagus tips, small hats and French perfume." Henry also discovered that she hated "Bach, spinach, comic strips and city noises." Each excitedly realized that the other relished "the country, books, quiet, and peace."

Dallas meant farewell. A "husband" could hardly depart from his wife without an embrace. Henry challenged her to "make it look good." She didn't need encouragement! With their goodbyes came promises to correspond.

The letters addressed to "Sgt. Henry E. Giles, 15042375, Co. A, 291st Engrs. Combat Bttn., A.P.O. 230, New York, N.Y." and "Miss Janice Moore, 1437 Hepburn Avenue, Louisville, Kentucky," would represent their entire courtship—a courtship that would transcend two continents and the maelstrom of a global war.

They intended to write daily but that proved impossible. There were 822 days between their meeting on the bus, July 12, 1943, and Henry's arrival in Louisville, Kentucky, on October 11, 1945. The Janice Holt Giles manuscript materials in Library Special Collections, Western Kentucky University, Bowling Green, Kentucky, contain 634 letters from Henry Giles to Janice Moore.

The first letter from Henry, dated July 19, 1943, acknowledges receipt of a letter from Janice with gladness to hear from her and a postscript of "Try to answer soon." The letters that follow are newsy notes of discovery and a continuance of the conversations begun on the bus, such as descriptions of things they liked or disliked.

In September 1943, the 291st Engineer Combat Battalion was ordered to sail to England. Janice Moore did not see Henry Giles again before he boarded the *Santa Elena* in Boston Harbor on October 8, 1943. It would be two years to the day before he again stepped on U.S. soil.

In Europe, Company A, Third U.S. Army, 291st Engineer Combat Battalion participated in many of the major actions of the war: the Normandy invasion, the Battle of the Bulge, and the crossing of the Rhine at Remagen. Throughout the European Theater, they dug foxholes, slept in pup tents, and worked under extreme conditions and artillery fire. They repaired roads, built bypasses, bridges, and culverts, cleaned up debris, and opened bombed-out roads. Because the unit was so mobile and the action so intense, it was very difficult for soldiers to save letters from home.

In the fifty years following the beginning of World War II, great volumes of battle stories and field action were written by noted historians and celebrated wartime leaders, including Eisenhower, Churchill, Bradley, Patton, and others. Memoirs illuminate the historical significance and specific happenings of the war under the direction of each writer. Everyday human experiences on the battlefield during the major events of those unforgettable encounters often become mere distillations of wordage in numerous texts stretching 400 or more pages.

The World War II letters of Henry Earl Giles reveal the everyday life of a citizen soldier, and he is representative of millions of other servicemen. The letters also tell a story of war. His writing provides insight into the suffering of painful separation, fear, and fatigue which had to be overcome with determination, courage, and family support.

Reading Henry's letters, one senses the agonizing isolation of being away from home that only those who experience war at the front can truly feel. Soldiers stood in every transport station to say goodbye to those they loved—not knowing the length of their expected stay and with the gnawing fear that there might not be a return.

To the soldier "across," letters received were a life support, providing a will to live, a touch of home, a boost to morale. One empathizes with the soldier's anguish of extended separation and his longing for a time "when war will separate us no more."

Through Henry Giles's irrepressible scratches on pieces of paper and the intimacy of his letters to Janice Moore, a friendship develops into a mutual recognition and admittance of shared love that soon leads to the trusted promises of marriage. He seeks as often as humanly possible to write assurance of his affection and well-being to the woman he loves and longs desperately to return to and marry.

One catches the excitement of this young country lad when he learns his city girl has visited his homeplace and admittedly enjoyed it. "From all indications, you did like your visit at home. I was hoping you would. Everyone liked you, just as I knew they would." He wants to take her quail and squirrel hunting and wants her to share his Mama's fried chicken and his bed. He laughs when she scratches her sun-burned legs in the briars and sneaks a cigarette when his family cannot see.

Here are the World War II letters of a 27-year-old man who, before enlisting in the army, had not traveled more than a few miles from the simple frame home where he was born in the hills of the Cumberlands. They are letters to a divorced woman, far from her childhood home, who is working to support herself and her young daughter. In a time of war, she has a soldier; he has a girl. The emptiness in each of their lives is quietly dispelled day by day through correspondence bearing endearing words that instilled hope for a happier future together.

Henry Giles's continual praise of her letters reveals that Janice Moore, who later became a noted Kentucky novelist, is already a wordsmith, capable of writing beautiful, descriptive letters. In his thirty-first letter to her, dated October 26, 1943, he wrote, "You know, I almost asked you if you ever tried writing poetry, or at writing stories of any kind, but somehow I decided not to. It seems *you could write almost anything*." What prophetic words! The letters give glimpses into her life before her writing career as Janice Holt Giles.

Although Henry Giles completed only eight grades, his letters are very legible and remarkable for his limited formal education. He confesses "I'm not much at writing letters. (Which you will soon find out.)" The letters prove quite the contrary. They are warm, humorous, revealing, and in sharp contrast to his tempestuous surroundings—a result of his trying "not to sound too gloomy when I write."

Because of strict military regulations concerning mail written during that time, Henry's letters contain relatively little strategic information. Readers who turn to this book as a substantive war history will find it lacking. A soldier could not give his location or describe any action of the battles rampaging around him. Section leaders or other appointed platoon officers censored each letter. In May of 1945, another soldier wrote home, "No real news here at the moment. If there were it would probably be censored so I never write any news." Censored information was blackened out or cut from the page.

Hello, Janice contains only one letter Janice Moore wrote to Henry Giles. It is a typescript of a letter she read into a recorder and mailed to him on a disc in a Christmas box. Her letters to him would be a delightful addition to this book, but they could not be saved. After being read, they were burned, lost, or scattered across England, France, Belgium, and Germany.

In editing Henry's letters to Janice, preference was given to those which share the most intimate writings of their courtship and the limited information of his surroundings. Once it was acknowledged, Henry Giles never failed to express his love to Janice Moore. He showed amazing ingenuity in these declarations, but was also repetitious. In a number of letters, the omission of these lines has been indicated with ellipses, but the reader can be sure they were always there. "I love you darling. Very deeply and with all my heart. I've told you that a lot, but it never grows old."

The first chapter presents, in its entirety, each letter Henry wrote before he was shipped overseas. With chapter 2 came the difficult task of choosing letters for deletion in order to reduce the volume for publication. Brief letters, written simply to say hello with assurance of his love and safety, were eliminated to reduce redundancy.

Members of the Giles and Holt families are noted throughout the letters. Henry introduces the reader to his friends and acquaintances as he shares them with Janice. Rather than footnotes, explanatory information follows a letter in smaller type.

Henry almost always followed his salutation with a colon and a dash, a feature of his style retained here. Also retained are his incessant vernacular spellings of alright and O.K. Occasional misspellings were corrected, limited punctuation inserted, his generous sprinkling of "ands" and ampersands frequently deleted, abbreviations spelled out, and days of the week included with the letter's date. The intention of the editing is to present a readable text without greatly modifying Henry's personal creativity.

Less than half of the correspondence is included in this book. A list of letters at the end of the narrative provides the reader with the frequency of his writing and the number of letters omitted.

From Henry's responses, we can imagine much of what Janice's letters to him contained. Fortunately, Henry Giles managed to write a letter almost daily. Fortunately, Janice Holt Giles carefully saved and stored them. *Hello, Janice* is their story.

1

"It was nice of you to write to me."

291st Engrs. Co. "A" / Camp Swift, Texas
Monday, July 19, 1943

Hello Janice,

It was nice of you to write to me. I was glad to hear from you and will now try to answer by first saying that I'm not much at writing letters. (Which you will soon find out).

Was glad to hear you were fortunate enough to get a seat to El Paso. I was afraid you might have to stand all the way.

I left Dallas around 7:00 o'clock. Had extra good luck and was in Taylor by 1:30. I ate lunch, looked around some and at five o'clock I went to bed and slept until Thursday morning.

I came to camp and still had until Friday midnight to report back (which I didn't know) so I went to Austin for a night. Well, so much for what happened to me.

I know it would possibly be out of your way to come by Camp Swift, and some trouble to you, but I'm asking you with a prayer in heart that you will try to, for (please believe me), I *do* want to see you again. Try to be here on a weekend, for so much of the time I am not in camp during the week. I'll keep my fingers crossed.

I suppose you did have to think fast when the two asked for "our" address, so I wasn't wrong in believing you were capable of thinking fast for you were way ahead of most people I have known, and far too smart for a green country boy like myself to try to interest or entertain.

Well Janice, I hope you have lots of fun on your vacation, so I'll stop here.

Just me, / Henry

Try To Answer Soon

———————————

Wednesday, July 21, 1943

Hello Janice,

Just thought I would write you a few lines to say hello. Just in case you were planning to come by Camp Swift, *Don't Come*.

Today it is rather hot here. I think I would rather travel (even by bus) than to work in the Texas sun.

I guess I'll stop here now. I'll write as soon as I hear from you.

Your friend, / Henry

———————————

Somewhere in Louisiana
Sunday, August 1, 1943

Dearest Janice,

I received your letter today and was indeed glad to hear from you again.

By now you have probably guessed why I told you not to come by Camp Swift. I left there last Sunday for maneuvers in Louisiana. I am now in east Texas. Tomorrow we move into Louisiana.

I'm sure you must have had a wonderful time fishing and hunting. It is always good when you can "get away from it all" and just relax and have fun. And about the 250 yard shot you made—I don't know if I could have done better myself. I don't think I would want to make you mad if you were armed. ha! ha! I always liked hunting, although I never hunted big game.

I was rather disappointed because I couldn't get to see you again, but sometime I will, if you are not married or something before I can get around to it.

Here's hoping you have had a good trip back so far and haven't had to stand. Wish I could have traveled with you, but I suppose a trip like the one I enjoyed only happens once in a life-time. It was lots of fun and I liked you quite a lot (if you don't mind my saying that).

You will have to excuse my "maneuver stationery." It's all I have right now. So far I haven't been able to go to any town.

I guess I'll stop now as I have some work to do.

From a friend, / Henry

The 291st Engineer Combat Battalion was designated on March 28, 1943, at Camp Swift in Austin, Texas, from the 2nd Battalion of the 82nd Engineer Regiment. Their tough and rugged basic training of intense drill, marching, calisthenics, inspections, rifle cleaning, and machine gun classes was similar to the regime of every new soldier entering the services during the onset of war.

The engineer Unit Training included instruction in map reading, bridge building, road building and maintenance. The soldiers were sent east to Louisiana for large-scale maneuvers which included landing practices on the Gulf Coast. The diverse group of men passed the Unit Training tests with an Excellent rating and the physical-fitness requirements with high scores. Their strengths and personalities had melded into a tough and readied battalion.

The commander of the 291st beginning in April 1943 was Lt. Col. David E. Pergrin, a twenty-six-year-old from Elizabeth, Pennsylvania. Pergrin was a graduate of Pennsylvania State University with a degree in civil engineering.

Somewhere in the / Wilds of Louisiana
Saturday, August 7, 1943

Hello Janice,

Was somewhat surprised to receive two letters from you but happy nevertheless. So now I'll try to answer.

First, I would like to say you can write *very* interesting letters. Not the type with just a lot of nonsense that would mean nothing to me or anyone else, but the kind one could read all day then "gripe" because they are not longer. Believe me, I enjoy *every* word of them.

I never think much of the past, but when I read your letters where you tell of the fun you had hunting and fishing, it makes me remember the times when the "gang" and myself used to get together on Thanksgiving and Christmas days with our shotguns and 22s and hunt squirrel, rabbit and quail, and have more fun than you could imagine. Better watch myself or I'll start dreaming.

I agree with you that Louisiana *may* have its good points, but so far I haven't seen any of them. So far as I'm concerned they could give it back to the Indians. (If they would take it.)

By the way, I'm Sergeant now, Weapons Sergeant, and right now I'm having it pretty soft, which I like, especially in this Louisiana hot sun.

Say, do you like movies? We were taken to Camp Polk last night. I saw "Gals Incorporated," a musical comedy. It was a pretty good show. What type movies (if any) do you like best? Musical comedies, I like best—and I'm crazy about cartoons.

I'll send this to Louisville. It will probably be there when you arrive home.

Bye for now, / Henry

As Weapons Sergeant, Henry Giles was responsible for the care and cleaning of all the platoon's machine guns to keep them in firing order.

Sunday, August 15, 1943

Hello Honey:—

I believe I called you that while I was with you so perhaps it isn't too much out of place here.

The heat here today is terrible, and I've not seen or felt the slightest breeze since being in Louisiana.

By the 23rd, we are to be in Camp Swift again. I like that, for since we have been in Louisiana no passes have been given anyone, and *I* like to be somewhere besides in camp all the time. It gets monotonous trying to "soldier" for too long without a break.

I suppose it was good to get home again. After all, home *is* a great place. I only hope *you* enjoyed your whole vacation as much as I did the few hours I was with you.

In reading between the lines of your letters I am inclined to believe that you would rather I wouldn't get too—I don't like the word "romantic," but something like that is what I mean.

I'm sure you wouldn't believe a "line" I would hand you anyhow so I'll not. I only hope we can be friends for a long time. You were swell and I am flattered in knowing I have met someone like you.

I trust you will not be offended in the way I write, for I too write just the way I feel.

The girl you spoke of riding with as you returned home. I have seen and heard of that type for quite awhile. Although I'm not an angel myself, I do detest such actions. For a woman like that, I have a feeling of something between sympathy and hatred. For that reason I'm sure I don't want a woman of my own, until after the war—if then.

If this letter has escaped the wastebasket up to now, I will try to write more sensible.

There are rumors that a cadre is leaving the 291st. If it does, I believe I will be on the list. I hope it will go east of Texas. Who knows, it might be Kentucky.

I saw the show "Dixie," but haven't seen "Coney Island." Friday night I saw "Mexican Spitfire and Her Blessed Event." You should see it. It's really crazy. The cartoon was good. Little Johnny is always "on the ball."

A steering wheel doesn't make a very good writing desk, so I'll stop now.

Yours, / Henry

Sunday, August 22, 1943

Janice Dear:—

After taking a nice cool shower (in my helmet), I'll now settle down in my easy chair (an ammunition box), in front of my apartment (a pup tent), and attempt to answer your letter that I was most happy to receive today.

Before I opened your letter, I was wondering if my letters to you were becoming troublesome or somewhat boresome since I always answer back so soon, but after reading the first page I decided that perhaps they weren't, since you had written an "in between" as you put it.—I *liked* that. Your letters are always a treat.

Since being Weapons Sergeant, I have a lot more time to write. I only have about six letters to write, but when I was Platoon Sergeant, sometimes I wouldn't find time to write even home for a week.

In about a week I will be back in Camp Swift.

Already we are counting the days until we can go to Austin. I've had lots of fun in Austin. It's getting dark (blackout) so I'll stop.

Yours, / Henry

I'll write more next time.

H

On August 26, Lt. Col. Pergrin learned that the battalion had been ordered to leave Louisiana and return to Camp Swift to prepare for overseas duty.

Monday, August 30, 1943

Dearest Janice,

Received two letters from you today so will now try to answer the last three.

First, I was glad you sent me a picture. I don't know why I hadn't asked you for one, but every time I would write it just slipped my mind until the letter was gone. Thanks a million. It was a good one. I have no way of keeping pictures for long so I usually send what few I get home.

I never like to have mine taken, but I am enclosing a "cartoon" of myself. Looks like I was drunk but I wasn't. For God's sake, don't show it to anyone.

I was in Austin for the weekend. Sunday I was with a WAC for a few hours. The first time I ever talked to one. She was friendly and seemed to be proud of herself.

Hope you can read this. I'm "kinda" goldbricking this afternoon and am trying to write fast.

Say, I think I'm falling in love with your letters. Each one seems to be better. They are just the type I like to get.

I agree with the gentleman that said I had the best girl in the world. You are swell and I hope I can know you for a long time.

Being in such a hurry I don't see how I will be able to write all I want to.

Your letter dated August 21, was waiting when we arrived Friday. Air mail just this far doesn't come any faster than regular mail. It almost has to be across country before it's any faster.

After a long week working in the city, it *is* always refreshing to spend the weekend in the country. Just be sure you always take the married couples along to *make* it "proper."

Perhaps you will think I'm crazy, (you don't have to say if you do or not) but if I should know of someone holding you in their arms or kissing you it would "burn me up." Don't ask why. I'm just like that. Well—

You were speaking of the deferment of ministers. I think that's O.K., if a man is a minister not for a selfish purpose to save his hide, and whose convictions are such that he thinks he will be of more value out of the service. (Here's hoping you will know what I'm trying to say.) After all, what or where would the Army, etc. be if it wasn't for the people outside.

Can't remember it if I've seen the movies you spoke of.

About the heat. Texas is like an oven still. Last evening, it rained a small shower and cooled things some for the night.

If I'm supposed to say how I like women, I would prefer the tailored and smart looking to the "fancy and feminine." I'm just plain myself and I feel ill at ease with too much fancy stuff.

Yes, I remember the steaks we ate in Nashville. I believe we just found out each other's name while we were eating.

I *do* like cookies. Especially homemade ones. I told the boys about what you said. They said for me to answer fast and tell you they all liked cookies. ha! ha!

This is all for now. If you can read this you are better than me.

Lots of Love, / Henry

P.S. The 3 bucks. I either don't have the change or the money every time I write. Right now I just "flat" don't have it. H

When they reached Dallas, Henry had 16 cents left in his pocket. He borrowed $3.00 from Janice.

The "cartoon" enclosed in this letter was a photograph. It is included in the photographs in this book.

———————————

Wednesday, September 1, 1943

Hello Sweetheart,

Just thinking of you so decided to write a few lines this evening. It has rained some yesterday and today but doesn't get much cooler.

Wish I could see you again Honey. Sometime I guess I will. Seems to me that fate would be very cruel indeed to deny me ever seeing you again.

I'm always looking for a letter from you so I'll just start writing oftener and perhaps I'll hear from you oftener.

I'm seeing "The Black Swan" tonight. It's an old picture but I've never seen it.

Guess I'll have to stop. I have a little work to do. Goodnight Baby.

Love, / Henry

By 1939, eighty million Americans, nearly two-thirds of the population, were entertained by motion pictures. That year alone, Hollywood produced such box office hits as *Gone With the Wind*, *Stagecoach*, *Mr. Smith Goes to Washington*, and *The Wizard of Oz*. The cinema was by far the most desirable medium of entertainment and expression of popular culture.

Recognizing the supreme importance of troop morale, the U.S. Army created a Special Services Department in 1941 to provide, among other things, recreational activities for troops in bases across the states and overseas. Setting up temporary theaters to show motion pictures at all military establishments became a high priority.

A veteran relates how a 2½ ton truck was parked in a "dished-out ravine" or "centered in a cantonment" with a couple of white sheets hung over the side of it for a makeshift screen. Around dusk, soldiers sprawled on their spread-out ponchos or in the grass, pulled up large tin cans, sat atop wooden boxes, or obtained chairs to await darkness. By that time, a generator was cranked up to power the projector for the cinema reel to begin rolling.

Another veteran said the best parts of the movie for him were the comments and whistles offered profusely in shouts and loud tones by his buddies all around him. In an era of strict social decorum—days when "movies were tame"—a soldier could, in the absence of ladies, relieve his anxieties through humor and crude remarks shouted out into the open night air. In such a context, movies were a proven prescription for lifting spirits and relieving fatigue.

Monday, September 6, 1943

Hello Darling:—

I was really happy to hear from my sweetheart again. I'm always "sweating out" the mail calls expecting a letter from you.

This Texas weather is burning me down. Seems like it just won't cool off.

Sorry I mentioned the WAC in the other letter. I'll never mention another date—even if I should have one. *I* always detested a woman that liked to talk of her other boyfriends.

You know, (I mean this) I think you are just the type of woman I've always wanted to know. (I'll try to explain what I mean.) Someone who is smart and clever and can also talk my language. I like you an *awful* lot too, Honey.

I suppose we were a little—(I don't like the word "fast.") Anyhow we were soon very well acquainted. I liked the looks of you when I first saw you on the bus. I've always been glad it rained so much in Columbia I couldn't start "hitchhiking." You are too nice a person to have never met.

What I am writing and have written, I *really* meant it. I trust you don't write like you do just to make me feel good or something. I wouldn't like that at all. If there's any one thing I admire about anyone, it's honesty, not flattery.

Please don't be offended at the way I write. I just like to be "on the level."

I'm living for the day when I can be in Louisville with you. I think that will be a long time (if ever), but I'm sure if I should be across, perhaps on the front, I could, in thinking of you, do most anything. I'll see you sometime, I'm sure.

There's so much noise I can hardly write. I guess I'll stop here baby. Answer *quick*.

Love, / Henry

X

Henry put a large X in the lower left corner of this letter, the only "kiss" he sent in this way.

Thursday, September 9, 1943

Dearest Sweetheart:—

Received the cookies and your letter dated September 5, yesterday. Also the other letter today, so this will have to be a double-header.

First. The cookies were fine. They were consumed in short order. You should have heard the "oh's" and "ah's" as everyone would eat one.

One fellow told me, if he knew someone that could make cookies like that, he would marry her as soon as possible. I thought that was pretty good. And—*not* a bad idea.

My birthday is June 23. What do the stars say about me? Right now, I would like to know.

I didn't get a pass last weekend. I guess I could get one every week, but I don't.

About the cadre I spoke of. That's a little "shaky" right now. I too, wish I could be sent to good old Kentucky. The only soldiering

I've ever done in Kentucky was as we went to Tennessee last fall, I drove through the extreme west corner.

Of course, I haven't lost anything "over there" but if I have to go, I don't mind. The only thing that would bother me, would be my Mother worrying about me. I tell her not to, but I guess that's the way mothers are.

The Engineer insignia is a castle. History says that the engineers captured a castle that all other branches of service had failed to do, hence the castle insignia. When I'm in town again I'll try to find some kind of novelty with the Engineer insignia. You can find them in most military stores.

I didn't even know when Labor Day passed. Everyday here is almost alike. Right now, I have a detail of men mopping the barracks. So, I thought now would be a good time to answer your letters. A letter from you everyday wouldn't be too many. Of course, I know you couldn't write that often since you have to work everyday. I know I couldn't write *every* day. I am crazy about your letters and crazier about you than I suppose I have any right to. Oh well, perhaps someday I can see you, then we can talk.

I'll admit I just didn't know how to ask you anything about the fellow you went to see, but have been hoping you would get around to saying something. If I had anything to do in causing you two to agree to "disagree; (as you put it), I have nothing to say. Well, I'm glad you're not engaged. I've been wondering up to now if you were. I didn't ask you, I don't believe.

I *hope* you're not "fooling," but I've seen a few women and I might as well tell you that I don't believe everything one says. I don't suppose you could, but I think I could learn to love you. I mean extremely. Could you say that? *Answer that question.*

Guess that's all for now. Answer soon.

Lots of love, / Henry

P.S. This letter's a mess. Hope you can read it.

Friday, September 10, 1943

My Darling Janice:—

Perhaps you are thinking I have gone nuts. Well, if I have I don't care much. I could never write to anyone as I do you. Just seemed I should write you a few lines tonight.

Wonder what you are doing Honey. Wish we were together. Oh! Darling how I would like to hold you in my arms again—and kiss you.

Say! Wonder what could be wrong? Do you believe a guy could meet a girl, say—on a bus and ride with her a few hours, then find he loves her? Do you think that could be possible? Well anyhow, it seems like you are always on my mind.

I have a "helluva" headache right now. Must be from some shots and a vaccination I took last night. By the way, the shots *were* injected.

I sent your picture home yesterday. I have no way of keeping pictures neat and clean.

Seems like there is nothing more to write so I'll stop here. Goodnight baby.

Forever yours, / Henry

P.S. Write me as often as you can without too much bother. H

[Postcard] / Port Lavaca, Texas
September 17, 1943

Hello,

This is all I have time to write, but will write as soon as I'm back in Swift. Received your two letters yesterday.

Love, / Henry

Camp Swift
Sunday, September 19, 1943

My Darling:—

So sorry I haven't written before now, but for a week I've been down on the coast for anti-aircraft practice and it has been next to impossible to write. Please try to forgive me.

While I was in Port Lavaca, I received two letters from you. I mailed you a postcard from Port Lavaca. I also had a letter from you yesterday. I'm always anxious to hear from my Darling and I only wish I hadn't waited so long to write.

I'm in Austin today and don't have your letter with me so can't write as much as I should, even though I'm trying to answer three at once.

You know Honey, for the past three weeks, I haven't written anyone but you. (And home.) I don't know, but it seems as though it doesn't matter whether I write anyone else but you.

Evidently I missed one of your letters, for in the one dated September 15, you said you had written me the day before, so I don't know if you said you loved me or not, but regardless of whether you do or not, *I love you*. Please believe me Honey, for I mean that from the bottom of my heart.

You spoke of there being a lovely moon. I sometimes try to imagine just what it would be like to hold you in my arms beneath a golden Kentucky moon. Darling, that is something *we* can look forward to, for sometime I'm sure we will be together again. A full moon over an Army camp seems terribly out of place.

I don't know why Darling, but when I try to write you, it seems that something wells up inside and words fail me when I try to tell you what you do mean to me.

Perhaps it should be strange that I write you like this since we have only seen each other once, but somehow it seems only natural.

Oh! Darling, it seems that there is only one thing I can think of to write now, which is only three words, *I love you*.

I'll stop now and write again tonight. Tomorrow *anyhow*.

Yours forever, / Henry

Sunday, September 19, 1943

Darling:—

I trust it won't be too much out of line if I write you twice the same day. After writing you this morning, it seems I didn't say enough since you are always on my mind.

Darling, I suppose you will think me crazy, but you are always the first I think of when I awake each morning and always you are on my mind. Before now, I have thought myself in love, but please believe me Darling, I know I've never loved anyone before.

Right now Honey, I can't offer you anything but love, but Oh! Darling just promise me (if you can) you will wait for me. For I want you for my own sometime and I'm sure, if you care, that sometime you'll be back within my arms to stay.

I won't be in Swift for another week. I don't know where I'm going but by the time you get this, I will be on my way somewhere. It isn't because I'm going somewhere that I'm writing like this. My emotions are never stirred as far as duty is concerned. It's just that I love you and I'm asking you if you could wait for me.

If only I had the money right now to buy an engagement ring, I'd do so and try to believe you would wait for me. If you will say Darling, that you will wait for me there won't be but three letters for me to write. You, my Mother, and sister.

Honey, it would be worth Heaven if I knew you could care for me as I love you. I suppose to a smart woman like you, a letter like this sounds silly and perhaps you amuse yourself in reading them. If you should be that way, I would like you to tell me and I'll *try* to forget, even though I know I could never.

Darling, *please* don't be offended at this very rude question, but I would like to know your age. Not that it would matter if you were two, or two hundred, I would still love you more than I can ever tell you. *Please* don't be angry at that question. *I love you Baby.*

About the ring you said you remembered me wearing. It's your answer that will cause me to wear it or not. I only wish I knew you were as honest as I'm being. I'm meaning *every* word that I say to you, and I would surely be sadly disappointed if I should find out you were only kidding.

For your happiness I would be willing for anything to go, but God only knows how much I wish that our life's happiness could be shared together sometime.

Darling! If only I could tell you just the way I feel for you. For you to be someone else's would be a tragedy that the world's best authors could never put into words.

It seems I could go on for hours and hours and never tell you what you mean to me. I'll stop now but don't be surprised if you get another letter that I'll write tomorrow.

"Write me lots of love and send me kisses everyday." Ever hear that song?

Yours *always*, / Henry

P.S. Part of this letter *does* sound silly but I trust you will take it for what I mean.

Henry

Sunday, September 19, 1943

My Dearest:—

I've just gotten back to camp and have been reading your last three letters that I've gotten.

In one you said "I'm not fooling a minute about the things I write to you." Darling, that makes me happier than anything I could ever hear.

Honey, I like to tell you how much I care for you and at the same time be practical and not write things that sound like I'm silly, for I am perfectly normal and not lonesome or something like that as you may be inclined to think I am. It's just that I love you, Darling.

You said something about drinking. Well, if I can get beer I never drink anything stronger, and I've been in several places and drank what I've wanted and have never gotten into any trouble.— Well so much for that.

I think I have a letter in the Company mail now. Some of the boys told me my name was called at noon so I'll get it tomorrow. Say the fortune was pretty good. I liked it fine, although I may not agree with all of it.

No, I didn't know just what day I met you on. If I thought of it I would have known. Anyhow—as far as I'm concerned it was a very lucky day.

I wrote you twice today besides this one, so for now I'll stop. I'll write you tomorrow night.

All my love, / Henry

Monday, September 20, 1943

My only Darling:—

Received your two letters dated 16–17 so will try to answer now, while I'm waiting. I'm still missing one you wrote last week but should get it by tomorrow.

I'm sorry I didn't write you any last week. I promise it won't happen again. Darling, I'm always so happy to get your sweet letters. They are just like a stimulant. When I'm feeling a little low or something your loving letters always give me a lift.

Yes, I too wish it were possible for us to talk together again. Sometime, I'm sure we will.

You were wondering what I was doing. Well as I told you yesterday, I was down on the coast last week. As we came back we stopped in a small town for supper (Yoakum was the town). I believe it was a tannery that was giving a dance for their employees, a few miles out of town. Upon knowing we were in town (24 in all), they changed the place and had the dance in the City Hall and we were their guests. I only tried the last dance for I didn't like their band much. I like swing music, but everyone they played they would "swing it." Even waltzes.

They were really courteous and kind to us, as we were the only men in uniform there. There isn't an Army camp close.

The Texas weather has cooled down quite a bit. In fact, we were forced to leave the coast on account of a storm, and the "squalls" (as they call them) have cooled the weather.

I went to Austin this weekend as you probably know by now. I wrote two letters to you while I was there. About what I do in town. As far as dates are concerned, I don't know a girl's full name in Austin. Of course, you could be thinking now that I know I could tell you that and you wouldn't *know* the difference, but that's the truth Honey.

Sometimes I go to shows. I usually go to bed early and sleep late, as it seems so good not to have someone come in and turn on the lights and yell. They only have about two places to dance and they are usually crowded so much I don't like to go. I don't like the "hop" they have at the USO either. But I can most always find something to do.

Don't be silly Darling. You know darn well I would want to see you every weekend and—every day if it were possible.

When I sent your picture home I only sent it to my Mother to take good care of it.

Honey, your letters *never* bore me, no matter what you should write. Since you are such a fine girl I'm sure your father *must* have been a very grand person.

I'll stop now Baby.

All my love, / Henry

John Albert Holt, Janice's father was born January 10, 1871, and died April 6, 1940.

Tuesday, September 21, 1943

Honey:—

Gosh! It's good to hear from my Darling everyday, even though I know it must be a lot of trouble for you to write so often. I'll hate myself for a long time because I didn't write any last week.

Please don't say anymore that you guess some of your letters are not worth reading, for Darling, I cherish every word you write.

Oh! Honey, I wish I could be with you again soon. Seems as though you are the only one I can think of. I still haven't received one of your letters. Perhaps in a day or so I will.

You know Honey, perhaps it should sound strange that I should be loving you, but somehow I do, even though we weren't together very long.

You asked what I remember most about us being together. It was as we came through Arkansas, when the moon was shining through the window on you. You had your eyes closed. I watched you for a brief minute and wished (but dared not hope), that somehow you might like me just a little. The beauty of you asleep in the moonlight was more to me than anything else. I'll always cherish the last few minutes we were together at Dallas. Remember you saying you could get awful fond of me? I told you just to like me and was at the same time hoping against hope that you could like me a lot. Honey, I could go on and on and never tell you just what you mean to me. Anyhow I love you. Try to believe that Darling, for I mean it.

Honey, by the time you get this letter I'll be leaving Texas. I don't know where to. If I should have to wait a few days to write don't worry for I'll write every chance I get from now on.

Darling, I don't have time to write anymore so will stop now. I'll write you again tomorrow night whether I hear from you or not.

Goodnight Baby.

Love, / Henry

Wednesday afternoon, / September 22, 1943

Sweetheart:—

It's wonderful to receive your sweet letters everyday. Each one seems better than the one before, although everyone has been a treat. I suppose today you got the letters I wrote Sunday. Anyhow, the card I wrote in Port Lavaca.

Don't ever worry about me, for I will be alright. You know— that sounds funny for *me* to be telling *you* not to worry, but you said you did. And I don't want anyone to do that.

If I should still be in the states in December or January, I probably will get another furlough. If and when I do, I'll probably spend a major part of it with you. I *would* like to be with you Christmas.

I heard a rumor a few days ago that sounded pretty good and a little authentic, but I'll not say anything about it now.

The weather here is pretty nice now. Just a little warm air in day time and a blanket is needed at night,

Honey, you don't know how much I do want to see you again. Just to hold you in my arms once more would be heaven.

I *do* like to hear what you do each day. A letter every day *isn't* too many.

I don't remember saying "you asked for it." Was it when we were together? Tell me what I said it about.

It wasn't a matter of whether I wanted to fall in love with you or not. It's just that I love you. I've tried to reason with myself from every angle but when I'm through I'm right back where I started. I'll admit it doesn't "add up." (Remember the man that said so much.) Sometime, you may think I sound like a kid when I write like this, but I think I'm old enough to know what I'm doing—and saying. You may think that I write to every girl I have met, like I do you. I don't. I very seldom ask a girl her name—and (not bragging), I've been with quite a few girls. Well—so much for that.

I'll stop here Darling. Don't forget: *I love you.*

Henry

I wrote this lying down. Hope you can read it.

Henry

Thursday afternoon, / September 23, 1943

Janice my Darling:

Here's hoping I can write all the things that I want to, but don't blame me if this one sounds "muddled," for I'm trying to answer *four* letters in one.

First of all darling, let me tell you I *do* love you, *more than ever* since I received the letter in which you said you *could* learn to love me. I quite agree with you that there wasn't any reason why you should have told me the things, when we were together, that you wrote in your letter. And if there is any one thing I admire most in anyone, it's honesty.

I wouldn't exactly say that I've been hurt at anytime. It's just that the girl I know at home did something very distasteful that I could never forget and forgive her for. I don't think it necessary to tell about that for it could never bother you, me, or her again. It does hurt to not be able to trust anyone, and like you say "love without trust is no good." In fact, it's rotten and rather disgusting.

Honey, I love you and since you are so frank in telling me the things you have, there's no reason on earth I can't trust you. I don't think I'm being selfish in always hoping I could know someone that could love me and I could call mine and someone in whom I could trust completely.

In all sincerity, I believe you are *the* one. Honey, I've *never* had the idea that there was anything cheap about you, and I *haven't* labeled you as just a woman. Please believe that. I swear I mean every word I'm writing you—and I believe you mean what you write. After all, I suppose we both have reasons to want each other to be honest and square. Well Dearest, I've tried to tell you that I love *and* trust you, so now I'll change the subject. (For a while anyhow.)

I arrived in town so late Saturday night, that all the military stores were closed. I saw a nice locket or something heart shaped with the Engineer's insignia on it. I'll get it as soon as possible.

Oh! yes, you asked what my religion was. It's the Church of God. (Headquarters, Anderson, Indiana.) For several years, before I joined the Army, I was song leader at my home church. On several occasions I've been to other churches (large ones) when their regular choir leader wasn't present or something and they "drafted" me to take the lead. I always loved to try to sing although I can't read anything but shaped music very fast. A fellow I know at home and myself used to go most every place not too far away and sing. Once we went to a town, by the name of Liberty, to an all day affair and during the day he, his little girl, and I sang thirteen songs. We also played guitars. Once, since I've been in the Army, I won first prize in an amateur contest, the only one I was ever in. What I like most is just to play or sing for my own entertainment. As you already know, I'm just a hillbilly and everyone doesn't like that so well. I don't like too much of it myself.

I think my father or mother either can (and do) talk more than I do. My mother is a grand person, always talking but she won't talk about people. I also have a very fine father. I had a letter from my sister in Detroit today which had been sent to me while I was at school.

Darling, your letters are wonderful—and *you* are wonderful yourself—every word is a treat. I haven't written to anyone but you for over three weeks. No one else seems important. That's the truth Honey, whether you believe it or not.

You do a neat job of analyzing my letters.

I guess that's all for now Baby.

Love and kisses, / Henry

Henry's family attended the community church on Caldwell Ridge. Although the small white frame church served all denominations, Henry's family claimed the Church of God as their faith. The church is now known as the Caldwell Chapel Separate Baptist Church and its adjoining cemetery is the final resting place for many members of the Giles families.

Henry (1916) was the oldest child of Bessie Hazel and Thomas Franklin Giles, followed by Irene (1918), Robert (1926), Cora Mae (1928), and Kenneth (1938).

Sunday night, / September 26, 1943

Darling:—

I've already written you once today but it seems I just had to write you again. I suppose some of my letters may sound silly, but Darling, I love you and am trying to tell you so.

Sometime I'm sure we can be together again—perhaps for a long time. Honey, that is a lot to live for.

Sometimes, it seems I still hear you talking. And at times it seems you are awful near me. Perhaps because I love you so is why I'm always thinking of you.

I don't care how much you "swamp"me (as you put it), with letters. I believe I'm doing O.K. in writing often. Believe me, I *never* wrote anyone as often as I do you.

I don't know hardly anything about Louisville but the description you gave of the French village, I'm sure I would like it fine. When I come to Louisville, we will look around some.

Right now I can't think of anything more to write. So I'll say goodnight Baby.

All my love, / Henry

Monday evening / September 27, 1943

My Darling,

Just received four letters from you, so I hardly know where to begin answering.

In one you mentioned that you would like to have something with the castle insignia on it. As luck would have it, I had put in the mail a locket (I suppose it would be called a locket) for you. Hope you like it, as it was all I could find.

Darling, I don't know how to tell you what you mean to me. I am always waiting for your loving letters.

I suppose you have by now received my letter in answer to yours of September 15. In case you haven't Honey, I *do* love you just the same and each day I still love you more. And it makes me happy when you say you will wait for me. That, Honey, is what I want more than anything else in the world, and someday I'm sure with you as mine, *my wife*, I know we can be happy for a long, long time. And I'll *never* be disappointed in you, for I trust you completely.

I had planned to call you tonight but wasn't able to get away. I will as soon as I can.

Some of my letters I guess sound screwy, but I'm one that likes to be sure of everything. I'm sure you will understand that by now Darling. Your letters have never indicated anything I didn't like.

My age is 27. I know our ages won't matter. My Grandmother was 10 years older than my Grandfather. She died at ninety-one years of age. My Grandfather was eighty years old when he died. They had almost sixty years of married life.

Oh! Darling, I wish I could be with you. My heart cries out for you both night and day, I love you so.

Honey, I don't know how many times I've written you since I've been here, but every chance I've had, I would write. Remember, that even though I may not get to write often enough, I will always be loving you and thinking of you.

Honey, I can't think of anything to write now so I'll stop.

Forever yours, / Henry

Henry's grandparents were affectionately known as "Muh" and "Pah." Mary Elizabeth Campbell Giles was born in 1844 and died in 1940. James Washington Giles was born in 1854 and died in 1938. They were married 56 years.

———————————

Tuesday, September 28, 1943

Darling:—

Perhaps now I can answer your letters I've tried to for three or four times.

As you can see, I've changed places but I'm not across.

Wish I could see you Honey, but I suppose we will have to wait awhile.

I don't have any of your letters, so will not be able to write very much. There's not so much I can write now, so I'll stop.

Just remember, *I love you Darling*.

As ever, / Henry

P.S. When you answer, use the address on the envelope. H

The 291st Engineer Combat Battalion left Camp Swift on September 24 aboard a troop train bound for Camp Miles Standish, Boston.

———————————

Friday, October 1, 1943

Hello Darling:—

As I'm thinking of you so much tonight it seems I should write you a few lines.

I wonder what my little girl is doing tonight. Wish we were together Honey. Oh! how I would like to hold you in my arms once more. I love you so much Dear, you are always on my mind.

I've just gotten back from a movie. I saw Montey Woolley in something. It wasn't very good.

You are probably wondering where I am. Well, I'm somewhere in New England. Very much alive and happy.

An old veteran made a talk for us today (a Major) and the mental pictures he could draw *almost* made me cry. (Something I haven't done for 15 years.) Believe me, he could really make a man see why we fight, what we have to fight for, and why we *want* to fight.

I hope you (and the censor) can read this. I can't write very well lying down.

None of your letters have reached me so far, since I left the west, but they should in a few days. So you see, I can't write so much since I don't have a letter to answer.

I guess I'll stop now Honey. It's almost time for lights out. I love you Darling.

All my love, / Henry

Tuesday afternoon / October 5, 1943

My Dearest:—

Received two of your wonderful letters today that had been addressed to Texas. By now, you should have my new address.

Honey, I've told you before that I'm always happy to hear from you, and every letter I like better. It's great to be loved by someone like you and Darling, I'll always believe in you, for I love you so much I could never care for anyone else, even if I should try. Believe me Darling, for I mean that from the bottom of my heart.

Yes Honey, it *will* be wonderful when we can be together, you and me—a long time. That is a lot to live for and someday I'm sure it will come true. Darling, I know I will never feel different towards you than I do now. Darling, I *do* love you dearly, more than life itself. *Nothing* that has ever happened could change my love for you.

You changed my heart Honey, and I in turn, *had* to change my mind. But I love the change.

I remember now saying "I asked for it." I must have been in a hurry or something when I read your letter you mentioned it in before.

Honey, I just don't have time to answer your letters as thoroughly as I would like to, on account of being stopped two or three times while I'm writing one page. But I'll do the best I can. There's not a hell of a lot to write about unless I do answer your letters in the proper sequence.

Well, this wouldn't have left here tonight so I've been to a movie. Saw a double feature. Neither show was so hot.

When I remember the wonderful few hours we had together, I too want to see *you* and hold you again in my arms. I'm *sure* I can find everything in you that any man would expect from a woman. I love you Darling, and one day I mean to make you *my own*.

Perhaps I had better give the censor a break and stop this letter.

All my love, / Henry
To my Darling Janice

Wednesday, October 6, 1943

Darling:—

Although I didn't get a letter today, I'm still writing you. It seems I have to, I love you so much. I think of you all the time and wish we could be together, but as we have said before, we will have to wait awhile.

I've just gotten back from a movie. I saw "Thank Your Lucky Stars," starring most everyone in Hollywood with lots of good music and songs.

Today I made an allotment of my pay to be sent to you each month beginning in November. ($40) You will get the first about December 1st. Keep it, and someday when we are together we will use it. I want you Honey, and *you* are the *only* one I would trust as far. I believe in you Darling, and am always dreaming of the time when we can be happy together. Just wait for me Darling.

I suppose that's about all for tonight.

Just remember—

I love you Baby, / Henry

Warner Bros. produced the musical *Thank Your Lucky Stars,* which presented a host of Hollywood's best specifically to entertain soldiers overseas as well as the families they left behind. The stars who appeared for charity in the grand finale of the film included Bette Davis, Olivia De Havilland, Dinah Shore, Ann Sheridan, Ida Lupino, Alexis Smith, Joyce Reynolds, Hattie McDaniel, Errol Flynn, Willie Best, Spike Jones and His City Slickers, Jack Carson, Alan Hale, and Jesse Lee Books.

Henry Giles boarded the *Santa Elena* on October 8, 1943. Early the next morning, it slipped out of Boston Harbor to sail for England. The 291st Engineer Combat Battalion arrived in Liverpool on October 19th and faced a grueling three-mile march to a train that carried them to Devizes. From there they traveled to Camp Stapley, in Taunton. Companies A and C were soon involved in building tent camps for other infantry units on their way to England.

Sgt. Giles's first letter from overseas was dated Wednesday, October 20, 1943, from "somewhere in England." It was written two weeks after his last letter in the states.

2

". . . across the distances
of time and space . . . ."

The following is a typed letter from Janice in the collection of Henry's letters. It was written Friday, October the 8th—the day Henry boarded the *Santa Elena*. Part of the wordage on the paper has been destroyed by insects. The first salutation, "My dearest Henry:" was penciled through and "Hello darling" written above it.

Hello darling:

In one of your recent letters, you said that there were times when you thought of me, when you could almost hear me talking. Fortunately, there is a way in which that can be made possible, if you are able to find a record player on which to play this record. For I am dictating this letter into an RCA transcription system, and as I speak into the microphone, my voice is recorded on the disc which you will receive. It occurred to me that you might know someone who has a record player, or there might be one available for the use of the men at some place you stop, and you could play this record and hear . . . instead of reading one. The voice is such an intimate . . . personality that I thought perhaps it might have s . . . actually to hear me speak across the distances of time and space which are now between us. I shall pack the record in one of your Christmas boxes, and I feel certain it will make the trip to you in good shape.

This is being written on Friday, October 8th. It is a beautiful Autumn day here in Louisville, clear and . . . sparkling freshness in the air. I am wondering, though, wh . . . things are crowding my thoughts these . . . are memories—with a lot of hope mixed in. There are . . . things, aren't there, when you start remembering? The chicken dinner that turned out to be steak, but was good anyhow. The man who couldn't make things add up. Heat and dust, and then moonlight, in Arkansas. Buying a ticket for you just about every two hundred miles. And then goodbye in Dallas. We crammed a lot of fun into a few hours, didn't we?

I went Christmas shopping at noon today, while I was out for lunch. It seemed queer to be buying for Christmas in the middle of October but boxes to you all overseas have to be mailed by October 15, and I discovered there were a great many people in the stores looking for gifts to be sent overseas. The packages are limited in size and weight, so everyone's first concern is whether a gift will weigh too much or be too big to pack in the regulation box. I saw one woman buy *three* money belts. I wondered if one fellow was going to wear three, or if three fellows were going to wear one. I didn't buy you a money belt. I thought I'd better just let you work out your own banking system! I also saw another woman buying a sewing kit. Remembering how skillfully your stripes were sewed on, I decided you already had more needles and thread than you can manage. So—you'll find the results of my shopping along with this record. No money belts or sewing . . . things I thought you'd like. It was fun buying th . . . and I won't even mind standing in line at the post office . . . . Henry, this isn't what we had hoped for Christmas—but we'll have those plans yet, someday.

I have something new to wear, darling. It's your locket—with an inset of mother of pearl. A tiny silver castle is fastened directly in the center. It's quite perfect, and you will know exactly what . . . put it on, I shall not take it off again . . . .

As I write this, it looks very much as if you will be on your way across very soon. Where you will be when you hear it is entirely unpredictable. Stay well—and happy—and safe. I shall keep on writing you every day, just as I have been doing. If there are long periods of time when there are no letters from me, you can be absolutely sure it is because they are held up in the mail, for the letters will be written without fail. Whenever you go, they'll follow you, and all my love will be with them.

Take care of yourself—for me.

Always yours, / [no signature]

Postal services provided extraordinary efficiency in handling staggering quantities of mail during the war years. Letters were usually exchanged within ten days except in times of intensive mobility. Amazingly, the letters "written without fail" would always follow.

Wednesday, October 20, 1943

Hello Darling:

Since it has been impossible for me to write you sometimes, I will now write you a few lines.

This leaves me fine and dandy. I'm now somewhere in England. Received the telegram before I left the states. It was sweet of you to do that and I love you all the more for it. I had planned to call you, but was unable to do so.

I miss your loving letters Honey, but I'm sure they will reach me before so long.

Darling, I wanted to see you so much before I left, but someday I'm sure we will be together again. Just you and me. That will be heaven itself.

I love you so much Darling. You are *always* on my mind. Words can't express my love for you and what you mean to me.

Honey, I can't think of much to write now as I'm in somewhat of a hurry. I'll write some everyday if it's at all possible. Just don't worry. I have good living quarters, comfortable and clean and eat the best. So for now—

All my love, / Henry

Saturday, October 23, 1943

Dearest Sweetheart:—

Another mail call today and still no letter from you (or anyone), so I'll just *try* to write this time. Perhaps I'm a little too anxious for my mail, for after all, it must be quite a long way from here to the good old U.S.A.

Darling, how I wish that I could see you. All the time I'm thinking of you and trying to imagine just what it will be like when we can be together again. And dreaming of the happy times we will have together, when you are mine—my wife, and a little home of our own. That will be Heaven.

England is rather a beautiful place. I haven't been to any towns but have seen some of the beautiful farms and nice looking farm houses. So far everything is almost normal, except I have heard that our cigarettes are to be rationed. I don't know how many for how long but perhaps enough. Uncle Sam looks after us pretty darn good.

I'll stop now Honey. Remember, I'll *always* love you more than anyone or anything in the world.

All my love, / Henry

Saturday, October 23, 1943

Darling:—

It was great to hear from you again. It was beginning to seem like ages since I'd had a letter from my Darling.

I have written you three or four times since I've been here, but you will probably get them all at once.

When you tell of the wonderful fall weather you are having it kind of makes me want to be back in old Kentucky—but someday when the world is free and peaceful again, I would like to start life anew with a little woman like you. Then we can really enjoy the great outdoors and the wonders of Nature together. Don't you think that will be great?

You said if there was ever anything I needed to let you know, well once in awhile you can send me a carton of Luckies. That is going to be the biggest problem. After I'm over here awhile I'll probably get along O.K. for I've already written home for some, and in the letter I wrote you yesterday I almost asked you to send me some but didn't hardly.

Honey I'll stop now. Space is scarce.

All my love, / Henry

Tuesday, October 26, 1943

My only One:

Needless to say, I was happy to get your letters today. (Eight of them.) First though, you can see the stationery you are sending will be a welcomed necessity. Right now this is all I have.

I suppose I have all of your letters that went to Swift. Three of them I got today were forwarded from there, the others to the one before my present address.

I'll be *very* glad to get the recording you are sending. I'll play it if I have to hunt all over England for a phonograph. Once while I was in California, I made about a dozen 6 inch records. Some were "talkies," others were singing with Hawaiian and Spanish guitars and any other musical instruments we could pick up. They still have them at home. Several of the boys I was with then said something in one of them. We had lots of fun making them.

Darling, I too have wished a million times that we could have been together once more before I left the states, but since that wasn't possible, we will just have to make the best of things as they are.

One thing we can always have is the memory of the few hours we did have together. I only wish we could have known then that we were made for each other, there would have been so much more to talk about. My Darling, as long as I know you are waiting for me, I'll be happy.

You are the only one I know that I could, and would trust as completely. I *do* love you and believe you are the one that will wait like a man wants his love to wait. I don't mind who you tell about me, or *us*, I should say.

Sgt. Hinkel is bothering me now. Trying to rush me so he can have the table to write on. He's trying to distract me by singing to his wife's picture he has in front of him. We often talk of how we will visit each other when this darn war is over. He's from Ohio. A swell fellow if I ever saw one. We have a lot of fun talking about the English money. It seems funny to ask if someone has change for a pound or a shilling or sixpence. Someone told of him weighing thirteen stones, whatever that means.

They call a saloon, a "Pub."

I quite agree with your and the professor's conclusion as to why now that men very often marry women who are older than themselves. The greater percent of the younger girls only want a fast time, and after a few drinks it seems that almost anything goes. Basically, I detest such freedom displayed by anyone. But I know it's true.

Darling, I'm glad I love *you*. And happier because I believe you love me.

I often think of how near I came to not even knowing your name. If you remember, you asked me first what my name was. Before then I had no idea of going any farther than Nashville with you. I'll always be glad that something made me stay.

Someday I'm sure you'll be back in my arms to stay.

I'm sure the song "My Shining Hour" must be beautiful. The words are, but I've never heard it.

You know, once I almost asked you if you ever tried writing poetry. Or at writing stories of any kind, but somehow I decided not to. It seems you could write almost anything. I trust you don't mind me saying that since I got one of your letters today where you mentioned that you *do* write some poetry.

Honey, I can't write everything tonight so I'll stop here.

I love you Darling. Always.

Forever yours, / Henry

S/Sgt. Paul J. Hinkel, Platoon Sergeant, 2nd platoon, Company A, shared living quarters with Sgt. Giles.

"My Shining Hour" was nominated for an academy award in 1943 as the best song from the musical *The Sky's The Limit*.

Friday, October 29, 1943

My Darling Janice:—

Received two of your loving letters a few days ago. I'm thinking that by now you have some of the letters I've written from here. I've written you everyday since I've found out my correct address. I love you more every day Honey. I'm sure life would have been very dull indeed if I hadn't found you and learned to love you as I do. I am unable to find words that will express my love or feelings for you.

If the bill you spoke of should pass, try *hard* to stay where you are. Make the WACs or WAVEs your *last* resort. I detest the thought of you having to be in either of those.

Baby, there's so much I would like to say to you and tell you that it's impossible to write now. When we are together again I'm sure we can find enough to talk about to last for hours and hours.

Just wait for me Honey, and when this damn war is over we'll find a little nest for two and just "let the rest of the world go by." (For a while at least.)

Too bad your watch broke. I remember you telling me about its history.

Good night Baby. Keep loving me Honey, and I'll be back.

My Love Forever, / Henry

Sunday night / November 7, 1943

Dearest Janice:—

Received two of your loving letters today and I thought the best way to answer them *now* was to use the blue envelope. I suppose you know why and how they are used.

First about the ring. Yes, I quit wearing it. I suppose you have a perfect right to ask anything you want to. I'm being just as honest and true to you as is humanly possible. I love you too much and want you too bad to do otherwise.

Along with your letters, I had a letter from two girls. They both wanted to know why I hadn't written for so long. Their letters have already been burnt. I promised to love only you. I believe one should be that true, don't you? I often remember what you said in one letter about believing that love was not to be thrown around as it sometimes is. I like that policy and I want (more than anything else), you to believe in me. And I'm rather sure you do.

I'll send you my Mother's address in another letter that will reach you sooner than this one.

I love my parents as much as anyone, but always when I would be joking about getting married they would freeze up, and the place would take on the atmosphere of a morgue. Probably because since I've been old enough I've supported most of the family, besides what we grew on the farm which never was so much. When I was only making $21 per month in the Army, I always sent part of it home. I now have an allotment of $25 per month sent to them. But I've always done it without hesitating and it's always been a necessity.

Honey, I love you so much. Someday I mean to make you my own. I'm sure something will work out. Anyhow, I'll repeat what you said once before. When we are married there won't be any in-law or family "squabbles" to cause us any unhappiness. If there's anything you want to ask after you get this, don't hesitate to do so. I'll close now.

All my love, / Henry

A lengthy letter could be sent in a blue envelope with an air mail stamp while the free V-mail was one page only and photographed. The following information was printed on the V-mail sheet: "V-Mail Service provides the most expeditious dispatch and reduces the weight of mail to and from personnel of our Armed Forces outside the continental United States. When addressed to points where micro-film equipment is operated, a miniature photographic negative of the message will be made and sent by the most expeditious transportation available for reproduction and delivery. The original message will be destroyed after the reproduction has been delivered." The photographed copy measured 4 x 5 inches!

The original letters were kept on file in case the copies were lost or damaged in transport. In the great bulk of mail sent from overseas, there were occasions when letters had to be re-photographed.

A veteran remarked how impersonal the V-mail letter was because the recipient did not receive the hand-held pages that had been inscribed by the sender. The smaller photographed copy supplied by the military services destroyed the immediacy of the handwriting, and the warmth and scent of the sender.

                                      Monday, November 8, 1943
My Dearest:—

Will try to finish answering your two letters I received yesterday. In one, you asked if I thought it a good idea if you bought a few things that would be useful to *us*. I don't think you should too much for there is always the one chance in a million that I won't get to use them. So—just use your own good judgement. Of course, I would have wanted to return to the good old U.S.A. anyhow, but since I've met you and love you so much it is *very* necessary that I get back. So baby, sometime we will be together again for a long, long time. You and me.

My mother's address is, Bessie H. Giles, Knifley, Kentucky. Don't forget to use the "H," for I have an aunt of the same name. Write her anything you care to. You will probably get the letter in the blue envelope by the time you get this.

Darling, I *do* write everyday that is possible, and of course there will always be times when I can't. Always remember Darling, that no matter where I am or what I'm doing, I'm still loving you with all my heart and thinking of you all the time.

I'll stop here Honey.

                                      Love & Kisses, / Henry

Henry's aunt was Bessie Mae Giles.

Thursday night / November 11, 1943

My Dearest:—

Will try to answer several of your letters I have received the last two days, including the three first V-mail letters.

Sometimes you probably think I don't want to answer some of the things you ask, but it's just that the letters don't reach me in the sequence you write them.

Yesterday, the one arrived in which you sent the letter your mother wrote. A week ago in one of your letters you said you had sent it. It was a *very* wonderful letter, and I can't find words to express my feeling of pride and happiness. Your mother must be a wonderful person. When you write to her (or see her) give her my best.

Having been in the Army this long Honey, it's actually *hard* to state one specific life I want when I'm out. One thing I'm sure I want, is you. Then together, a few weeks of peace and quiet.

Darling, I wish I knew how to tell you "I love you." Those three words alone seem very small, and rather weak when I try to tell you what you mean to me. I *too*, am sorry we couldn't have a few days of happiness together. For you to have waited as my wife would have been more than wonderful. When I'm back, Baby I don't *want* you to ever be away from me. And we *will* have a little home of our own. I've wanted that all my life. A little wife like you to come home to after a hard day's work is all any man should want.

Honey, this is all I have time to write now. Just as soon as I can I'll write more.

I love you *truly*, / Henry

Sunday, November 14, 1943

My Dearest:—

Today is Sunday and as usual I'm thinking of you an awful lot, and loving you more all the time.

The allotment I was sending you wasn't approved of, due to the fact you were no blood relation to me. I was told yesterday. So I'll send it to my mother. I still don't understand why a man can't do as he pleases with his own money. There must be a reason though.

In one of your letters (October 22), you wanted to know what I planned to do or what kind of life I wanted when I'm out of the Army. I believe I told you in one letter before this that after being in the Army this long, it's actually hard to state one certain thing. One thing I'm sure of, is I want *you* no matter what I decide to do. I know Darling that we want the same things as far as a home is concerned, peace and quiet and above all, love and faithfulness. I've known for a long time that I don't want to go back as far in the "sticks" as I came from. It's *too* quiet. I trust you will understand that it *is* difficult to be exact.

I don't think there's so much difference in V-mail and air mail. The reason I like air mail letters is because more can be written at once.

Darling, I *do* think of the time, *all* the time, when we will be together and *never* be far apart anymore. Honey, that's what I want more than anything in the world.

You said you liked Gabriel Heatter as a news commentator. Everyone at home thinks he's a wizard. To me he is a big bag of wind. *I* don't like him.

Honey, I love you, and while I wouldn't want you to—shall we say "chain" yourself until I'm back, it does make me very happy to *know* you are not dating *anyone*. I believe in faithfulness to even the smallest *nth*. I guess there's nothing a man likes more than to *know* he is loved that much.

I'll stop now and write again soon.

Loving you *always*, / Henry

Gabriel Heatter (1890–1972) was an American journalist and radio commentator.

Wednesday, November 17, 1943

Darling:—

Will try to write you a little tonight amidst discussions, arguments and what not. I'm thinking of you tonight Honey, as usual, and wishing I was with you.

Today, I rounded out forty months in the Army. I only hope that it won't be that long until this damn war is over and I'm out— with you.

I received your letter of November 2. Evidently you were getting the letters then that I had written before your first letters had reached England. (Sounds like double talk.) Honey, I *know* you write me often enough and I'll get them eventually. Now I'm doing O. K. Some of the fellows have suggested that I divide some with them. I love you Baby and someday when this waiting is over, we'll be happy together. That's worth waiting a long time for.

I'm sure there will be things that we will do before talking so much when that time comes that we meet again. I'll never let you go again Darling.

This is all for tonight Honey. It's late.

Loving you always, / Henry

Tuesday, November 23, 1943

Hello Darling:

I'm thinking of you tonight Honey and wishing I was with you. I love you Darling.

Tonight I received the package with candy, nuts, the St. Christopher medal and the pen, which I'm using now. It's just right, not too fine or too coarse. I'll wear the medal Honey, for you. A swell time was had by all when the candy and nuts were opened. I hardly know how to thank you, but anyhow, I appreciate everything a lot and thank you *very* much.

I wish there was some way in which we could count the months or days or something but as it is, all we can do is wait and hope for the day to come as soon as possible. Then we'll be happy—together, for a long time. I *know* I could *never* tire of you Darling, loving you as I do. Honey, you mean everything to me.

Well, the conversation among the fellows tonight seems to be women (as usual) and there's so much loud talk and interruptions that I'll have to stop here. Remember I love you Honey *always*.

Forever yours, / Henry

Janice asked a friend to have her priest bless a St. Christopher medal for Henry; St. Christopher was the patron saint of travelers.

Thursday, November 25, 1943

My Dear:—

Just received your loving letter and Darling, it makes me want to see you awful bad every time I hear from you.

Today is Thanksgiving. Although I didn't spend the day as I ordinarily would have, we did have the traditional turkey for dinner along with other good eats, and tonight we are going to town perhaps to have a couple of beers. Perhaps next year we can celebrate the day together. Anyhow we can hope so.

I love you Darling, and want you more every day. Just wait for me and keep on loving me. Someday, we will be happy together.

I don't have time to write more, so for now I'll stop.

I *Love You* Honey, / Henry

3

". . . when war will separate us no more."

Sunday, November 28, 1943

My Dearest:—

I'll *try* to answer the letters I received yesterday. Nine of them from November 1st to the 8th. I'm always happy when I hear from my little woman. And now that I have your picture you will be nearer me all the time. I don't know when I'll be able to hear the record. It's possible they have a record player at some of the Red Cross places. I'll try those first.

Thanks a million for everything. The lifesavers were a treat and several of us enjoyed the fruitcake immensely.

Before we go any further: I love you Honey and am thinking of you all the time. You mean *everything* to me. I'm glad my letters reach you without too much delay. Seven days *is* a short time. I too, like air mail because you don't have to stop when there happens to be more you want to write.

Yes Darling, it's possible this could be a long separation. But—I'll *always* love you and trust you completely. I could never doubt but that you are doing just as you say you are. You see—Honey, I believe in you extremely.

Honey, you were talking about some of the things that occurred while we were together. They are memories to me that are very precious. I suppose it was just for us to meet as we did. I remember how I wondered if you would *really* write to me. I'll always be thankful that you did.

I only wish it could have been possible for us to have been together again. Since it had to be otherwise, we can always love each other and wait for the day when war will separate us no more. That will be great, won't it Honey?

I had a letter from my Mother yesterday too. She is sending me some cigarettes, so it looks as if I'll have plenty of smokes. So far I haven't been short.

In my opinion, the fellow who had his ring returned is far better off to know it now than later. The same thing happened to a fellow I know. He has a lot of fun talking about it with the other boys. It seems that most men in the Army just have that "don't give a damn" attitude about things like that. I believe I've said before that we have the same ideas about loyalty and faithfulness.

It seems that food prices are soaring. In England eggs are rationed to *one* per month. That is hard to imagine, but an Englishman told me that.

I guess this is all now. I love you Baby. Don't ever forget that.

All my love / Henry

The collection includes two letters to Janice from Henry's mother, Bessie H. Giles. The first one, as follows, is postmarked November 30, 1943.

Dear Friend,

Will write you a few lines in answer to your kind and welcomed letter. I really appreciate the way you feel about Henry, as he is just the kind of boy you seem to think he is. Yes, he has written to me about you and how he came to meet you and sent me your picture to keep for him. I like the looks of the picture and the way you write, for I always hoped if he ever married he would get somebody that would be good to him. He has always been a good boy and always been good to me.

It looked like it was almost more than I could stand when he had to cross but I'm only trusting the Lord to keep him safe. He always tells me not to worry about him and I always write to him cheerful. But God only knows how much I worry about him. I hope this terrible war will be over soon and the boys will all soon be back home.

I'm glad you write to him often. It was sometime before he heard from home after he crossed but said he heard from you everyday. I guess I've written about all I know to write. Write to me again sometime.

Your friend / Bessie H. Giles

Following receipt of this letter from Bessie Giles, Janice began writing her each week to share her news from Henry. Mrs. Giles frequently responded.

Wednesday, December 1, 1943

My only darling:

Have just been thinking that there never was anyone that I ever tried to write to everyday until now. It's easy to try it everyday, though I know some of the letters must be washouts. I like to tell you that I love you, for Honey, I want you to know that beyond *any* doubt Darling. Having your love and loving you means everything to me.

You know, I just happened to think of the three dollars that you let me have in Dallas. I've put it off so long now that I can't send it. We get paid in terms of pounds and shillings, etc. You probably know about the English money. So—the three bucks will just have to wait awhile.

Honey, I don't know how I ever got along without your pictures. I'm often looking at them, and wishing we were together.

It's been two or three days since I had a letter from you, but I always know they are coming so I don't worry for I'm always sure you are writing. It's just that the mails are a little slow. It takes about an average of ten days for your letters to reach me.

Darling, you will never know how I long for you each day. No man could love a woman more than I love you.

Well Baby, as you have probably guessed by now, there's nothing to write about. So for now—bye now.

Yours always, and / all my love / Henry

Thursday, December 2, 1943

Darling:

Two letters from you today and Honey, do I feel great. Oh! it's wonderful to hear from you Darling. I think I've said that every letter from you gets better, but Darling the two today were *wonderful* and every word thrilled me so, I hardly know how to start writing. Anyhow, first, I *do* love you. You are dearer to me than life itself. Each day I love you more.

I'm only living for the day when "you'll be back in my arms to stay." Ever hear the song, "When My Blue Moon Turns to Gold Again?" Listen to it sometime and think of me during the chorus. I don't think I've sent a letter by regular mail since I've been across. If I have I can't recall it now.

I wrote to my Mother about you some time ago. *That's* something I've never done before is write home about a girl I may have happened to have met. But I've told you before that *you* are different.

I honestly can't think of a single good reason why Mama shouldn't like you. Of course she never wanted me to marry anyone but that's beside the point. I love you and someday you'll be mine *regardless*. Won't you Darling? And nothing will mar our love for each other. I'm *sure* we will be happy together. Darling, I love you and before you, I had never thought I could ever believe in and trust a woman completely, as I do you. I thought it an impossibility and something people only thought they did. I believe in you Honey, and (don't think that I believe it could *ever* happen to us) for a love and trust such as I have for you to be betrayed would be the most heartbreaking tragedy imaginable by me.

By now, you must have the letter in which I told you the allotment won't be approved of by Headquarters. I have since had it sent to my mother. The same amount.

Due to the time it takes our letters to reach us, it's amusing how they cross each other. In one letter you will mention that I haven't written anymore about different things, which, since you had written *that* one, I have mentioned it. (Hope you know what I'm trying to say. It sounds like double talk to me) and of course my letters are like that too, to you.

I *did* get the cablegram. It was about six days in reaching me. Your letters today (dated November 23 & 24) were eight and nine days in coming.

I'm sure Mama will appreciate the gift you are sending her, but she won't know hardly what to think, since this is the first time anything like that (or this we might say) has ever happened. I'm writing to her tonight. It was quite alright for you to send her a Christmas gift. I'll write another letter on that subject in a few days.

No, baby, I *don't* mind you saying that you wish for me, and imagine I am with you and my arms around you. In fact I *like* it. I'm sure our happiness together will exceed all imaginations we may have had.

Well Darling, it is rather late, so for now I'll have to stop. Keep remembering that I love you.

Forever yours, / Henry

P.S. Have just finished writing to Mama and told her about us— everything this time. Goodnight baby. H. G.

In the next letter, dated December 3, Henry shares: "I'm writing to my sister and telling her about you and me. She lives in Detroit. Has three kids, Kay Frances (1938), Shirley Ann (1939), and I don't remember the boy's name, or how old any of them are. Kay is probably about six. She's the oldest." Henry is referring to his oldest sister, Irene, married to Charlie Scott. "The boy's name:" Gary Louis (1942).

Saturday, December 4, 1943

My only Love:

Today your letter written November 12, reached me. A little late, but sweet and welcome.

. . . You said you were afraid the letters you wrote while you didn't know where I was, were not too cheerful—Believe me Baby, *anything* written by you is *always* cheerful and welcome. I love every word you write and I want you to *always* love me and tell me you do. That's the greatest and most important thing.

I remember the song "Night and Day." Did Dinah Shore sing it in "Thank Your Lucky Stars?" Somewhere I've heard it. It's lovely.

I can hardly wait until the picture you are sending reaches me. At times I find myself gazing long at the ones I have now. It seems that you are so near to me that you should speak when I look at them.

Irene is the only one of my sisters I've mentioned before. I have another sister, Cora Mae at home. She's 15, cute but shy.

Robert is 17. At nine months of age he was a victim of Infantile Paralysis and has never been able to walk. You should hear him play the guitar. He sort of showed me up when I was home last July. Kenneth is a little squirt of 6 years. He's always at my heels when I'm at home, and can out-talk an auctioneer.

No Honey, I'm sure there will be no need of "chaperones," for the first thing we do (and I *do* mean the first) will be get married.

I mean in record time. There won't be a moment lost from the time we see each other, until you are mine, in black and white. Isn't that what you want too?

I just remembered one stanza of a song that I think is good. Here it is:

> Your lips that used to thrill me so,
> Your kisses were meant for only me.
> And someday they'll live again Sweetheart,
> And my blue moon again will turn to gold.

Like it? For several months I have.

Yes, I remember the bus ride with you. At one place I was *so* sleepy I couldn't even get off, after I finally went to sleep.

You know Darling, I like the way you usually close a letter when it says, "Your own." Those two words to me mean an awful lot.

Well Honey, it's a little late so for now I'll stop and see you in my dreams.

Remember

I Love You, / Henry

Monday, December 6, 1943

My only Darling:

Today there were six letters from you and two from home— and a Christmas card. How's that? I think they are doing O.K. They were from November 15 to 20 inclusive and I had already gotten two dated November 24 & 25 but they are all good, in fact lovely, and I cherish every word you write regardless of how long they are in reaching me.

I didn't know the fruitcake you sent was made to order but one thing we all knew, it *was* exceptionally good, and someone did remark that we should have had some wine. They have lots of beer (if you could call it that), some wine (I *don't* like wine), and cider, and a *very* little whiskey, but being short doesn't bother me any. I can drink it or not.

I didn't know that I had written as sad a letter as you said I did. I didn't mean to sound so melancholy. It's just that I miss you so much and want you so bad, and love you as I do. Honey, you mean everything to me, and I *know* you love me and will be waiting for me when I get back. You are the only woman that I could actually believe and *not* doubt at all. Loving you Honey is all sweetness which makes everything better.

No Honey, I *don't* mind if your mother announces our engagement. In fact, I would like it very much, for I want the world to know you are mine. If you haven't already, I would like for you to.

No Honey, I *never* cared for anyone enough to write every day. In fact, not to even think of more than once a day. You, I think of all the time and love it.

Well Baby, I've answered about three of the letters and it's late so I'll stop.

Remember I love you.

[no signature]

The following announcement appeared in the Ft. Smith, Arkansas, *Southwest American*, on Sunday, November 28, 1943: "The engagement of Janice Holt Moore to Sergeant Henry E. Giles of Knifley, Kentucky, has been announced by her mother, Mrs. John Albert Holt, 501 North Thirty-ninth Street. The wedding will take place when Sergeant Giles returns from foreign service where he is with an engineers unit in England. The bride-elect is secretary to Dean Sherrill of the Louisville Presbyterian Theological Seminary at Louisville, Kentucky."

Tuesday, December 7, 1943

My only love:

How are you tonight Honey? The time I write you every night you are probably just having lunch, but I still seem to be near you when I'm writing.

. . . We have just been talking of the treacherous thing that happened two years ago today. I remember we were building roads in California when we heard it. That night, our Captain was giving us a pep talk and of all the people that shouldn't pass out, one of the first aid boys fell out. We laughed about it afterwards.

Last night, another fellow (another Weapons Sgt. incidently) and myself were having one of those talks of home and he was telling me (or trying) how much he loved his wife and what a joy it had always been being with her. How they loved each other, etc. Of course I was boasting of you also and what *we* believed love and a happy married life should consist of and all that. He's from

Louisiana and his wife is chief operator of the Southern Bell Telephone Co.—Well, someday *we* will know the sweetness of married life of two that are deeply in love, won't we?

I remember July 12, how I cursed the rain and everything that held me up when I was trying to get back to camp, but it was a *very* lucky day, and I'm happy that everything happened as it did. It is still, (and I know always will) mean everything to me.

Too bad about your mother being ill. Here's hoping her a speedy recovery.

I'm sure I've told you before that I had to send the allotment home. And it is for our home that I'm saving it. I had never even thought of trying to save for anything before I met you—but you changed a lot of things for me, and I love it.

Yes, I remember the Bible passage you wrote. In fact the whole verse. I don't have an Old Testament but (I'm not so sure), I believe it's Ruth. I don't remember who she said it to, but I know she was the one. I like it too.

Well Baby, there's nothing to write about.

I'm O.K. and still loving you more all the time. As the English say "Cheerio."

All my Love, / Henry

The "treacherous thing" was the bombing of Pearl Harbor by the Japanese on December 7, 1941, which thrust the United States into war with Japan.

In the Old Testament book of Ruth, chapter 1, verse 16, Ruth responds to her mother-in-law, Naomi: "Intreat me not to leave thee, or to return from following after thee: for whither thou goest, I will go; and where thou lodgest, I will lodge: thy people shall be my people, and thy God my God."

Thursday, December 16, 1943

My Dearest:

Four letters from my baby today. A *very* welcome treat, which I enjoyed so much. Sgt. Hinkel is at it again. When I'm trying the hardest to think, he starts some long drawn out conversation.

Oh yes, all the packages have reached me. They were, and are still being enjoyed,—by all.

Darling we both are hoping the same thing, in that by next Christmas we will be together. That *will* be wonderful.

Darling, I love you, very dearly. You are everything that makes life happy. Although we don't know how much, but surely every day *must* be bringing us closer together.

I've just read the parts of the Sunday School quarterly you sent. It make me feel pretty big to see your name in something like that. I'm sure "The Candles of Christmas" will be a beautiful program, or service. Next year, perhaps we can see something like it together.

Here's hoping the cold you had is well by now. Glad you have Dr. Sherrill to watch you.

The reasons you mentioned were why the allotment wasn't approved of. All told (as you said) it *is* a good policy.

Yes, I've tried to begin at the start of the bus ride, and think of everything. And I remember a *lot* that before I wouldn't even have thought of a second time. And *don't* worry about my "wandering hands." They're completely under control.

I suppose Mama would send some of the records I made to you. When you ask for them, tell her just the one's with music and singing. They're not so good unless played on a machine with controlled volume. I'll write her tomorrow.

I'll finish tomorrow night. Goodnight Baby.

Love, / Henry

P.S. By the way, what is your middle name?

Saturday, December 18, 1943

My only Darling:

Two letters from you today. A little delayed (November 27 & 28), but sweet and welcome, nevertheless.

Yesterday, I had a V-mail from Mama. All she wrote about was the letter she had from you. I wish you could read it. She said she *liked* the way you wrote. She is sure she will like you or she wouldn't have written *anything* about you. Well that's good, but if it had been the other way around I would still love you just as much, and that is an awful lot. All there could be. My love for you is so great that Darling I can't find words that will begin to express it. Oh! Honey, I love you.

I don't know why the letters I've written don't reach you any faster. I've only missed one day in a hell of a long time. And—I don't know why the letter in the blue envelope hasn't come through. (I've written you twice in blue envelopes). Perhaps soon, you'll be "swamped" with letters. By now you may already have. But *don't* worry when a letter doesn't come when you think it should. I'll be O.K.

Yes, I did get the letter in which you sent the one your Mother wrote you. In time you'll get the one I wrote in answer to it.

I think I'll stop soldiering altogether when I'm out of the Army. One fellow said if he ever saw one of his kids step off with his left foot, he'd disown it. That *may* be a *little* on extremes. Maybe you'll be able in a couple of years to teach me to be a civilian.

It does seem a long time since we were together, but actually the time has gone pretty fast. Those of you are precious memories and I cherish every one of them, and every moment with you was very dear to me. Your kisses I'll *never* forget.

So, Darling this is all for tonight.

All my love—*forever*, / Henry

Tuesday, December 21, 1943

My only Darling:—

Not only did I have a letter from you today,—but I heard you talk!! Yes, I played the record you sent, at a little cafe in a town where I was working.

Several of the fellows heard it, and while they were making remarks as to how good it was, and how well you talked etc., it had a far greater meaning to me. It was hearing you speak, the one I love. The voice I remember so well.

Darling, how my heart cried for you as I heard you talking, bringing back memories, happy memories, of the few hours we were together. The hours that have since meant so much to me. Always (before I met you) when I was riding a bus or train, I made it my business to ride with a woman. Of course I wasn't looking for a wife, but I'm glad and will always be thankful that I found you.

If you remember, I wanted you to stop in Memphis with me. When you let me know that was *definitely* out, I began thinking about you from a different point. Of course you knew then it wasn't for church services I wanted to stop.

I started thinking that you were *really* the type you had seemed to be from the start. I'm glad Darling, that I have found out you *are* just as I hoped you were, then. Someone I can love and trust *completely*, and you love me too.

While the record was being played, one fellow asked if you were a college professor. Others wondered *why* a woman like that would have anything to do with me. Of course, I didn't know the answer to that one.

Darling anything you write, I like it. The more you write the more pleasure it is for me. And you *won't* be "more silent" when I come home.

Goodnight Baby. I'll write more tomorrow.

All my love, / Henry

I LOVE YOU DARLING is written in large letters across the back of the last page of this letter.

4

"Well, Christmas in England hasn't been so bad."

Christmas Day, / Saturday, December 25, 1943

Dearest Darling:

Well, Christmas in England hasn't been so bad. We had our turkey with dressing, and quite a bit more good food that goes to make up a Christmas dinner.

It's about three o'clock here, so I guess you're just beginning your Christmas day. I was thinking of you just about the time your "open house" (as you called it) party must have been at its peak and of course, wishing I was with you.

Perhaps before next year Adolf will give up, (the dirty son-of-a-_____) and it will be possible for us to be together.

I just had a letter from Mom yesterday. She said she had already sent you the records. I trust you weren't expecting too much when you heard them.

I love you Darling. Each day you are dearer to me, and mean more to me.

Oh yes, Mom also said she liked your letters fine. And—she said you must be an awful fine woman. How's that? I had already told her that.

I wish I could think of more to write, anyhow you know I do love you. That's the most important thing, that we do love each other—and always.

Well Darling, goodbye for now.

All my Love, / Henry

Tuesday, December 28, 1943

My *only* Darling:—

There were three letters last evening at mail call, after the two I had already gotten when the mail was being sorted, which I answered last night. So you finally received the one in the blue envelope. You should have another by now.

Darling, I *did* do what I wanted to about the other girl's letters. I didn't answer either of them. Darling, there's no room for *anyone* else since I found you. I'm happy with the best, so why should there be any time or space for anything more. *You* are the one I love and shall, *always.*

Honey, there's one thing I've been wanting to ask you for, for a long time, but didn't know if it was proper, or whether I should. *I* don't see why not. Could I have your Mother's address and name? I can't think of a logical reason why I shouldn't.—So, if it is O.K. I *would* like to write to her.

I could never see a wife of mine working. I believe it's a man's responsibility to do the earning and providing. Don't you, really? I would be ashamed to be seen if my wife had to earn or even help earn a living for us. I mean so far as working for wages is concerned. A wife, to me, would be a lot more than just a woman to live with. She's something very precious, to love, and cherish and care for. I trust you see it the same way.

I like the way you and Mama get along. If she *hadn't* liked you, she would have told me just as quick, and you would never have gotten a letter from her. You know,—it still seems odd to be writing you about Mama and her and me writing about you. I've never done that before.

I guess this is all for now. Goodnight Baby.

Love and kisses, / Henry

Wednesday, December 29, 1943

Hello my Darling:

. . . I'm alone tonight and I like it that way best when I'm writing. It seems you are nearer. Oh, that I could hold you in my arms tonight. Darling, I love you so much that at times it hurts to be so far from you. But sometime, when the days of waiting are over and we are together again, we *will* start life anew and we both know that it will be the happiest part of our lives.

Darling, we *are* starting our life together as soon as possible. When I'm in the city limits of Louisville, the shortest time it will take us to be married will be far too long. I mean, we will be busy until the ceremony is over.

I quite agree with you that we have more than we did before. To me, it was nothing then to *everything* now. Darling, you are my whole life. Without you—well we've been over that before.

Right now I'm not sure who the "bloke" was that wrote "Hello" on the back of my letter to you. I've an idea, and when I find out for sure he'll tell me *why* he was messing with things he had no business in.

Your letter of December 18 was short but sweet nevertheless.

Darling, I love you and am lonely without you. It seems I'm at a loss to write more now so will stop. So—Goodnight baby.

Love always, / Henry

Thursday, December 30, 1943

My only one:—

No letter today but I did receive the cablegram for which I thank you from the bottom of my heart. I only wish I could have been in position to at least send you a Christmas present, but I was not and am still unable to do so.

Darling, I do love you, more every day. I've thought an awful lot at times of how much I wanted you for my own (for *keeps*) before I left the states, but it seems we waited a little too long. I am sure though that you will be waiting for me when I'm back again. That's a great consolation, and the only thing I'm living for now. You are sweet Darling, and I'll always love you.

I told Sgt. Hinkel of the song you said was so good, ("My Shining Hour.") He immediately wrote his wife about it, and tonight he had a letter from her telling him what a beautiful song it was. So far we haven't heard it.

In town, where we eat lunch when working there, we hear some songs we know, and believe me they sound good. I also heard some of the President's speech on Christmas eve.

Well Darling, I'm out of anything to write, so—I guess it's cheerio for now.

Goodnight baby.

All my love, / Henry

Wednesday, January 5, 1944

My only Love:—

Today there were four letters and each one was tops, since there hadn't been one for three or four days. . . . The letters were dated December 13–24, 25, & 27. That's pretty fast isn't it? At the same time, I have one from your sister in Arkansas dated December 18, (a Christmas greeting) which I shall answer presently.

The letter of December 13 *was* a love letter if I ever had one. And—in one place you did make some *very* logical suggestions. That is concerning *where* we would be after we are married. It is very possible that 1437 Hepburn will be the address for some time. Anywhere with you would be home. When I'm back Honey, I don't want you to *ever* leave my side. This is long enough to wait and I *won't* be without you any longer.

I'm glad honey, that you had the letters for Christmas since they mean as much to you as you say.

I'm glad you liked the gift Mom sent you. It still seems funny for a girl of mine to be writing about my mother, and she about her. I said *"a* girl of mine," but honey, *you* are the *only* one. It just never happened before.

Yes, I got the engagement announcement too. Several of the fellows have read it, and congratulated me. The picture *was* O.K.

Goodnight baby. I'll write more tomorrow.

All my love, / Henry

Janice's sister, Mary Catherine Holt Sullivan, nicknamed Petie, lived in Fayetteville, Arkansas, with her husband, Claud, and their son, Dan.

Wednesday, January 5, 1944

My Dearest:—

Still no letter today, but I hardly expect one *every* day for they usually come two or three or more when I do get them.

About the first thing I usually like to tell you is, I love you Darling. We have written that more than anything but it never gets old or tiresome. Does it? I do want you to know I love you, even though it isn't possible to say how much. Love isn't measured in any way, but Honey, if it was, the love I have for you would exceed *all* imaginable calculations.

Sweeter than all baby, is the fact that you love me. I remember after I left you in Dallas, I was afraid that all I would ever hear of you any more, would be just a few casual letters then nothing more. If that *should* have been the case, I know I could never have forgotten you. I'm sure we both knew before we parted, that there was something different, but were afraid to mention it.

I've had a couple of letters from Mama the last three days. I think she's in love with you too. She writes more about you than anything else, but I like it.

No, you don't have peculiar ideas about being married. In fact, they are just what I had hoped you wanted. *I* don't want to be bothered with any formalities or timing or be a part of a "show" (as you said). Just you and me and the necessary witnesses is *all* I want. Of course, there will be a minister too.

I'm sure you have thought what *I* know, that to begin, you will *have* to do most all of the planning since you are more accustomed to civil life. Regarding colors—anything but Khaki or O.D.

You will have the wide gold band as a wedding ring.

I've been reading about the sinking of the Scharnhorst. Neat maneuvering on the British Navy's part.

Honey, I guess this is all for now.

I love you very dearly, and I'll *not* forget that I'm an officially and formally (and happily) engaged man. I *am* conducting myself accordingly.

Goodnight my darling, and—

All my Love, / Henry

O.D.: Olive drab uniform.

The Scharnhorst, a 26,000-ton German battle cruiser, fitted with nine 11-inch guns and with a speed of 29 knots, was faster than any British battleship. On

Christmas Day 1944, British cruisers, later joined by their destroyers, exchanged fire with the *Scharnhorst* and successfully annihilated it. Only 36 of the 1,970 officers and men aboard the German ship were rescued.

Monday, January 10, 1944

My only love:—

. . . Someone here has a record player and a few good records (some are hillbilly and mountain ballads), they play in the kitchen. It's pretty good to hear a few songs and some music from the states. The British seem to be several years behind in a lot of things.

The censor called me into his office today and told me that I was one of the few in the company whose letters he didn't bother to read anymore. I can write more than I want to at times and don't, but still not write anything that shouldn't be written. I thought that was a lot of trust he put in me, one which I couldn't betray.

I'm writing this just before mail call, and I'm expecting a letter from you today. In fact, I'm always looking forward to the wonderful letters you write me.

Darling, it will be the most perfect day of my life when we meet again. I guess this is all for now baby. Remember I love you with all my heart. All there is.

My love and kisses, / [no signature]

Tuesday, January 11, 1944

My only Darling:—

I'm thinking of you a lot today, and loving you still. I didn't get a letter last night but I know they will get here eventually.

Today is another "nawsty" one (as the British would say) rainy and foggy. We didn't work this morning, due to the downpour. I'm glad it doesn't rain so much, so often.

Honey, I love you so. You'll never know how much. I will always be thankful for the day we met. Life would have been very dull indeed if it hadn't been for loving, and being loved by you.

The day couldn't come too soon for me, that Adolf gives up. That would give better hope of seeing you sooner.

Darling, this is short, but it seems all there is. So—bye for now.

Loving you—*always*, / Henry

Saturday, January 15, 1944

Hello my Darling:

Two *wonderful* letters from my baby tonight, and I'm happy.

Don't blame me if this letter isn't so good. There's quite a mob of jerks they call sergeants in here and everyone is trying to out-talk the other.

I *don't* mind you telling me twice in a day you love me. In fact I like it. I haven't gotten the letter you wrote Wednesday, December 29, only the one written Wednesday night, but it was sweet and *every* letter from you, honey, is tops.

I told Mama about the difference in our age, and there's always the best time for everything, not that it would matter with me if it did with her. I'll tell her in time that you have been married. After all that's a very small thing, as far as I'm concerned.

Honey, I love you all there is and always, and it's a consolation to know you love me. You will *never* be sorry you did.

My love forever, / Henry

At age 18, on November 27, 1923, Janice Meredith Holt married Otto Jackson Moore of Fort Smith, Arkansas. A divorce decree was granted September 19, 1939. In an unpublished manuscript, Janice Moore wrote: ". . . In the years we were married I never once found anything within him I could reach. I don't know what sort of man he was, for we couldn't even talk to one another. If we had been persons of different nationalities, we could not have been further apart. We never meant the same things when we talked. We could never get through to one another. I had the constantly frustrated feeling of ramming my head against a stone wall, doubtless he had much the same feeling."

"When the marriage ended some years later, it was as if I had spent them with a stranger. I knew what foods he preferred, how he liked to dress, what his creature comforts were, and that, literally is all. Not once did I ever have a clue to what his deepest emotions and thoughts were. He didn't read, he didn't like music, he didn't like the outdoors. Those things wouldn't have mattered if I could have discovered one thing at all he did like, except too much liquor too frequently, and penny-ante poker. He worked hard all day, came home to eat and sleep, and lived in a world of his own which was entirely closed to me. We produced Elizabeth, and she was the only thing we had in common."

"There are marriages which carry the seeds of separation in them from the beginning. This was one of them."

Henry's hesitancy to tell his mother that Janice was a divorced woman was indicative of the social attitudes toward divorce through the 1940s. Prior to World War II, only 8 percent of marriages ended in legal dissolution, with the greater percentage of those being in urban areas as opposed to rural.

Hardly a wedding was solemnized without the vow "Til death do us part" and the admonition of the minister, "What God hath joined together, let no man put asunder." A divorced woman bore an imaginary "D" as prominently affixed as the scarlet A of an earlier time. Without consideration of the circumstances, she was viewed as having failed pure and simple and was, in the eyes of society (especially mothers), a risk to future suitors.

Sunday, January 16, 1944

My Darling Janice:—

Starting that way seems a little funny since I've never used your name since the first few letters I wrote you. But I somehow just happened to start that way.

Once when I was addressing an envelope to you I wrote Janice Giles. It looked good but I tore off the stamp and used another envelope. I love you Honey, with all my heart. You are everything to me.

No letter today, but Sunday is one day when it seems there's never much mail.

I hope a V-mail will be sufficient tonight. I can't see any point in using a stamp and stationery for as small a letter as I'm writing tonight. I don't like them myself but it seems I have to use them sometimes.

This is all tonight Honey. Remember—I love you baby, *forever.*

All my love, / Henry

Friday, January 21, 1944

My Darling:—

It seems that V-mail is getting to be a habit, but I can tell you what there is to tell on one of these sheets. Each day you are on my mind and I'm constantly wondering when we will be together again.

I've just been thinking that my replies to you, when you asked what I intend to do when I'm out of the Army, must be a little disgusting to you. Perhaps some can, but I find it hard to just exactly know what I want to do, etc. One thing *I know, I want you*. Then I'm sure *we* can work out some of the things that for a long time have seemed very remote to me.

This is all baby, for now.

All my Love, / Henry

Wednesday, January 26, 1944

My only love:—

Tonight is a very dismal one outside. The wind blowing, raining, it's foggy and everything that goes to make up a very disagreeable night, but inside it's rather nice and warm. Three of us are writing letters, and our main topic of conversation is home and the ones we love, and why we *have* to get back there sometime.

I love you Darling, and I'm thinking of you all the time. Someday Honey you'll be mine forever. I'll never let you leave my side, for after waiting this long nothing else would do. You'll be with me *all* the time. Count on that.

I sometimes try to imagine just what it *will* be like to have you with me all the time. I'm sure we will have fun, and you are going to be the most perfect little wife in the world. We will *never* be sorry we loved each other. I know that.

Do you remember what you said when I asked you if you loved me? I believe we were going through Arkansas when I said that. You didn't know (or I) that you were speaking so much truth when you said, "This is awful sudden, isn't it?" Well the whole thing has been sudden, and full of surprises. Sweet surprises. We will just stop trying to figure out why it happened, but always be thankful it did.

You are everything to me and I love you with all my heart. Well, goodnight Baby. It's about bedtime. I'll see you in my dreams.

My Love always, / Henry

Sunday, January 30, 1944

My *only* Love,

I somehow like to begin a letter with those three words. They seem to mean more than a long letter even. Early mail call today, and a *wonderful* letter from you. I only hope I can write an answer that will somehow express my feelings and love towards you now. It was the most perfect description of what I think a happy married life should consist of.

You were speaking of the "little things" there might be for our likes and dislikes, and it seems that we do "click" on almost everything. All my life, I had wondered if there could be someone who thought or had the same ideas I have. (Which I think are sensible and essential in any marriage.) In you Darling, I have found exactly those qualities.

In the things we don't agree on, I know we *are* going to have fun "thrashing" them out. The major things you spoke of, darling, we are quite agreed upon. Unfaithfulness is one thing I wouldn't dream of. I am now and shall continue to be just what you expect of the one you are going to marry *and* to be your husband. Believe me Darling, I *will never* do anything to hurt you or cross you. I love you too much.

As for drinking, I've always drank what I wanted (which is nothing to be proud of) and have been a few places but have never been "called down" by any law officer. Military or civilian.

Gambling, in almost any degree, is in excess. Basically, I mean. I do sometimes play poker or blackjack if there's a low limit. I mean low. It's usually done for want of pastime.

Honey I'm proud of you, and madly in love with you, and in quoting you, *I* am sure we will "get along." You will *never* be sorry you loved me, *and* married me. My love for you is so great, I would go to the end of the world to *keep* you happy.

You will always be mine darling and I'll see to it you are never disappointed in me.

Flash: We had chicken for dinner today. And I had a leg besides the usual neck. G.I. chickens are usually made of wings and necks.

So long for now baby. I love you and am coming back to you—sometime.

All my love forever, / Henry

Monday, January 31, 1944

My only Love:

Today there were three wonderful letters! It goes without saying, that everything is just about O.K. Your loving letters *always* brighten up everything.

I love you darling. Each day you are dearer to me. If only there was *some* way of knowing how long this waiting will last. Not knowing that, we *will* make the best of it. Won't we, Honey?

In one letter, you said you "felt guilty" for sending the letter you had from the fellow in Oklahoma. You shouldn't and it wasn't anything to ask me to "forgive" you for. I hadn't thought anymore about it. So—forget it.

By the way, just what *do* you write, or have written? Two or three times recently you have spoken of writing, so I just wondered what. Do you mind a question like that?

I think that perhaps before so long I can have some pictures made.

I don't think I remember the song you mentioned. I'm sure it must be good. The words are.

Yes Honey, we *are* going to have a lot to make up. As for ever getting "caught up"—I don't know.

Yes, *I* think it would be the right thing to do, to accept the things your Mother wants us to have, and we *will* find a place for them. I thought I had told you before that now you do know more of civil life than I, so for that reason you can do more planning, etc. But we'll get adjusted soon after we start together. We *will* be happy together Darling. *I* have no doubt of that.

Oh yes baby, a kiss from you I would always like. Regardless of the time of day.

You know, I like the way you usually close a letter. The way you write "your own" gives me a great feeling of security in knowing you are mine.

Well, I guess I'll have to stop here.

All my love forever, / Henry

5

"Somehow it seems you are very near me."

My *only* love:

Tonight there were four letters! That just about makes the day end perfectly. So tonight I'm happy and loving you *very* much. All that is possible.

No, if you need glasses of course I wouldn't mind, although I never especially liked them. You *would* take them off when we retire at night, wouldn't you? O.K. No offense Darling, I was only kidding.

You almost spoke for me when you said you must have at least *thought* you were in love once. I know *now* I was *never* in love before. No, I never before wrote every day (or nearly so). I never wrote home about anyone, and say the things I do of you. Perhaps before, I've mentioned someone, but that's all. I'm happy now that I know what loving someone is. I wouldn't have missed it for anything either.

I too, hope Charlie doesn't have to go to the Army. I wouldn't like that at all.

The things you sent Cora Mae are O.K. Since you asked me if I minded you doing these things, no, I don't. Whatever relations you may have with the folks at home I consider none of my business.

I think Darling by the time I'm home you *will* have everything lovely. Even if it were tomorrow and only *you*, I would be happy. Yes, the happiest man in the world. Everything sounds lovely, and a new bed *will* be safer to begin with. See? I trust my kidding isn't *too* ———— . I'm not so sure if I'll mind you kicking the covers loose around our feet or not. If I don't like it, I shall wrap them tight. How's that?

Goodnight baby. I love you with all my heart. Remember that.

A lot of kisses and *all* my love. / Henry

Charles "Charlie" Scott, husband of Henry's oldest sister, Irene.

Friday, February 11, 1944

My only Love:

Tonight there was no letter (for some reason the mail didn't come through) but with two for the last two nights, I can't afford to grumble.

I love you my darling. You are more to me than the entire world. For you I live and breathe. I only hope that we don't have to wait so much longer.

In one of your letters last night you spoke of Frank Sinatra, and you said you *didn't* like him. I've never heard him (or much *of* him) but according to newspaper articles, cartoons, etc., every female is supposed to swoon when he croons. I saw a cartoon where a Chicago hotel manager was "bawling him out" because the women were fainting in every place they saw him.

Tomorrow I'm going on a 24 hour pass. I'm going to the Red Cross and try to find out where my cousin is located.

Well baby there's nothing much to write for now. I'll have to say "Cheerio."

All my love *always* / Henry

Tuesday, February 15, 1944

My Dearest,

Again I'm happy, for there were two letters today. Good ones, postmarked January 17–18. I wouldn't have squawked if there hadn't been any after fourteen for the last three days. You know what your letters mean to me. I've told you that before.

One letter had the stamps in it and last night I got thirty air mail envelopes, so I'm pretty well fixed for a time at least.

No darling, I haven't missed writing you every night but the three I've told you of. That was Christmas and one since. I *will* write to you *every* possible chance I get, no matter where I may be. You can count on that. I also know that *our* life and *our* future depend on each other. *I* will only find happiness with you.

I shall never forget the trip to Dallas and on to camp. I could only think of you—just wondering. Now I'm the happiest fellow in the world since the things happened that weren't logical for me to even hope for then. *That* was the beginning of happiness for us, the day I first saw you on the bus, but we didn't *exactly* know it then. Now we know the things that then were a little confused. We will have fun talking of the trip to Dallas when I get home, where we will never part again.

The cartoon was good. Once I was on convoy when we came to a R.R. crossing where a long freight was passing. (Rather fast.) In order to not slow the convoy down we *built* an overpass. (*Over* the R.R.) And the convoy continued on as the freight passed below. That may sound a little *fast,* but *we* were good.

Well Darling, I love you with all my heart and for all time. Goodnight and—

All my love, / Henry

Thursday, February 17, 1944

Hello my Love:—

By the time Sgt. Hinkel and I finish writing at night, we usually have enough clothes off to go to bed. I don't know why but we start undressing when we begin writing.

Honey I'm loving you *very* much tonight. Somehow it seems you are very near me.

There were four letters today! Someone has gotten "on the ball" and they are really coming through. I *like* that. I must have had at least twenty letters the last week.

In a few days I will get another pass, and all I'm going to do is hunt for a studio and have some pictures made. That's a promise.

I didn't hear from home today. I'm anxious to know if Charlie passed for the Army.

My shoes are off now.

Yes, of course I was only joking when I asked you on the bus if you loved me. Even at that stage the answer wasn't really negative. Was it?

What was put in the letter you wrote first on the seventh? Evening in Paris? It was a much lovelier perfume than the Lifebouy I use.

I wrote to my cousin **about** three weeks ago and he hasn't as much as answered. If he **doesn't**, I don't give a damn if I see him or not.

You were speaking of Dr. Sherrill. It must be terrible to anyone who loses their eyesight. I always felt very sorry for anyone who is in such condition.

While I was at the P.O.E. I tried several times to make it to the Exchange to call you, but always I couldn't get in the door. The last few days we weren't allowed to.

Darling, I don't know if I've mentioned it before, but there are two words you always write, that to me mean more than I can ever tell you. The way you always say "your own," Janice. I love those words and what they mean.

So for now goodnight baby.

I'll love you always, / Henry

This writing looks like hell tonight, but I always try to write too fast. H

Because of macular degeneration, Dr. Lewis L. Sherrill began losing his vision in 1943.

P.O.E.: Port of Embarkation.

Saturday, February 19, 1944

My Darling:

Well here I am writing you again, and I love it. It's the only time of day I can have a little "visit" with you. Then you are nearer.

I had a V-mail from home tonight, evidently in answer to the one I had told Mama your age. She seemed a little surprised, because your picture doesn't look it.

Well Darling, if we were together now, we would probably be going out for the evening since it's Saturday night. Not that it would be necessary to go out to have fun, for *any* place with you would be the best place in the world. We are going to have some wonderful times when that day comes that we are together again. Aren't we Honey?

I'm writing to your Mother tonight. Once I wrote in answer to the Christmas greeting, but I didn't get an answer. I trust I'm doing the correct thing.

I'm lonely for you tonight my Darling. And I love you *very* much, in every way there is for a man to love a woman.

Honey it's bedtime so for now—Cheerio.

All my love, / Henry

Monday, February 21, 1944

Darling wife of mine:—

I say "wife" because you *should* be my own in that respect. You will be some day anyhow. I like those words so much I thought there would be nothing wrong in beginning a letter in that way. O.K. Honey?

Oh yes baby, there are going to be a lot of ways we will have fun. Where or what we eat. What type of shows, etc.

No, I don't like concerts, but I do appreciate the art and talent displayed in one. I saw one in Swift that was good. When you want to see one, *we* will see it. We will learn to bowl and do anything *you* want to do. You will find I'm not hard to get along with. The greatest thing of all will be the fact that we are together again.

I like the things you are doing for our future and (I shouldn't curse), I wish to hell there was something *I* could do to help. Right now, I seem helpless.

Yes, you were right when you said I would probably say for you to get what you liked best.

Goodnight my love and remember you are mine.

All my love, / Henry

Saturday, February 26, 1944

My Darling:

Tonight as usual I'm thinking of you and loving you with all my heart. Everyone is quieter tonight for some reason and it isn't so hard to write.

Today was when I was *supposed* to go on pass, but due to circumstances passes were cancelled the middle of the week.

Tonight I am a little tired again, but next week probably won't be so hard.

Have been reading this week's *Yank*. Ever read them? It's an Army weekly magazine. "By the men, for the men in the service."

There was no letter today but tomorrow I guess there will be.

Well Honey it's late, I've been interrupted several times since I started this.

Goodnight Honey.

I love you, / Henry

P.S. Tonight I played a guitar some. The first one I'd had in my hands since I left the states.

P.P.S. Send me a fruitcake.

Sunday, February 27, 1944

My Darling:—

. . . Honey, I'm sure I know you well enough that I can understand your letters quite well. Such as the one in which you asked what I planned to do when I was out of the Army. I knew what you were meaning. I also know that you would *never* want to offend me, and the same goes for me. If I have ever written anything that you may have thought didn't sound right, I assure you I've never meant to. I love you too much to ever do or say anything to hurt you.

Yes, I knew when we left Swift that we were sailing. If I could have been home once more, we *would* have been married now. I've wished an awful lot that I could have come to Kentucky just once more.

I will have some pictures made as soon as I can. I've said that several times before, and it may sound as if I'm not trying to.

It's lonely without you Darling, and I miss you an *awful* lot. Someday baby, we will start life again together. Won't it be wonderful?

Honey, I guess I'll stop here.

All my love & kisses, / Henry

Thursday, March 2, 1944

My Darling:—

Last night, I was unable to write you. I've told you before that there would be times when I couldn't write. I love you just the same honey, with an ever increasing love that grows with each passing moment.

There were three letters today. In one you were telling of the rug you had bought. It *must* be beautiful. I'm getting terribly anxious to see the things you tell me about. First though, I want to see you. I've told you before that I only wish it were possible to help you now, to do the things you are doing.

Sometimes (or should I say at all times), *I* want to *hold* you in my arms, so badly that my heart aches. The thrill and contentment there will be in having you near me is worth waiting for (if need be), a long time. Then *we* will begin living.

I'm "bucking" for another pass, then I *will* have some pictures made. You have been very patient, but honestly I have done the best I could.

No, "Merrie old England" isn't so merry now, nor it *actually* hasn't been, but of course there must be worse places.

It does kinda make my mouth water when you tell of the chicken, mashed potatoes, etc. The last letter I had from Mom, *she* was telling of the same things.

I remember eating a sandwich while I was waiting for the bus in Bowling Green. I also bought a half pint of Old Taylor, but it was gone before I saw you.

Goodnight my dear. I love you with all my heart.

Love—and forever yours, / Henry

On March 1, 1944, the 291st was sent with the First U.S. Army to Highnam Court in Gloucester to begin training in earnest for the inevitable invasion. They also began grueling exercises in what would become one of their primary missions—erecting Bailey bridges. The bridges, constructed with prefabricated panels, each weighing five hundred pounds, were named and designed for Sir Donald Bailey. In addition to bridge–building, men in the 291st were instructed in the procedures for detecting, laying, and clearing mines.

Saturday, March 4, 1944

My Dearest.

There was a lovely letter from you today, which I was very happy to receive. I always "sweat out" every mail call, and try to get close enough to the mail clerk that I can see what he has in his hands, and in looking at the stack of letters he usually has, I sometimes see the corner of one of mine, several letters before he calls it.

. . . No, I haven't heard from home that Irene and Charlie had gotten back. It seems that I get the news from home, from you, sooner than I do from home. (Sounds like double-talk).

Yes, honey, I too would like to buy a little place, (not too small) and we could have everything we wanted. We'll probably do that.

Well Darling, I guess I'll say goodnight now. I love you honey in every way you can be loved and I'll *always* remember you love me.

Love always, / Henry

Tuesday, March 7, 1944

My own darling:—

Well this is about the umpteenth time I've started to write this so now I'll try to carry through.

Six letters today, wow! I hardly know how to start, but first, I love you my Darling.

. . . I would much rather you wouldn't worry about me, but suppose it must be the normal thing for you to do. Just take it as easy as you can. I'll write as often as I can. You *know* that.

It is a little strange that we both were loving each other before we knew how much we thought alike. But since *those* facts already were—I suppose it must have been only natural for us to love each other.

No, I won't mind you writing after we are married. You should since you like it. And with me to help you—No, never mind that.

I remember that song you heard in the movie. "I'll Get By" and I'm afraid you *will* always have me. Yes, I'm sure you will.

Darling, if I should be wounded or something, I *will* come back to you. I promise you that. *You* promise me one thing, (perhaps there's no use saying this) that your love for me will never turn to pity in such a case. Not that I think it would, but I wouldn't like that.

Well, goodnight my love, and all my love—

Forever yours, / Henry

————————————

Friday, March 10, 1944

Hello my darling:

Again there was no letter from you, but I had two from Mama and she was telling me that Cora Mae thinks a lot of you, and that everyone always likes to read your letters, so hearing *of* you is next best to having a letter. I guess you have noticed I don't say much about Dad. Well there's no particular reason for it, it's just that I always wrote to Mama and Robert, and would ask or say something about Dad to them. He's a fine old boy, the best I know of, and I remember the first time I went home on furlough he nearly cried. So, that's it.

Oh yes, I love you with all my heart, in *every* way there is. I am constantly thinking of you, and wondering when we will be together once more. That will be the happiest time of my life. Then,—"I'll never let you go little darling. I'll never let you say goodbye." That's part of a song I used to know.

Goodnight my love.

Forever yours, / Henry

————————————

Sunday, March 12, 1944

My only Darling:

Today, it has been eight months since we met and learned to love each other! These eight months have been the happiest part of my life. Since the first day we met, I have known what true love really means. Darling, I love you *so* much. My heart cries for you all the time.

Today is Sunday and I slept late and missed a fine breakfast which was "sunny side up" eggs and hot cakes, (or flapjacks they are sometimes called) and at lunch I was so hungry, my stomach thought my throat was cut. We had a fine chicken dinner with everything that goes with chicken.

Sgt. Hinkel and I are thinking of taking in a movie later this afternoon if we can find one we think we will like.

There was no letter from you today at noon, but tomorrow I may have one that comes in the evening mail call.

I guess I'll stop this now, so cheerio honey and all my love always.

Forever yours, / Henry

Tuesday, March 14, 1944

My darling Sweetheart:—

. . . It makes me a little "homesick" when you tell me of the happy home we are to have and the way you are planning and preparing it. Oh darling, it's going to be the most wonderful thing in the world to be at home with you. Yes, the happiness we have wanted so long. It's hard to wait, but someday it will be over, then there will be happiness.

You know, I've begun to wonder what a lighted city or town looks like. The average person doesn't know what there is to be thankful for in the good old U.S.A.

As for what nationality I may be, I don't know. Strange, but I don't. I've heard my grandfather speak of his grandfather, but Cumberland County, Kentucky, seemed to be the only other place he knew of. So—that's that.

If I had known at first that you felt as you did, it would have saved me a lot of anxiety. You didn't give me a hint that you cared, but between the lines, I soon decided I might have a chance, so I told you I loved you. I have, since you told me you loved me, been the happiest person in the world. We are so agreed in the things it takes to make a happy married life, we just can't miss.

Oh my darling, how I love you. It's late, so for now I'll close and see you in my dreams.

My love forever, / Henry

Wednesday, March 15, 1944

Darling:—

There were *five* letters today! March 1, 2, 3, 4, 5. How's that. All in rotation, and I love every word of them. You are wonderful darling, and each day I think of you, and love you more. Never doubt that for a second.

I was only kidding about your glasses and why *"suppose"* what would have happened *if* you had had glasses on? You didn't have any on, and I *didn't* go on by, so that's that. Anyhow, now, you would look good to me with *only* the glasses on. (That sounds a little rude.)

So—you think my story of the overpass sounds a little "fishy."—Well it does.

I'm writing this lying down, so I'm not responsible if it looks even worse than usual, but anyhow you will probably get the most important part. I love you, and I *never* tire of you telling me the same thing.

I'm going to have it hard trying to say just what I want to here. You said you were afraid I was giving you qualities you don't possess. Well, (don't think me sarcastic) however that may be, I'm still not afraid of my own conclusions, and listen baby, you *will* be the most perfect wife in the world. I've thought of *everything* that you could have possibly thought of and I'm still convinced that we will be the happiest two persons in the world. Now,—don't get in *that* mood anymore, because you read something in a book. I'm *not* expecting too much of you. Don't mention *that* again. O.K. honey?

I don't suppose we will ever forget the little things that happened on the trip from Bowling Green to Dallas. You asked what I was thinking of you during our last hour together. Well—if I hadn't been thinking the best of you, I wouldn't have been with you any farther than Memphis. Remember? Then was when I decided you *could* be one of the finest women in the world. In Dallas, I was wondering more than thinking, and wishing I could hope, but was afraid to. Remember you saying, "I could get awful fond of you?" (Or words to that effect.) I kept wondering if you *really* meant it or just happened to say it. Now, I think you *did* mean it. When you left, I missed you more than it seemed I should.

Well baby, it's a little late so—

You telling of playing midwife to a cat etc., made me think of once when Irene got two kittens somewhere and gave them names suitable for a boy and girl. When they were grown it was the "boy" that had the kittens. We had a lot of fun about that.

You know, it's funny when you think of little things like that. It seems like centuries have passed since then. It's so strange that it only seems they were dreams.

Well, goodnight baby. Remember I love you with all my heart.

Forever yours, / Henry

Friday, March 17, 1944

Hello Darling:—

. . . So you saw Carmen Miranda. I've never seen her, but when I was in California, I did see quite a few radio and movie stars. Once I saw some "stills" taken of Carmen Miranda that were rather unique.

We do have lots of fun when some of us guys are together, and sometimes it definitely wouldn't be the right place for ladies to be.

Yes, I've been kidded about writing as often as I do, and only a couple of days ago, one fellow said, "If it wasn't for Sgt. Giles, the mail clerk would have to find another job." However true that may be, I still want every letter I can get from you, and only extreme emergencies will keep me from writing you every day. I love you so much, it's only the natural thing to do.

Goodnight my darling. I love you with *all* my heart and in *every* way.

All my love, / Henry

6

"You mean more to me every day. . . ."

Sunday, April 2, 1944

My darling:

Today I hit the "jackpot." Four wonderful letters that I was certainly beginning to need, and I love every word in them. You mean more to me every day and all the time I love you more. I only wish we could have been married before I had to leave, for there is more joy in loving you than anything I have ever known.

Had a fine lazy Sunday today. Slept until 10:30, got up and dressed and because we didn't have chicken for dinner, went into town and ate at the Red Cross. A good meal for one and three. That's about 25 cents. Went to a show and came back early to see if there were any letters and found the four.

From the description, I'm sure I shall like Hepburn Avenue quite a bit.

I believe we have done a very complete job (just writing) finding out everything about each other. More than I thought could be done. You don't have to ever worry about there being someone else. Even very casually.

You did a very neat job in "telling off" the woman who thought war love affairs were so romantic. I liked that, and I think you were quite right in telling her as you did.

Well Honey, I'll stop here. I love you with all my heart, for always.

Forever yours, / Henry

Monday, April 3, 1944

My only love:—

Three *very sweet* letters again today. After having four yester-day, I wasn't expecting such good luck again today, but everyone is welcome, and I love every word you write. I believe the first time we ever mentioned "love" was when I said I was falling in love with your letters, and in reply you said, save some of it for you. Remember? Well Honey, you are loved as completely as any woman *ever* was. Never forget that for a moment. And that *will* be the first thing you will be told when I see you again. *When* I get around to saying anything.

The alligator gag was pretty good. I should like to have seen you three "uncaging" it. Once when I was in California, in the fire department, with only about twenty-five fellows, someone had a stuffed horned toad which I didn't know of, and one day they put it in my bunk. That night I didn't notice it until I was well in bed, then I felt it, very prickly between smooth sheets. At first I froze stiff, then I was in the middle of the floor, bunk and all. Everyone had a big laugh and *I* had to fix my bunk again.

From the number of letters you have gotten since the an-nouncement, it seems that quite a few people know of our engage-ment. Well that's good, but only you and I know of the real happiness there has been in learning to love each other so com-pletely, and the continued joy there has been since, and all there is to be later. I love you with all my heart, darling.

I haven't heard from your Mother yet. I will write her again soon. I still don't understand why she didn't get either letter I wrote.

You asked if I would like your hair. Listen baby, I would be crazy about you any way you happen to be. If it was only with a garter on. How's that?

There was one thing you left out when you were speaking of the "colors" of breakfast. Eggs sunnyside up, with brown country sausage as a background. By the way, these new fangled pow-dered eggs don't show up so good. I prefer the old fashioned type that have to be broken and you can hear them crackle.

Sgt. Hinkel just told me about his wife buying her Mother a rug and paying $175 for it! He said he wrote and asked her if she was sure she didn't buy rugs for the entire house. We have been talking of what it will be like when Adolf gives up. Oh, we have a lot of things planned. Of course, the first thing will be getting back to our wives.

So your nice beautiful weather changes quite a bit. (March 19) Well, maybe we *will* go Florida if we decide we like it warm all the time.

I'll be looking for the candy, and the fruitcake should be here pretty soon. A few more of the fellows are "sweating out" the arrival of the fruitcake and they ask at every mail call when it should be here.

Mama keeps telling me when I want anything to write for it, but there's nothing much I care for except something good to eat, but that's a lot of trouble for anyone.

So you are learning to drink beer. Say, did you ever drink a Zombie? Better wait until I get back before you try it, for only one is almost a certain derailer. Schlitz is a pretty good beer but Pabst was always about the best, I think.

Goodnight baby and I love you with all my heart.

Forever yours, / Henry

Tuesday, April 4, 1944

My only darling:—

Everything is rather quiet now and it's a good time for our little "visit." Although you are probably still working, it seems you are very near. Sometime, it will be possible for us to be together physically as well. *That* is the time I'm living for now.

. . . About the pictures I had taken. I haven't heard anything from them as yet. Honey, I know the same old story is tiresome, but I *will* send you a picture when I can.

My job consists mainly of the maintenance of, and teaching the nomenclature, employment etc., of the weapons we have.

I still have a Red Cross sweater that was given by the Pasadena chapter in California. One fellow married the girl that knitted his. Mine didn't have a name in it.

I should think you *are* pretty well disciplined, to knock on the door, wait for an answer, then be sorry to bother someone to report a fire. That's pretty good.

Darling, this is about all for now. You know how much I love you and what you mean to me. It's wonderful loving you as I do.

Goodnight my darling. Remember—

I love you, / Henry

The 291st Engineer Combat Battalion was composed of three letter companies: A, B, and C. There were three platoons in each company with a total of more than 600 officers and men in the full battalion. Each platoon had a weapons sergeant, a weapons carrier, and a four-ton troop hauling truck with a .50-caliber machine gun. As Weapons Sergeant for Company A, Sgt. Giles was responsible for the firing of the machine gun, as well as other duties described in his letter.

———

Thursday, April 6, 1944

Hello Sweetheart:—

Two wonderful letters today and one of the boxes of candy was enjoyed by the three of us. Sgt. Wall, Loftis and myself.

I am writing your Mother tonight. I still can't understand why she hasn't gotten the others I wrote. They weren't returned to me.

It looks as if we will be pretty well set up for housekeeping when I get back. That I am very grateful for, but I would have loved you just as much if it had been any way otherwise. In fact, I would have liked to have helped you to have done everything from the start, but since it makes you happy doing the things you are now, I'll love it. Everything.

I do love you my darling with all my heart, in every way, and each day you are dearer to me. Never forget that.

I'm writing in every direction tonight. Lying flat on my stomach (in my underwear) probably has something to do with it. Anyhow, I'm pretty comfortable.

Sgt. Hinkel has been in tonight, and we've been reading some comic books his wife sent. Superman, Bugs Bunny, etc. I guess I'll always like funnies. I even laugh to myself when I read some of them.

His wife must get a lot of letters from him, for everytime I see him he is writing or tells me he has just written. When we were in the same tent or room he *had* to write her darn near every night. *And,* he also had a very nice box of chocolates that were *very* good. He liked the fruitcake I had.

It's a little late, so for now—By now.

All my love always, / Henry

Sgt. Arlie Wall, 1st platoon, and Sgt. Jack Loftis, 3rd platoon were the other two Weapons Sergeants for Company A.

Sunday p.m., April 9, 1944

My only love:—

Four letters today already and that makes it a better Sunday. I slept very late today and enjoyed it tremendously.

It does hurt to have to be away so long though. What you said about the mattress and the lazy Sundays, etc. sounds wonderful and I know everything will be just as near perfect as anything has ever been. Oh Baby!

Come to think of it, I believe you are right in saying my folks weren't as set in me getting married, as they were who I might marry. I'm glad now I *thought* as I did anyhow or I probably would never have met you. After all, "Pap" and "Mom" are pretty hard to fool anyhow. In fact, I never could fool them in any way.

About the blood test we will have to have. I'll get one a few days before I'm turned loose and you can have yours too. We can almost get married the first day I'm there. I really think we can.

I agree that twin beds *are out* for us. We'll be together day *and* night.

Yes, I remember the way we held hands when we were together. I remember a lot of little things that happened.

The snapshots came back but I wouldn't even keep them myself. You will just have to wait until I'm in town in uniform. I'm tired of having to tell you that so much but it's just that way and there's nothing I can do about it.

Goodnight darling and—

I love you, / Henry

Tuesday, April 11, 1944

My only love,

A good letter today that makes everything just about right. There *is a great* difference when you hear from the one you love and everything seems brighter than when there is no letter.

There is always the sweetness of knowing you love me and you are waiting for the time when I shall come back to you. *That* makes life far easier. I know we shall be *very* happy when that time comes. And for a long, long time. Yes, always. I think *we* will get the idea rather early in the game, when we begin "showing" how we love each other.

Darling, the things we are getting and what you are doing doesn't seem as farfetched and trivial to me as you may think. In fact, they do seem very real and I shall love everything. The things you mentioned are just what I've wanted for so long. Love, home, children and all of the other little things that go to make life so beautiful. One thing we have already started. Love. That should be first and everything will follow. Seems that this is all for now darling. There's no news as usual.

So goodnight baby.

I love you, / Henry

———————————

Wednesday, April 12, 1944

My only Love:—

Tonight I'm loving you more than I had ever thought it possible to love a woman.

It's been nine months today since first we met and of course began loving each other, even if we didn't know anything about it at first. I shall never forget it. Every little thing that happened during the trip is a sweet memory.

No letter today, but I'll not say so much about that. They do mean everything to me now, since it's the next best thing to being with you. After a while, we will have each other, then everything past will be just memories.

Goodnight my love.

Yours always, / Henry

———————————

Friday, April 14, 1944

My only love:—

I hardly know how to begin this one, for today there were *nine* sweet letters from my darling!

First though, I do love you with all my heart in every possible way. One of the letters was rather amusing, for first I had read the one where you "apologized" for writing the one when you didn't feel so good. It's O.K. baby and I love you just a little bit more anyhow, for it wasn't as bad as you painted it in the next one. You were a little "bluer" at the time you wrote it. And—don't you ever write me and then destroy it and not send it to me.

We both seem to be pretty near the same when there is no letter. Just not as happy. Tonight I *am* happy, and I love you so deeply it hurts.

Sometimes I like to be read aloud to but promise I won't bother you so much. O.K.?

Today the other little box of candy arrived and the three of us enjoyed it immensely. Thanks a lot honey.

When you asked if I had a favorite comic strip, I thought of Dagwood and Blondie, even before I had finished reading the paragraph. They are my favorites too. With Popeye next.

It's late, so goodnight baby and—

All my love, / Henry

7

". . . my love for you will be my source of strength."

Saturday, April 15, 1944

My Dearest:—

After nine letters yesterday, I wasn't expecting any today, but there was one (April 6) and it makes everything better still. I love you so darling that I'm always hungry for just any word from you.

The things I spoke of once and others, do seem remote and far away. No matter how rough the storm may be, it will be your face I will see. And you will always be near me and loving me. Those things and my love for you will be my source of strength. I do love you darling, want you, and miss you so much it hurts. Never forget that.

I had a letter from Mama yesterday and she was telling of a kid getting married. When I left, she was only a kid and it does seem strange that she is old enough to marry. Well, there have been several things that have happened in nearly four years.

I'll close now baby. Don't forget—

I love you, / Henry

Sunday, April 16, 1944

My only Love:—

I've just come in. I've been out on pass and it may be the 17th by the time I finish this. I had another good letter today (April 9) and it only took seven days to get here. I also had a V-mail from Cora Mae. She said you must be a fine woman and how she liked your letters and the things you sent her.

I went to a couple of pubs, drank a little rough cider, some beer and one shot of Scotch. The last in the bottle. Then it was time to come in. Not that I think you will, but don't ever write anything about me drinking any, when you write home. It would hurt them if they knew it. O.K.? I don't drink so much. Very little compared to some fellows.

I've written too far before telling you I love you. Well I do, with all my heart. And I think of you *all* the time. You are everything to me darling, and I will always be glad I found you. Someday this mess will be over then we can *really* start our life together.

Today I met the Lt. that was platoon commander when I was platoon Sgt. in Texas. He left the outfit some few weeks before we came across. I talked to him some and we decided this must be a pretty small world after all. I was glad to see him.

This isn't a very good letter but I'm *so* sleepy I'll have to stop.

I love you baby, for keeps, and always.

                                        Forever yours, / Henry

---

                                        Thursday, April 20, 1944

Hello Baby:—

. . . O.K. since you say you will get even, *maybe* you didn't trick me into loving you. Anyhow—something made me love you. I guess it was just you. It is the most wonderful thing in the world to love you and to be loved in the same way by you.

We have discussed about everything there is and now we know each other probably better than if we could have been together three or four months. Don't you think so?

Honey, I *wish* I could have some pictures made. I've checked every studio in town on Sundays and I can't get off during the week. If I ever can, I will.

Yes, I *am* very fond of chicken. In fact, I don't know if steak runs a pretty close second or not. I do like steak quite a bit. As for ham. I like it fried, at home preferred. You should eat some of the chicken Mama can fry. We will sometime.

Oh yes, the time I wrote I was falling in love with your letters. I was, and with you also. Mostly you. I thought an answer to that might give me an idea of the way you felt. It did. I got the results I wanted, but I didn't *know* you meant it. You see, I didn't want you to *know* I loved you until I was sure you did me. Even though you didn't say it first, (or write between the lines but darn little) I knew I loved you when I wrote it and was pretty sure of an affirmative reply. You see, if it had been one-sided, I didn't want you to know it.

Now we know what love can really be and we are already having a lot of fun. And, oh yes, I will keep you warm if you get cold.

Well, this letter is a little lengthy. It's a little late and I'm pretty darn sleepy, so for this time, I'll say Cheerio Baby.

All my love and Kisses, / Henry

Friday, April 21, 1944

My own darling:—

Again there were three more letters. Of course you know the difference in moods when there is a letter and when there's not. The three today were a little late. They were written April 2 and two the third. But *any* letter is always *very* welcome and I live for them and the time I'll be coming back to you. Darling, I love you so much. Never forget that.

The pattern you chose for monogramming our linens and other things is O.K. I like it and it will look good on anything you have it on.

I don't know who is worse. You or Mama for wanting me to write for something. O.K. send me a dish of ice cream. Banana flavor with nuts. How's that?

Seriously, there are some things I would like to have. You know, just something to eat. So you can send me some candy. Nothing fancy. Something like Baby Ruth, etc. Be sure and get something with coconut in it. We get two bars each week and a pack of gum. This week, I happened to get my favorite gum. Juicy Fruit. I like gum but don't crave it so much.

Well, I guess I've done about all the damage I can in this letter so I'll close. I love you with all my heart for all time.

All my love, *always*, / Henry

Saturday, April, 22, 1944

Hello Baby:—

Today, everything went O.K. There were *six* wonderful letters! They were postmarked April 4, 4, 4, 5, 6, & 8. Darling, you are wonderful and the thrill of reading your letters is something I can't describe. Everyone, a *special* treat.

It does make us blue or pretty low when there isn't a letter for two or three days, but all told, I guess we don't do too bad. If there should be a time when I can't write as often, you must still remember that I'm loving you and thinking of you no matter where I may be. You *won't* forget that, will you Darling? And I will always know you are loving me and waiting for me.

Had a letter from home today. Mom said Kenneth was tickled over the Easter box you sent. My cousin finally wrote home. He told them of hearing from me and that he was going to see me if he could. So far, I haven't seen him.

I also had a V-mail from Irene. She was pretty blue it seemed, for Charlie had left that day. She said Kay & Shirley were "tickled crazy" over the Easter box you sent and of you she said, "She's a swell kid, we all think."

That was just like Kenneth to ask if you didn't say anything about him. I believe it was last summer when I was home, he went with me to see one of my uncles and on the way we found some huckleberries that were ripe and for thirty minutes he was telling me all about them. What color they were first and how they changed before getting ripe and where you would be more likely to find them and everything. He's some kid.

Yes, I *am* rather certain of myself once I make up my mind about something. Just for example, you *are* going to be the most perfect wife in the world. I knew what you were meaning when you wrote about it once before. In fact, I think I understand you pretty well.

I've just looked at my identification card to find out just what color eyes I *do* have. It says here, Hazel eyes, Chestnut hair. The nutty type, no doubt.

You are a sweet little girl honey and made for me to love. Which I do with all my heart. You *know* that. I do remember something of the way you looked. Even if I can't mention any one thing.

So you wonder what kind of civilian clothes I like. Well, I like sport clothes mostly. I very seldom wore a tie before I came into the Army. Guess I will quit it when I'm out too, except on some occasions. I guess the only reason I had for enlisting in the Army was that I just wanted to try something different. It was a few months before Selective Service.

Guess this is all for now. Goodnight—

with *all* my Love, / Henry

The procedure in the United States for determining who was to be drafted was called the Selective Service System. A draft was used during the Civil War and World War I. It was discontinued after the armistice in 1918 but re-instituted in the Selective Service Training and Service Act of 1940 as the first peacetime U.S. draft. The system delivered almost three million men to the service in World War I and ten million during World War II.

Henry Giles enlisted in 1939 and entered the service July 16, 1940.

Monday, April 24, 1944

My only darling:—

It's Monday again, but not so blue, as there were two loving letters from you my darling. Everything is about as bright as can be here.

. . . The two letters today were written April 9 & 13 and as I have said before, it seems every letter is just a little better. That perhaps is because I love you more all the time. I love every word you write. Of course there are things you write, that I can't say anything about when answering. You know, things like the research work you do for Dr. Sherrill, etc. But I still want you to write *everything* you can think of. Incidents such as the little boy on the bus that only asked you your name and gave you a jonquil. It's interesting, but what is there I can say about it in answering. See what I mean? Now listen baby, I don't want you to shorten a letter *one word*. I do answer everything you ask me. And I like to know what you have been doing and everything. See?

Sgt. Loftis had some letters from his wife and she was telling of one time it was two weeks between letters. He said, "I would go crazy if I ever had to wait that long." I agreed that I probably would too. It was a terrible wait when I first got here. Well, I just can't think about it. You mean more to me than I'll ever be able to tell you.

By the way, the address you sent of your mother's is the one I used and it came back. I'll try it again. Tonight. I remember now, I used Fayetteville instead of Ft. Smith.

It was just like Kenneth to think he should send you some money for the Easter candy.

Well, goodnight honey. Remember I am loving you more each day and sometime I'm coming back to you.

All my love, / Henry

Janice's sister, "Petie," lived in Fayetteville, Arkansas; her mother, in Ft. Smith.

Tuesday, April 25, 1944

My only love,

Today there were *six* loving letters and I'm just about as happy as could be. They were postmarked April 12, 16, 17, 17, 20, & 21st. Imagine it only taking four days for one to reach me. The ink was scarcely dry. Anyhow, I am very happy tonight and loving you with all my heart and wishing it were possible to hold you in my arms. Well—someday that will be so and you are going to have a hard time ever getting away from me.

Sgt. Hinkel just came in and is he crying the blues because he hasn't had a letter for three or four days. He has a way of saying things that keeps you laughing all the time.

You said when I was back with you, that you would always do everything to make me happy. Funny, but *I* have the same ideas about *you*. When you are happy, I'll be happy too. I know we shall be the happiest couple in the world.

The things Petie wrote are very nice. She must be a swell person. Very thoughtful, I know. I appreciate everything she said. As good as it sounds, it is a little too early to make a definite answer. Of course, you didn't expect that.

No my darling, you *don't* write me the "craziest letters." I've told you before that anything you write, I like it.

There you go bawling me out again for not asking for something. Well, I sent an "order" to you a couple of days ago. That should do for a while.

I had to laugh when I read of the way you said Dorothy told Lloyd how we happened to meet and "just like a bolt of lightning." That's pretty good.

I'm glad you wrote me about what Mama said of that girl at home. In the very few letters I wrote her after I met you, I didn't mention your name, but you know the old grapevine system of how everything gets around. All the time, I've been afraid that she would write you. I said "afraid." Not really of what she could write, but she had a way of being very insulting when she wanted to and I don't want you to be insulted or something, from someone like her. I probably know more about her than anyone, but it was just like Mom not to say anything "ugly about anyone," no matter what she knew. I will always be glad Mama wrote you as she did. She and Dad will never know *why* I thought they didn't want me to marry. As far as "breaking us up" is concerned, there wasn't but *darned little* to break up. Now and for all time to come I'll love only you, with all my heart. If I *never* see or hear of her again, that will be a million years too soon.

I know you believe me darling, but I wish I could write my feelings and really tell you what you are to me and how I love you. No one else will ever come between us.

I wrote your Mother last night and sent it to Ft. Smith instead of Fayetteville.

It's nine-thirty and there is still a baseball game in progress outside. I've been going out and in watching it. I like baseball. I read the standings every day in the *Stars & Stripes*. Today, the Reds are third place in the National League. I don't remember the American. When the Reds are not doing so good I don't keep up with it so well.

Goodnight darling. Remember I love you with all my heart. Only you, for always.

All my love, / Henry

Dorothy and Lloyd A. Naveaux, friends of Janice's lived across the street on Hepburn Avenue.

Wednesday, April 26, 1944

Hello Sweetheart:—

Tonight I'm missing you terribly honey and loving you with all my heart. You mean so much to me that there just aren't words to explain it. Someday though, when this waiting is over, we can *really* begin living.

I've just finished pressing Sgt. Hinkel's and my trousers. I washed a shirt and tried to press it dry, but it won't work. I'll just have to wait until it dries and then use a wet cloth on it. Be glad when I'm out of the Army, so someone else can do my laundry and pressing. Although we don't have so much of it to do—just sometimes.

Had an air mail from Mama today. She said she was always glad to hear from you and was telling of you wanting to know when Kenneth's birthday was. And again, she was wanting me to write for something. Think I'll write for some hot biscuits with butter on them.

I wrote your Mother the night before last. I think I told you that last night.

This is all for now. Goodnight my darling and don't forget—

I love you, / Henry

Friday, May 5, 1944

My only darling:

I'm still thinking of you constantly, loving you with all my heart and wishing we were together.

Darling, it's hard to be away from you for so long. But honey you must always remember that you are on my mind, no matter where I am or may be doing. You will *always* be near me.

There was a *good* letter today, as only one can be from you. Every letter is always full of love, life and plans for the future that will bring so much happiness for us and *I love every word* you write.

You can paint some *very* beautiful pictures of spring too. The dogwood and redbud in bloom and the young maple leaves.—Oh well, next year we will enjoy them together. My grandfather always talked of "dogwood winter" and another I believe was "blackberry winter."

Hope the pictures won't be too long in reaching you. After all, it has been a long time since I promised them, but they're on the way now. I'm sending Mama two, in a day or so. Sgt. Loftis got hold of the other one and I can't get it back.

You asked if I thought of you at night when I went to bed and wished we were together. Oh baby! Well, I'll show you sometime just how, why, and when I think of you. Just wait. O.K.?

I read an article in the *Stars & Stripes* today of how everyone was waiting for the man in Radio City to press a button and make the big announcement. It told of the "Invasion Jitters" that most everyone has.

Guess this is all now. I'm going to get a long night of sleep.

Goodnight baby and all my love, / Henry

Sunday, p.m., May 7, 1944

Hello Honey:—

It's a beautiful day and I've just gotten back from chow and now I feel pretty good. Had fried chicken again.

Sgt. Hinkel is in with me now and is writing to *his* wife too. He's some fellow and a swell guy.

You know, I *really* like my watch. It keeps perfect time and is admired by everyone. Thanks a million honey. It's the most useful gift I could have gotten for my birthday.

You know, sometime just before I come home, I'll have to know what size ring it will take for you. I would like to have everything ready to get married as soon as we are together. Unless you had rather be along when the rings are bought. Whatever you like and the way you want it. I've thought about it quite a lot. Well baby, this is about all for now. Remember I love you with all my heart and in every way.

All my love, / Henry

In his letter dated May 3, Henry wrote "The watch came today and it's a honey. Just what I wanted. Thanks a lot darling. You must have had to pay more than a dollar or two for a 15 jewel Swiss make."

Monday, May 8, 1944

My only darling:

It's right now midnight and I've just come in off pass, but I still have to write to my darling. Oh I miss you honey and think of you all the time. And I love you with all my heart.

Had a wonderful letter today. It's funny, but in the letter I wrote last night, I said something about the wedding ring and today in your letter *you* were talking of it. When I was on pass, I was looking at some wedding rings. They too, were narrower than I had supposed you wanted. I don't know much about what they should be priced at, but the ones I saw seemed too cheap. I believe fourteen pounds was about the highest priced ones I saw. We'll *get* what you want, but I would rather you would wait until we are together to get it. O.K.?

I read the results of the Derby today and it seems the favorite didn't show up so well.

Goodnight darling. I'm sleepy now. I love you baby and wish we were together.

All my love, / [no signature]

The 1944 winner of the seventieth running of the Kentucky Derby was Pensive, owned by Warren Wright of Calumet Farm. The jockey was Conn Mc-Creary. The favorite, Stir Up, ridden by Eddie Arcaro, placed third.

Thursday, May 11, 1944

My darling:—

It isn't really the eleventh, for it's two o'clock past midnight, but I'll still call it today. I've just gotten in and had pie and hot coffee, so I'll try to answer the *seven* letters I had today. Hope I don't get too sleepy to finish.

It's very quiet and I feel very near you. Have your pictures in front of me and I'm sure that just now you must be thinking of me. Darling, how I long to be with you. I love you so much and it's so hard being away from you so long, but it's wonderful to know that you are waiting and loving me as you are.

I've been thinking, when did I ever come in at all hours of the night and sit down and write to a girl! Never. But you are not just "a" girl. You are *the* girl and that has made several things different.

Sorry Honey, I'm just too darn sleepy to finish this letter. Will write tomorrow (or rather today) and answer the letters. Goodnight baby and remember—

I love you, / Henry

8

"There is loneliness unless there's letters."

Friday, May 12, 1944

My only darling:—

This is the twelfth and ten happy months have come and gone since first we met. Happy in every way, although there is loneliness in having to be away from you for so long. I wouldn't have missed you for the world. You are everything in the world to me and I love you so much it hurts. Oh darling, how I want to be with you.

Last night (or rather this morning) I started to answer the letters I had yesterday but got too sleepy. So—I'll try now. They are wonderful letters darling and so full of love. Love that I'm sure very few know of.

No honey, I don't think I will be a Presbyterian, but what you want to be, I consider none of my business.

I won't surprise you when I come home. You will probably know where I am all the time, from wherever I start from, to Louisville. If there are layovers, I'll call you. Funny how we think of everything like that, but we do.

I remember the first "in between" letter you wrote me. Kind of a surprise, but I *did* like it. And I still love everyone you write, *every word*. I shall never tire of you telling me you love me for that is exactly what I want to hear. Often. And I think we do a pretty good job telling each other.

So you won't send me a dish of ice cream. I think you could have frozen it hard enough to send it over here without melting. According to the atmosphere when you wrote about it. Rather frigid.

What you wrote of the fellow who came back with his arms off and the reception his wife gave him really makes your blood boil. I would like to name the punishment for someone like that.

In one of the letters you said I should soon be getting my watch. I believe that was the day I got it (May 3) and it *is* what I wanted.

So—you call a V-mail a lazy man's letter. Well, whoever started that probably doesn't know what it is to be rushed or not have the time you may want or need. *I* think they are pretty handy.

Well honey, this is about all for now. No news. You know I love you with all my heart.

Goodnight my darling and—

all my love, / Henry

Sunday, May 14, 1944

My only Love:—

It's a beautiful Sunday and I'm outside writing and wishing we were together. Bet we could think of a lot to do and maybe do a lot. Think so?

We're only having two meals today. The one at ten, I've already had (I slept up to then) and we have chicken at four. I'll like that.

A good letter today. And one from Mama with ten air mail stamps, so I'm pretty well fixed now.

. . . Try not to let the word "invasion" get you down. Wait until it starts anyhow, before worrying. Possibly it won't be as rough as everyone thinks.

I'll be looking for the candy and I'm sure it will be good.

Well honey, this is about all. Remember I love you with all my heart in every way.

All my Love always, / Henry

Wednesday, May 17, 1944

My only darling:—

. . . Had a letter from Irene today and she says Charlie is terribly homesick. She also said she had a letter from you. Here's what she said: "I think she is a swell person. I know we all like her. I'll be so glad when you can come home so you two can be married." How's that? Everyone doesn't only "approve" of us but they are anxious for us to be married. Well, that's good, but I would have loved you just as much and as deeply, if it had been otherwise.

Yes, I read of the Derby in the *Stars & Stripes*. I would like to see it sometime, although I don't know anything about horse racing. I agree that everything will seem unimportant when we can just be together. And we won't need anything more to make us happy. Oh, it *will* be wonderful darling.

Say, you're pretty good at "sounding off" when you don't like something. Such as too many V-mails mostly. You leave nothing to the imagination. Come to think of it, I believe I *will* use air mail from here on.

Honey, you are the best in the world at painting mental pictures. I'm referring to what you said you were thinking while in bed one Sunday morning. (May 7) It was beautiful. I too, had thought City Hall would be the first place we would go. Maybe we *will* stay at home the first night or so.

Don't ever expect me to write for money. *That* would be the last straw. And now we aren't allowed to write home for money anyhow.

Oh my back! Here's some more about V-mail. Well—I've said enough about that already. By now you should have the pictures I sent. They were mailed around the fourth or fifth. As rough as it was, it *was* made for you. If I had had the "hash mark" or shoulder insignia showing, I couldn't have sent it.

Well honey, it's rather late, so for now, I better say goodnight. So—I'll see you in my dreams.

Goodnight Sweetheart and—

All my love, / Henry

Monday, May 22, 1944

My only darling:—

Today there were two sweet letters that I needed pretty bad, and even before reading one I always know that everything is going to be a lot better, for you always write just the things I like most. There's never the fear that you may have changed or something, for our love is too deep for either of us to do that.

You mentioned what I said of wishing we were in position that I could show you how much I love you. After I already had it written I noticed it, but thought you would know what I had in mind first. You did, and also the second, and that isn't such a bad thought in itself, I agree. And I *do* like you being realistic. You are a sweet little girl honey and we are going to have a *lot* of fun.

Yes, if you can get a picture of your family, send it along. And, oh yes, I have to laugh everytime I read what you said everyone had said of the picture I sent. Imagine there being something sweet about me. The ribbon you don't know is for service before Pearl Harbor.

By the way, Sgt. Wall and I went home with a fellow yesterday (yes, from the Pub) and stayed two or three hours. There were he, his wife and another gentleman. He had a phonograph and some pretty good music. You should have seen me in a dress uniform the older fellow had worn a few years ago as an expert rifleman. It was a little tight on me but Wall fit it exactly. There must have been a hundred buttons in the front. He said the last time he wore it, was in escorting some queen through some city. The whole thing was red and white, with a little yellow. The hat was a killer. They had a piano but no player. When we were ready to leave, they gave us a "spot" of tea and sandwiches and wanted us to come back.

Well baby, it looks like this is all for tonight.

You know how I love you. So much that words won't express it. Goodnight Sweetheart.

All my love, / Henry

Thursday, May 25, 1944

My only darling:—

There was a letter today. A *good* one (as they all are) written May 15 p.m. You said you couldn't write the night before, but I've already had the one written on that Sunday afternoon. It's alright honey. I love you just as much and as deeply. Those days are bound to come when either of us may not be able to write. You *have* done a wonderful job writing. I remember thinking to myself and wondering if one *could* write every day, when you said you would. I've since been convinced that it can be done and *you* have done it. Yes, every day for a long time. And you haven't missed *once* as yet.

By the way. Do you remember the bet I made with you as we left Nashville? When you called it, I backed out. I suppose we both remember most everything that happened though. The bus driver asked me as I got off in Memphis, "Did you and your wife make it alright?" Well we *did* fool some of the people anyhow, but little did we think that some day we actually *would* be husband and wife.

Well darling, I'd better stop here and get a little sleep. Remember I'm thinking of you and loving you with all my heart.

All my love, / Henry

Monday May 28, 1944

Darling,

. . . It has been a lovely day and I'm outside with my shirt off and *really* comfortable. It's about nine-thirty.

You told of a beautiful wedding you saw and then you mentioned what *we* wanted. I too, am glad that we both want the same thing. Just the two of us and whoever we need as witnesses. It's going to be wonderful. And with the love we have, I know we will be the happiest two people in the world.

Yes, the place you spoke of in Indiana sounds awfully good. Well, we both want the same thing and I believe you can do a good job finding it. O.K.? It *will* be perfect when we can be together. Alone—in a world of our own. With you in my arms. Oh darling, it's hard to wait so long, but one day—it will happen.

I had a letter from Mama today. She said that the pictures I sent her had reached there. And she told me about hearing from you again.

Went to town awhile today but came in early. This is about all for now honey.

I love you with all my heart in every way.

All my love, / Henry

"The place in Indiana" was Spring Mill State Park. Established in 1927, it contained 1,319 acres in the southern Indiana hills. The park provided a swimming lake, beach house, small caves to tour, a restored pioneer village of log structures, an operating grist mill, and hiking trails. In 1939, a 75-room inn, built of native limestone, was opened for tourists.

Tuesday, June 6, 1944

Hello Sweetheart:—

. . . I'll not say anything concerning the events of today, for you probably know more about it than I do. Anyhow—I'm O.K. darling and *don't* worry.

Guess I'll write home tonight too. You know, just to keep up the home front morale. I think I've started in the month of May again. In the letters I've written you this month I believe I've used May instead of June in some of them. [*Just this one was dated May*]. But it means all the same, for what I try to tell you most is how I love you. And as much as I've tried to, I've never expressed to you just what you mean to me. I do love you darling and you are everything in the world to me.

Oh yes, there were two letters today too. Sweet ones, but you were a little blue because of not having any letters. I know the feeling perfectly well. There is loneliness unless there's letters. You can be sure darling that they are coming. As long as I can, I'll write every day.

The candy is gone now. It was in good condition too, when it reached me. I told you I got the cookies. I'm not so sure I said anything about the silverware. The pattern you suggested is O.K.

Well goodnight baby. Think I'll go to a movie and it's nearly time. Remember I love you. Now and for always.

Forever yours, / Henry

During the last week of May 1944, the Allied High Command prohibited travel between England and Ireland and halted mail from American servicemen to the United States to prevent security leaks of military information to enemy agents.

"The events of today" referred to the invasion, or D-Day, under the command of General Dwight D. Eisenhower. Planned for June 5, but postponed due to extreme weather conditions, Allied naval and air forces landed troops on the northern coast of France on Tuesday, June 6, 1944.

Eisenhower told his men: "You are about to embark upon a great crusade"—a crusade that assembled men, munitions, and supplies on a monumental scale and deposited them on the five invasion beaches along the northern coast of France. The first troops waded ashore through the murky predawn hours supported by 5,300 ships and smaller landing vessels, and 12,000 aircraft.

At home, President Roosevelt spoke to the American people from the White House and prayed: "Almighty God, our sons, pride of our Nation, this day have set upon a mighty endeavor, a struggle to preserve our Republic, our religion, and our civilization and to set free a suffering humanity."

The following letter is the second one from Bessie Giles that Janice saved; it was written the day after the invasion.

Wednesday, June 7, 1944

Dear Janice:

Your letter came today but I was not surprised to hear from you. I just thought I would hear and was glad to hear from you. Yes, it was one of the terriblest days yesterday I ever spent and I don't feel much better today.

I was getting breakfast and Frank, as he always does, got up and turned on the radio and I kept thinking the news went different but couldn't understand, so stood in the kitchen and was afraid to go in and listen or ask anything. I sat down twice to eat a little bite and yet hadn't called any of them to breakfast. I just got up and went to milk and came back in before anything was said.

It just looked like I couldn't stand it but maybe we shouldn't feel like that as long as there's nothing worse. I'm just trusting in God to take me through this and to take care of Henry. We know there will be many come back and many that won't.

Yes, I'm just so glad to be in touch with you and to hear from you often. You feel near to me since we have been writing and if I should hear anything, I will let you know at once. Henry always says something about you in every letter.

I have been looking over his letters today. The last one I got, he said he had a fine long letter from you that day and asked me to send him some more razor blades and shaving cream and I got them started just as quick as I could.

I have heard them tell twice about the American engineers running bulldozers over the battlefields but they were heavily guarded. Maybe Henry has not gone over there yet. There's lots of Engineers.

Janice, you must eat every bit you can, not try to work and not eat. I don't want anything to eat but I just try to eat anyway. I'm so bad to get nervous. I'll be so glad when we can hear from Henry again and when we can get a letter dated after the invasion started.

I know you hate for your Mother to go back. I sure wish she could have stayed with you awhile. But I'm glad she's been with you at this time.

I guess this is all for now. Write anytime you can and we must make the best of it we can.

Love from / Bessie

Thursday, June 8, 1944

Hello Sweetheart:

Another day has come and almost gone, that (in a small way perhaps) brings us closer to the time that we will be together again.

I love my darling, and I've thought of you many, *many* times in the last few days. Knowing that you *are* worrying now and there's nothing I can do about it. I only wish there was something I could do, but I guess all there is, is just for me to keep writing and eventually you will get them.

There was a very sweet letter today, written May 29, and you still hadn't had any letters for a week and as a result you were pretty blue.

Honey, I'm sure we'll get along O.K. as far as housecleaning is concerned. On Saturday's inspections, I may "gig" you once in a while, but not every week. How's that?

I've been playing ball this afternoon. Volleyball. I don't like softball, but volleyball, I could play all day. Maybe sometime we'll have a team of our own when our kids are old enough. Of course, that is only a—shall we say, postwar plan. But it only takes twelve to play. We'll think of that later.

It's been some time now since I wrote your Mother. Surely the last one I wrote reached her.

Darling, I know you are loving me, just as I am you and there's never a doubt but that you are waiting in just the way I always thought a woman should and I love you *so* much darling.

Goodnight honey. I'm going to bed now. A little early tonight.

All my love for always, / Henry

Saturday, June 10, 1944

My only darling:—

There were three loving letters tonight, which I was very glad to get. Two you had written as you were waiting for your Mother.

I love you honey. More each day, and I hope it won't be so many more days until I can come back to you. You mentioned that your Mother called you from Nashville and that the name brought back pleasant memories. It does. And *very* sweet ones too.

You did a very good job accounting for everything that happened there, although I don't recall the shoes you mentioned. The steaks were good. I remember that very well. I don't think the trip standing was any more tiresome for me than you. Oh, it was fun and the beginning of something very wonderful and sweet.

Had a letter from Mama today and somewhere, someone had "lipsticked" a kiss on the back of the envelope. It wasn't Mama for she never used it. If who ever did it ever knows what I said about it, there won't be such a laugh, if it was meant for some type of joke.

The letter written the third, after the false alarm, sounded as if you were a little scared. Don't be darling. I'll be alright. I felt the same as you about it being a mistake.

Goodnight darling and you will remember that I'm loving you with all my heart—

Always, / Henry

On June 3, 1944, Joan Ellis, a young British Associated Press teletype operator practicing on a teletype machine, punched in an erroneous announcement that the Allies had landed in France. The flash appeared on the AP's direct London printer in New York and was distributed around the world.

Less than two minutes later, a message from London, "Bust the Flash," was transmitted but not before the report was broadcast throughout the United States. NBC, CBS, Blue Network, and Mutual all interrupted programs to carry news of the invasion. When the announcement was made over the public address system, baseball fans in New York stood and observed a minute's silence. Newspaper and radio stations were flooded with inquiries.

Tuesday, June 6, 1944, the *Louisville Courier-Journal* published the actual happening in a three inch headline on the front page: FRANCE INVADED.

Thursday, June 15, 1944

My only love:

I've just been to a little church service and now it's time to write. . . . Today there were three letters. The two written D-Day, and one the seventh. Wonderful letters darling, but it hurts to know how you must be worrying and the strain you are under-going and there's so little that I can do about it. I can keep on writ-ing as often as I can, and you will know that I love you and that regardless of the situation, I will be thinking of you and you will be with me. I know that.

Our love is the most wonderful thing I've ever known, but I agree that it doesn't guarantee complete happiness.

Was with Sgt. Hinkel awhile ago. He told me that today is his wedding anniversary.

Listen baby. No more "cracks" like the one in which you said I would be "terribly ashamed" of you on a farm for you "would be so dumb." *You* will "do alright" any place. I know you do O.K. on a bus. And I am reasonably sure you will do alright in,—shall we say, a—bedroom. Anyhow, we will try it someday. (Or night). How about that? Guess my mind is wandering some tonight but it isn't too strange for a man to think of things like that.

In your letter written the seventh, you were a bit more cheer-ful. Maybe by now you have had some of my letters. They should help too.

Well, it seems I've run out of anything more to write so will have to say goodnight Sweetheart.

All my love *always*, / Henry

Friday, June 16, 1944

My only darling:—

There was no letter today, but I shouldn't gripe, because I've been doing pretty good lately. Always though, it's better when there is one since that is the only way we can "visit" now.

I'll be glad when I get your next letter saying you have heard from me. I know it must be just plain hell, sweating it out as you are.

I haven't heard from home since D-Day, but I should soon. And that reminds me that I must write home. Tonight. I think I shall write your Mother right away too, even if I don't get her letter.

Today, I have forty-seven months in the army. Eleven more than I bargained for. But I would never have met you if I had gotten out on schedule. Well, sometime we will be able to forget all the dark spots there have been and begin life anew. *That* is worth fighting for.

Well honey, it seems there is no more to write. So goodnight darling.

All my love, / Henry

On Wednesday, June 21, Company A boarded a transport ship to sail from Carentan to Omaha Beach in France. Storms delayed their departure and docking. They arrived on June 23, Henry's twenty-eighth birthday. Although it had been over two weeks since the invasion, the aftermath of those devastating days was a living hell to see. The beach remained littered with burned out vehicles, abandoned equipment, and supplies. These sights were a reminder of the high rate of casualties among those who had fought savagely to secure the beachhead.

Company A traveled inland, unloaded, and began digging the first of many foxholes and trenches. Henry's responsibility was to see that all the machine guns were kept clean and in firing order. The 2nd platoon had a .30-caliber machine gun for each squad and one .50-caliber which Henry operated.

The 291st reassembled at Vierville to begin their first wartime mission. They were to help maintain a thirty-mile heavily traveled main supply road between Carentan and Ste.-Mère-Eglise. Company A was in charge of the first ten-mile stretch, which included Tucker Bridge; Company B, the center; and Company C, the last ten miles. As they worked, the soldiers were subject to constant bombing raids and heavy German artillery fire.

9

"Somewhere in France"

Sunday, June 25, 1944
Somewhere in France

My only love:—

I love you my darling and I've been thinking of you even if I have been unable to write for a few days.

I'm in France now, but don't worry honey, for I don't think the bullet has been made with my name on it, and I'm not worried about those addressed "to whom it may concern," and since my name isn't Smith or Jones, there shouldn't be any mix-up there. So—just take it easy. I'll be back and I'll be thinking of you every day and loving you with all my heart, until the day that we can be together again. Then we will know the real happiness that we have wanted so long.

I'll write as often as I can. I didn't have time to answer the last letters I had from you. I also received the birthday cards from you and your Mother. I'll write her as soon as I can.

In your last letter you asked if I knew what it was like to go eighteen days without a letter. Not as well as you I'm sure. I always know (or I'm reasonably sure) that everything is still alright, while you have to guess.

I'm sure you will suit me, too, even if you should "sound off" occasionally. Yes darling, you are just as I want you to be. Guess I'll have to write home tonight too.

There's not a hell of a lot to write about France. I wouldn't like it in peacetime. Their language is all Greek to me. In fact, everything is just plain "Snaffer."

I'll close now honey and write again as soon as I can. Remember, I love you with all my heart.

Always, / Henry

"Snafu" is military slang for confusion.

Friday, June 30, 1944

Hello darling:—

Yesterday, after writing you, the mail came through and there were *ten* letters from you and two from Mama. Darling, I can't tell you how thrilled I am to get the letters after the few days without them. I love you honey, with all my heart and in every way there is to love a woman.

Yes, I hope you and Mama are doing a good job cheering each other up. Anyhow, take it as easy as you can and I'll be back.

I'm looking forward to the cookies and as much as I love you, I still wouldn't want you to be here, even if you could "tuck" yourself in the box and come along. After the war we will open a new front ourselves. It may be a "blitz" (for a short time anyhow). What do you think!

I'm pretty well fixed for postage stamps now. I got the ones you sent, and Mama sent some too. In all, I have about fifty. Pretty good.

Darling, I'm doing a bad job trying to answer all the letters at once. They are sweet though and mean everything in the world to me. By now you should have one written after D-Day.

No darling, there isn't a chance that I will ever write saying that I have found someone else, or that I think I have made a mistake. I've not been looking for anyone and I'm fully convinced that I've not made a mistake. I'll love you always. Just you.

Honey, I've tried to answer five of the letters. It's late and I'm *so* sleepy. Goodnight darling.

All my love, / Henry

Saturday, July 1, 1944

Hello Sweetheart:—

It's almost a year now since first we met, and started loving each other. Little did I know a year ago now, as I was on my way home, that I would find the girl of my dreams. The one that is everything that a girl should be.

. . . Oh yes, I still have some letters to answer. In one, you were speaking of the things we may say first when I get back. And maybe you have something when you said we *could* spend two or three nights (and of course the days too) at home and begin catching up on some of the things we have been missing so long. Including our talking. Regardless of where we may be, everything is going to be perfect. There will be a lot to do but we will have the time to do it *when* we want. We'll go to Arkansas when you want to.

Goodnight honey. I must get some sleep.

All my love—always, / Henry

Monday, July 3, 1944

My only love:—

. . . Loving you is the most wonderful thing I have ever known and knowing you love me in the same way makes everything perfect.

By the way, I saw Generals Eisenhower and Bradley today. Just a fleeting glance of course, as they passed. I was so busy trying to execute my best salute when I saw the four stars, that I didn't have time to get a very good look.

The mosquitoes here are almost as large as blackbirds and since I've been writing this they have been flying in formation and strafing me something terrible.

If you were *here* I'll bet you wouldn't be sitting around with just a pair of shorts and a (have to see how you spell it) brassiere on. And if *I* was there you wouldn't either. Fresh, eh? Well, I don't know of anything better I could be thinking of.

Say, what breed of mice do you have in Louisville anyhow? The one before was using an electric iron I believe, and this one, typing. Rather unusual for mice, but when I come back, along with everything else, I'll also keep the big bad creatures away from you, if I have to get you a shotgun.

I had a letter from Mama and I had better answer her's tonight too. I wrote to Robert a few days ago.

Guess I'll say goodnight now honey. Remember, I love you with all my heart in every way.

All my love always, / Henry

Tuesday, July 4, 1944

Hello Baby:—

There were three *good* letters today. Just the type that always gives a lift, despite the fact that you still hadn't heard from me since D-Day, and you were still somewhat anxious.

Try not to worry honey for I'll be alright and I'll be thinking of you constantly and loving you with all my heart. You won't forget that, will you? I know you won't and you will never be far from me. Sgt. Hinkel said his wife had gotten the letter you wrote. He and I are rooming together—in a pup tent.

About eight or nine of us got our picture taken today by a correspondent. I don't know for what new service and if it will even be printed or not. He saw us with some white straw hats on that we had found and thought it would be a good picture.

By the way honey, if you should go to Arkansas for your vacation, don't get too friendly with anyone who may suggest riding with you. I'm only kidding baby. I know better than that.

It's so dark, I'll have to stop. Will write more tomorrow.

All my love—always, / Henry

The Associated Press Wirephoto appeared on the front page of the *Courier Journal*, Louisville, Kentucky, July 13, 1944.

S/Sgt. Paul J. Hinkel was wounded on July 9 by incoming artillery fire at Tucker Bridge. He was taken to a hospital and sent word for Henry to take care of his belongings until his return.

Monday, July 10, 1944

Hello Sweetheart:—

. . . There is lovely music coming from another field nearby and it kind of makes me lonely. Beautiful but it seems to do something to you. No letter again today, darn it, but there should be a stack of them when they do come through.

I've just been eating some very good steak that we bought at a meat market and fried ourselves in our mess kits.

Once again, let me remind you not to worry about me for I'm O.K.

Goodnight my darling and remember that I love you with all my heart for always.

All my love, / Henry

Tuesday, July 11, 1944

Hello Sweetheart:

Early mail call today and there were three loving letters. I also got the cigarettes Mama sent sometime in May. Two cartons of Luckies and I already had nearly two cartons, so I'll not be short on cigarettes for a long time. Mama had "accidentally" wrapped them in some paper that you had sent something home in.

Oh, I love you darling and the letters today are about the sweetest you have ever written. Of course, all of them are *good* but these weren't so tense. It is good to have them. I suppose by now you are "sweating out" my leaving England. Well, one day it will all be over and all these long days and nights of waiting and anxiety will be over. By next year at this time, perhaps our dreams will be realized.

No, I don't suppose our honeymoon will be of any unusual length of time. Anyhow, I'll bet they won't be thinking, "why don't we do this more often?" Remember? I've never tried it, but come to think of it, maybe I could make it a little interesting in a pup tent with the right type of bunk mate.

Yes, if you have one, send me a picture. The ones I have are O.K. but a new one wouldn't hurt a thing.

I was only kidding about you "sounding off." I think you know that by now. And believe me honey, you have *never* touched a sore spot. There aren't any. I have never been provoked in the least, at anything you have written.

Well, cheerio Sweetheart and remember—

I love you, / Henry

Thursday, July 12, 1944

Hello my darling:—

Yes, one year ago it started. Loving you. In a small way at first, of course, but in a year, that love has grown very deep, and bigger each day. And the beautiful part is knowing you love me in just the same way.

So, the fellows say you might as well have married me before I left, since you are so much "out of circulation" anyhow. That in itself makes me feel awful proud. Honey, I too, have wished many times that we could have been married. I haven't received the letter that you said something about being married in Fayetteville.

I had a letter from Mom and Robert last night too, and Mama sent me Charlie's address. I'll write him in a day or so and if *he* doesn't answer, I swear I'll never write to anymore relatives or fellows I know.

Wish I could fly over sometime when you only have about two garments on. (Wonder where Superman could be?) I agree that the temperature won't matter. I'll probably soon get use to a bed and to sleeping with someone.

It's so dark, I'll have to stop here. Goodnight baby and—

All my love, / Henry

Sunday, July 16, 1944

My only love:

For two days, I haven't written. Sorry honey, but it couldn't be helped. I've been thinking of you all the same and loving you with all my heart.

There were three letters, written June 24 & 25. A little late, but sweet and *very* welcome. *Any* letter from you honey is always good even if they are late. I'm glad you did keep writing when you weren't getting any letters from me. Of course, it never occurred to me that you might not write. I *knew* you would.

No, Sgt. Hinkel isn't a father. I guess his wife is just hoping.

I have already had the letter in which you said to forget about the idea of being married in Fayetteville, so I guess there's nothing to say about it.

Today, during lunch hour, I went into a big church. It must be a very old one, but inside it was still beautiful except for quite a bit of dust. There were several altars (I guess they were) and a lot of statues. Must be a Catholic Church.

I'll be glad when I hear from you saying you've had some of my letters from France.

Goodnight my darling. Remember, I love you.

All my love always, / Henry

Monday, July 17, 1944

Hello darling:—

Another day almost gone that has brought us one day closer together. I love you honey and I'm longing for the time that will mean no more parting for us. Just to be near you all the time will be the most wonderful thing in the world.

I believe it was in *Yank*, I read an article called "Morale Booster." It was a collection of letters that men in service had received from their wives and girl friends. One woman had written her husband and told him not to worry about her being true, she only went out with servicemen anymore. Only the night before, she had been out with two soldiers and a marine Sgt. She said, "We drank until my knees were a little wobbly, then they brought me home and out on the back porch they took turns with me— dancing." The Sgt. says tell you not to worry. The situation is well in hand.

It was funny to read such as that, but there would be nothing funny about actually having letters like that. But I know every time, before opening one of your letters, that it is going to be a very sweet one, always full of love, the type that makes a man proud of his one and only. Until I get back, your letters are going to be the most wonderful thing in the world. Darling, I love you so much.

Yesterday, I had four years in the Army. I hope by the time another year rolls around I will have been home, with you, for quite sometime.

Well goodnight baby. You will remember how I love you, won't you?

All my love—always, / Henry

In *First Across the Rhine*, Col. David E. Pergrin, commander of the 291st, wrote: "Beginning July 18, [1944] the engineer missions of the 291st were many and varied. They included clearing minefields, building bypasses around blown bridges, operating quarries, filling craters in the roads, and patching road surfaces. We were tasked with removing American bodies from the battlefield as well. The fields were also strewn with German bodies, but we avoided them out of reasonable concern over booby traps. The men of the 291st were now seeing war at its worst"

Saturday, July 22, 1944

My only love:—

Today, there were two letters and that makes everything a lot better and of course, me a lot happier. I have no doubt but that I get the sweetest letters of anyone. Always so full of love and cheerfulness.

Yes, of course, when I'm within five miles of Louisville, it will seem like ages until I get there, the last five minutes, etc. If I remember right, we were very well acquainted in the first five hours. Weren't we?

I've just been reading about the invasion in the *New York Daily News*. A fellow found a paper printed in Russell, Kentucky and gave it to me and I've read that too. A little old, but it was something to read. It was dated May 29.

I'm going to make a little request here. (*Don't* laugh). Send me some comic books. (That's right, *comic books*.) I like to read them and everyone else does. Not so many, and most any kind will do.

Well goodnight darling. I love you with all my heart, in every way there is to love a woman.

Always yours, / Henry

P.S. I couldn't write you yesterday. Sorry I couldn't. H

Monday, July 24, 1944

Darling:

Just about time for a V-mail tonight. There was no letter today, but I love you just the same, and with all my heart very desperately, and I know the letters *are* on the way.

I wrote to your Mother last night. There wasn't much to say, but I managed to use one V-mail sheet.

I'll be darn glad when this war is over. I want to come home to you darling. I think of you so much and miss you terribly. Well,

Adolf will get it in the end, and I'll bet he will wish he had never heard of war.

Goodnight honey. Keep remembering I love you in every way—*only* you.

All my love, / Henry

———————————

Thursday, July 27 (I think), 1944

Hello Sweetheart:—

I'll start writing earlier and perhaps I'll be able to finish. I love you darling—one more day than yesterday—and I'm terribly lonely for you.

One day this eternal waiting will be over, and then we shall know the fullness of our love. Although I'm sure there has never been a more perfect love than our's this far.

There were *four* wonderful letters today, and that makes everything better. I had to laugh at what you said about having to hold my hands—Well, if you had been any other way, I probably would be just remembering you now as some woman I rode with on a bus, and you would have forgotten it now. But—you were just what a woman had to be. Sweet and lovely. I don't remember the men passing so close to us.

I was a little surprised at you going home for a few days of your vacation, but darn glad you are (or *did*, it will be when you get this). Wish to hell you had made up your mind sooner, I could have given you a few pointers, since you are going to be too modest (or something) to even smoke at home. I believe Cora Mae would have been a real pal to you, and if she is like the rest of the girls were at her age, would have helped you "sneaked" an occasional cigarette *and* had one with you. I'm anxious to know what you think of my neck of the woods.

Here's hoping you all the fun in the world on your vacation. Remember, I love you with all my heart, always.

My love forever, / Henry

Henry's folks had written and invited Janice to visit them at their home in Adair County, Kentucky. She traveled by bus from Louisville to Campbellsville where she was met by Henry's sister Irene. His parents paid a friend one dollar to transport Janice the remaining twenty miles by car to Knifley.

Monday, July 31, 1944

Hello darling:—

I've missed two days writing, but it couldn't be helped. Saturday, there were four wonderful letters that I will answer now.

First, I love you darling. With all my heart and for always. And the quickest way back to you is too darn slow. But I'll be back.

You were wondering what I was doing the Sunday you wrote one of the letters (July 9). Well, unless I hear someone say it is Sunday, I can't tell it from any other day. They're all alike.

No honey, it never occurs to me anymore to tell you to wait for me. I know you are. Just the way any man would want his one and only to wait. I too, think we will get to keep our wedding date and before April. As far as going to another theater after this one, I've never worried about it or thought of it much.

You must know by now that it was my mug you saw in the *Courier-Journal*. I wrote you about it the day the picture was taken. I got a V-mail from Mama yesterday and she was all excited over it. She said everyone knew my picture. Well, I guess I just look like that anywhere. I've already seen the picture. The fellow on the extreme left got one from home, New York.

Well honey, guess I'll stop here. Remember I'm loving you with all my heart, always.

All my love, / Henry

Wednesday, August 2, 1944

My only darling:—

Tonight, I'm thinking of you, as usual, and wishing it were possible to be with you. I love you more every day honey, and long desperately just to be near you.

Guess what—I saw Sammie today. (That's my cousin.) I first saw a truck from his outfit and asked the driver if he knew him. He knew him well, and said he would bring him out to see me in the afternoon. We were together for about an hour and a half, and talked of about everything we could think of in that time. Of course, I told him of you and that we were to be married, etc. He isn't exactly the kid I saw him as last. Nothing wrong, of course, but twenty months of overseas duty has aged him quite a bit.

There are four or five other fellows in his outfit that I've known all my life and I've already been told that I can go see them tomorrow and spend the day, or most of it, with them.

I honestly don't think I was ever so glad to see anyone as I was him today. Said he unloaded a truck all by himself so they could get started as soon as possible.

Wish I was with you tonight darling. You must be at home by now. Well—we will be together before so long perhaps. And the quickest way is too darn slow.

Guess I'll stop here. I'm pretty sleepy. So—goodnight darling and—

All my love, / Henry

Sammie Giles, Henry's first cousin, was also from Knifley, Kentucky.

Sgt. Henry Giles,
Gloucester, England,
May 5, 1944.

Janice Holt Moore,
Christmas 1943.

Above, the Greyhound station in Bowling Green, Kentucky, as it appeared in July 1943, when Henry Giles boarded a bus and sat down beside Janice Moore. Below and right, when Janice and Henry returned to the bus station in Nashville following their dinner together, there was such a crowd Janice thought she would have to return to Louisville. In spite of the priority of "Service men first," Henry promised her she would have a seat. He put her on a special soldier's bus and posed her as his wife.

Janice Moore moved with her daughter, Libby, to 1437 Hepburn Avenue, Louisville, in August 1941. Their upstairs apartment was in the back part of the dwelling.

In the letter she dictated on October 8, 1943, Janice describes the locket she is wearing, which Henry had sent to her. A tiny castle, the Engineer's insignia, is centered on the mother-of-pearl inset. Christmas 1944.

"The Moore gals" in the side yard at 1437 Hepburn Avenue, Easter 1944.

Married only a few weeks, 1/Lt. Nash Hancock and his bride, Libby, visited his family on their farm in Finchville, Kentucky, just before he was shipped overseas. August 1944.

Sgt. Henry E. Giles, Camp Swift, Texas. This photograph is dated August 1943 and is believed to be the "cartoon" of himself that Henry mentioned enclosing in his letter of August 30, 1943.

An Associated Press photo of a group of American engineers in Carentan, France, on the 4th of July, 1944. It appeared in the *Louisville Courier-Journal* on July 13. Henry is on the extreme right.

Henry and Janice a few days after their wedding, with his mother, Bessie, in Knifley, Kentucky, October 1945.

Henry and his brother Robert, October 1945. Henry is playing the mandolin he sent home from Europe.

Above, Janice holds
her first grandchild,
Bartlett Neal Hancock.
Also pictured are
Great-grandmother Lucy
McGraw Holt, Libby,
and Henry. Louisville,
October 1948.

Henry and Janice view
her first book, *The
Enduring Hills*, displayed
in W. K. Stewart's
department store
window in Louisville,
April 1950.

10

"Another day, and another letter to you."

Hello Sweetheart:—

Another day, and another letter to you. I'm always anxious to get started on your letter. It's like being with you for awhile. I love you honey, in more ways than I know how to tell you. Very deeply and *for always.*

I've been to see Sammie today, and I saw five or six other fellows I knew at home. Was with them for about five hours. We talked about everything we knew of. Ate chow with them, and one fellow who was from Wisconsin asked Sammie who I was. After telling him, we talked for awhile and when I left he gave me a carton of Lucky Strike greens.

I showed Sammie your picture and of course told him some more about us and he read our engagement announcement. He showed me a picture of a girl he used to go with in Louisville. Evidently, he thought quite a lot of her, for he said she was the finest and nicest girl he ever knew. But said not knowing if he would ever get back or not, he never answered any of her letters after he came across. Said he was going to see her if he did get back. I saw a letter with her name and address on it but all I remember was, her last name was Fraser and I believe, Fourth Street. A redhead. You probably never heard of her.

Well, so much for that. You are at home tonight if everything went as you had planned. I wrote home tonight and told them I was anxious to get the "reports" of your visit, from you, and from home.

Of course, I wish I was with you. I'm sure we could think of something interesting (and amusing) to do. Don't you?

Goodnight my darling. I'm thinking of you constantly and loving you more every day.

All my love, / Henry

Saturday, August 5, 1944

Hello Baby:—

Another day that has ended O.K. for there were two letters. Sweet ones as usual and I had one from home and one from Irene.

. . . Mama said that if Charlie was where he thought he was going, it would take 32 days to get there. I wrote him a few days ago telling him how lucky he was to stay in the U.S. I certainly wish he could have stayed in the states. But that's war, and part of the hell Sherman must have meant.

I'm still laughing at Dagwood. I think he gets better all the time. Especially when he's a little mixed up, like when he wanted his shoes scrambled on toast and his eggs half-soled with rubber heels. After Blondie told him he was taller than her when he was standing on a ladder, it soon occurred to him that he would also be shorter than her if he was standing in a hole. Well, so much for the funnies. I really get a kick out of them.

Oh yes, I like most any kind of meat, but I don't think anything can beat fried chicken. At home, we usually ate chicken (or most any meat) for breakfast with hot biscuits and gravy. Say—I'm getting hungry!

As soon as I can find something suitable, I'll send you something and Petie too. I guess the trouble with me is, when I start looking for something, nothing seems good enough.

The other day I was reading in the *Stars & Stripes* (evidently a few days old) of the capture of a town and when I finished, I looked up and we were riding into the town.

Let's see—I should get that new picture sometime next week. I'll be looking for it. You didn't say if the poem you sent was a song or not. If it isn't, it should be. It's beautiful.

Goodnight Sweetheart.

All my love, / Henry

On August 11, 1880, William Tecumseh Sherman, Union general of the Civil War, stated, "There is many a boy here today who looks on war as all glory but boys it is all hell."

Monday, August 7, 1944

Hello Sweetheart:—

Couldn't write you yesterday, but I had a very sweet letter, that I will answer now.

I love you darling with all my heart, and every day you grow dearer to me. Perhaps before so long there won't be an ocean between us. I'm more anxious every day to keep a wedding date I have with the most perfect girl in the world.

Today, I was taking a bath (in my helmet) and was just in a big way washing myself, when about fifty feet away, two women were walking by just looking at me and apparently carrying on with whatever they were talking about. My first impulse was to jump in my tent (or crawl as it were) which I shouldn't have done, for it was then they must have gotten the southern view of me going north. They were old women, probably walking around to keep down funeral expenses, but I was really caught.

Well honey, I guess I'll stop here. You know how I love you and I'm living for the time that I can come home to you.

Goodnight darling.

All my love, / Henry

Sunday, August 13, 1944

Hello darling:—

This will probably be a very short letter, as I can't think of a single thing to write. Of course though, there is *always* one thing I can write. I love you. And with all my heart in everyway you can think of.

I've just had my hair clipped all over. I've been doing that for about three months. It saves the trouble of carrying a comb and is easy to keep clean. I told someone it would be just my luck for the war to end the next day after a "baldy" sometime. Lt. Hughes told me once he would like to have a picture of me with my hat off, to send to a certain girl he knew of.

Hope you can read this. I'm lying down and the paper slides, and everything together makes the writing bad.

I guess this is all. Remember darling, I love you with all my heart.

All my love, / Henry

Tuesday, August 15, 1944

My darling:—

Received your letter yesterday, written August 1st, and I've waited until today to answer so as to be sure of what I wanted to write.

First, I love you darling and I'm sure, more than ever before. And—*only* you—always. *You* are the one I'm coming back to. *You* are going to be my wife, the sweetest little woman in the world.

I *am* going to tell you *frankly* what I think of your not telling me of Libby.

In the first place, there was no earthly reason for you not to, and you caused yourself a lot of "sweating," (pardon the slang) there was no use of. Trying as you did, you failed miserably to present *one* good excuse for your silence. And evidently, you wouldn't have said anything about her until we were married, had she not married, causing you to feel so alone. Darling, I too wish I could have been with you to tell you everything *is* alright. You love me and because you thought of the possibility of my re-actions, you forgot Libby and thought only of yourself, which was a little selfish. Even though she told you she thought you were doing the right thing, deep down there must have been other thoughts. Thinking only of you and her, I *definitely* don't think you did the right thing. And I believe *you* should be sorry for saying you were sorry to "dump" a ready-made family into my lap. You wouldn't want her to know you said that, would you?

I love you darling and nothing that has been can keep me from wanting you for my own. Don't let the way I started this letter mislead you. I knew what I wanted to write but wanted to use what I thought was the proper sequence. This is the only letter there will ever be anything in about your not telling me about Libby. And there will never (and I mean *never*) be a "flare up."

To me darling, you are still the girl I loved yesterday before I had your letter. The one I shall continue to love, and soon, as my wife. If I should get home before Libby's husband, as far as I'm concerned, I see absolutely no reason for her to get an apartment of her own.

I could never see myself writing you a letter like this and I won't make any excuses for it. I told you in the beginning I was going to be frank. And this will never be referred to as an incident. You can answer this letter as you like. Perhaps you don't think it, but I'll swear I haven't meant to offend you. I've told you what I think. I've not been offended or provoked at you in the least, but somewhat puzzled.

I guess this is all. Give Libby my best.

And remember, I *do love you more* than ever before and I long desperately for you. You are my life and it's hard waiting for you so long.

All my love, darling, for—

Always, / Henry

Elizabeth Ann Moore, "Libby," was born September 28, 1924. She married 1/Lt. James Nash Hancock of Finchville, Kentucky, on Sunday, July 30, 1944, in Tucson, Arizona, where Nash was stationed at the Davis-Monthon Air Base. Years later, in an unpublished manuscript, Janice shared their story:

Libby's Prince Charming did not come riding up on a snow white charger. Not at all. He came zooming out of the wild blue yonder in a Cub training plane, and she didn't even recognize him!

It was fall of 1941 . . . .

It was March of 1942 when Nash left Louisville, and it was January of 1944 when he [returned] . . . .

When he left, Libby had one of his lieutenant's bars and the letters started flowing, and the phone started ringing, from Albuquerque, from Lincoln, from Tucson . . . .

When he was first commissioned he had chosen heavy, military aircraft . . . . When he was sent to Tucson it was the final stage before leaving . . . .

He called one hot July night and he and Libby talked with their usual leisure . . . . I was in the bedroom and when Libby wandered in after hanging up, "Mom, Nash wants me to come to Tucson, and I want to go."

I knew then. "When?"

"Now. He can't get another leave, and there's just a few weeks left."

"O.K."

In all the whirl of Libby's hurried packing and getting away, in the mad confusion of that last morning when she scrambled out of her shorts and old blouse and left the pins from her hair scattered over the top of her dressing table, in all of that and in all of our excited, laughing talk, I knew the time had come. Not that there was a word said about it. But I knew just the same.

I said goodbye carelessly and gaily enough. Like it was just another trip. Like it was an everyday occurrence for her to take off so suddenly for Tucson. Like my heart wasn't tied in a tight knot. "I'll be back in ten days," she said, waving to me as she went down the ramp. But I knew better. I knew she would never be back! Not the way she had always been. I knew she was getting out of *our* life forever. I said goodbye to nineteen beautiful years with her, said goodbye to my daughter and let her go to become a wife.

For she did, of course. They like to remind me that they themselves didn't know they were going to be married then. I don't argue with them about it. Maybe they didn't know it. But I did. And when I went back to the lonely, solitary emptiness of the apartment and saw her faded, worn little shorts, and the ragged, discarded old blouse, and the scattered pins and the old, un-wanted hair ribbons on top of her dressing table, it was like seeing the still warm, still shaped garments of someone who had just died. For a way of life *had* died . . . a beautiful, precious way of life.

But even as I went completely to pieces and clutched the shorts and the blouse to me, and sobbed my heart out, I knew I wouldn't have had it any other way. For if our way of life was dy-ing, Libby was starting a new way, her own way, and it was right that she should. The currents of life are forward, and I would not have kept Libby from going with them!

Her letters came every day, full of things they were doing, places they were going, people they were seeing, fun they were having. And as the end of the visit drew near there was no men-tion of its being prolonged. "I'm flying home," Libby wrote, "and I leave Thursday evening. Will be home early Friday."

But Friday morning came without Libby. I hadn't expected her. But I did expect the call that came that night. "Do you mind if I marry your daughter Sunday evening?" Nash said.

As ready as I thought I was for it, it stopped the very beat of my heart. But I like to think my voice was quiet and steady as I talked to first one of them, then the other. "Mom, we didn't decide until I was ready to leave last night! Mom, is it all right?"

"It's perfect!"

"Oh gee, mom! Gee, we've been going in circles! We've already got the license, and we're going to be married in the Little Church of the Hills, and we've already talked to the minister, and I'm going to wear a suit! I bought it today. Mom, it's pale blue, and I'm going to have white things with it, and just a little veil on the hat."

Just a little veil! She was always going to be married in the seminary chapel, with white satin, and a long veil! And Dr. Sherrill was going to marry her! And there would be six bridesmaids, and a flower girl and a ring bearer. All the trimmings. That's what Libby was going to have!

"It sounds lovely, darling. What time Sunday evening?"

"Oh! Oh, of course! Seven-thirty. And we made it Sunday because Nash can't get off Saturday. But he has Sunday and Monday off. Mom, we've got seven weeks before he has to go."

Seven weeks! But what a great pride I took in them both. A pride in their daring and their courage in facing the grim, hard facts which lay before them. A pride in their hope and in their faith, not only in themselves, but in life. I also took pride in the fact that they expected me to have as much courage as they!

How could you bear to have Libby married so far from home, people asked me. How could you bear not seeing her married? How could you bear not being there? How could I bear it? Why, I was there. I was there the whole three years they were being married, for that little ceremony in the Little Church of the Hills was only the final ceremony. Libby and Nash were being married when they quarreled and bickered that first winter in our little apartment. They were being married through all the letters that came and went during the two years he was gone. They were being married each time he phoned. And I was there.

But I was there, too, at that final ceremony. That Sunday afternoon Dr. and Mrs. Caldwell, the seminary president and his wife, drove by. "We've come to take you home with us for dinner," they said. But they understood when I said I'd rather be alone. Dr.

Benfield, the Vice-president, also understood when he called to ask if I would like to spend the evening with them. And Dr. and Mrs. Sherrill understood when I borrowed his book containing the marriage service. I didn't know about the fly that settled on Nash's nose and almost spoiled the dignity of the occasion, but, keeping my place in the marriage service, I followed them through their responses. Oh, yes, I was there. But because I was also alone in the twilight of the living room, I didn't have to put up any brave front before people. I didn't have to pretend. I could cry just as forlornly as I wanted to!

Friday, August 18, 1944

Hello darling:—

Just received your letter in which you were telling of your hand, and the operation you were to have. I don't care if it isn't any more serious than you say, I'm still a little uneasy. I won't rest so good until I have more news of it.

I love you my darling, very deeply and with all my heart. It's hard to have to wait so long to get back to you.

Yesterday, I had the rest of the letters you wrote at home. Four of them and one written the seventh. It was amusing to read of your account of being there. You going after Dad and making him eat as the rest of you did. And Kenneth's lecture on "wildlife." Once when I was home, he told me all about huckleberries, from early spring until they were ripe in the fall. I believe you did like your visit. You say you found out quite a bit about me. Well, you still have some more to find out. But of course, that will only be between you and me. Know what I mean?

Oh yes—I also had a letter from home too, that was written while you were there. Mama said you two were doing a lot of talking. And she said, "We sure do like her."

Darling, I hope you didn't have to stay in the hospital long, for aside from everything else it would be a hell of way to have to spend even a part of your vacation.

Goodnight my darling and remember—

I love you, / Henry

Janice had surgery to remove a bursa at the third finger of her right hand on August 11, 1944.

Saturday, August 19, 1944

Hello Sweetheart:—

I'm writing early today. Before mail call. I'm anxious for another letter to see how your hand is doing.

. . . I *hope* you got to go see your folks during your vacation. Seems like that hand could have waited another month anyhow.

I *wish* Adolf would give up. Seems that by now he could see he's playing a losing game. Maybe it won't be so long until we'll be together again. I'm terribly lonely for you darling. I hope this letter doesn't sound *too* blue. It's just that I love you so much that I'll never be contented until I can be with you.—

A couple of hours later.

We have had mail call, but no letter. Tomorrow, I'll probably get some. I got a letter from Mom and she was telling me again how everyone liked you. She also told me how you left on the truck with the goats, etc.

Darling, I guess this is about all for now.

You *know* I love you, and living for the time that you will be mine *forever.*

All my love, / Henry

Janice describes the load on the truck for her return trip from Knifley to Campbellsville in *40 Acres and No Mule.* She rode with "six goats, a cow and two pigs!"

Monday, August 21, 1944

My only love:—

I couldn't write yesterday, but I got your picture and I love it. Thanks a million honey. It makes me more anxious than ever to get back to you. Oh, I love you so much darling, it hurts to have to stay away from you so long. But—one day.

There were two good letters today too, written when you first noticed your hand hurting. I've already had the typewritten one, written after these. I'm terribly anxious for some more word of the operation. I also had a letter from Irene. She said, "Just to let you know how much all of us thought of Janice," and too, she added,

"She's the best person I ever met, I know." She went on to tell how much fun everyone had and several more things.

Yes, I too, suppose it will seem like we're dreaming when we are together, and no camping trips, for we will stick to beds. After some of the "luxuries" of life, I'm sure we will know we're not dreaming.

I love you honey, and with all my heart for all time. I'll have to stop here so— Goodnight and

All my love, / Henry

Tuesday, August 22, 1944

Hello darling:—

Another day that we don't have to "sweat out." One day nearer you and the life we long so desperately for. I love you honey, so much that it's hard to wait so long. But one day, before so long, I'm coming home to you.

No letter today, and for that reason everything isn't exactly up to par. But I'll try not to sound so blue.

I did a little laundry today. French style. A pond of water and a board alongside. Rubbed the soap on and I used a brush instead of the paddle affair they use.

Wish there had been a letter today. I'm *so* anxious to know more of the condition of your hand. Well—tomorrow—surely.

Why couldn't Libby write to me? She probably would if you told her I would like for her to and I think it would be a pretty good idea to get somewhat acquainted. What do you think? In writing to you, I'm at a total loss in thinking of something to say about her and (I can't remember his name) her husband.

I haven't heard from your Mother either since I left England.

I read a piece in the *Stars & Stripes* tonight entitled, "Total War." Herb Caen on a trip to Normandy spied two *foxes* digging a *manhole*.

Well honey, this is about all for now. Wish it were possible to be with you tonight, to kinda cuddle up close and keep warm or something.

Goodnight baby.

All my love *always*, / Henry

Thursday, August 24, 1944

Hello darling:—

A note today that Rynthia had written the day you were out of the hospital, and I guess you must be O.K. for she said you even looked better than before going to the hospital. Morale lifter anyhow. I don't know why your letters have slowed down just at the time I'm most anxious to hear from you. I said "most" anxious. I'm always eager for your letters, but you're going to the hospital added some.

. . . Oh yes, I got a little box of candy too. You sent it July 27. It *really* hit the spot. I've already eaten it all. By myself. Thanks sweetheart.

Had a letter from Cora Mae too, in answer to the apology I wrote her about the lipstick kiss on the back of the envelope. It was postmarked August 14 and one from August 12.

Goodnight sweetheart. And you won't forget—

I love you, / Henry

Saturday, August 26, 1944

Hello darling:—

Couldn't write yesterday, but I love you all the same, and I'm living for the time that we shall be together again.

No letter yesterday *or* today, and as you know, that isn't so good. I'm not "griping" for I know they're on their way. There *was* another package of candy. I *really* like it, and thanks a million.

I was lucky in getting this paper. Most of the company had gone through the line for rations, but for some reason Lt. Hayes had this one tablet left for me. I suppose it was because I was the only one who said they needed some paper, when he asked. He laughed when I was the only one that needed it.

I saw a little tobacco growing today. First I've seen since I've been here.

I wish I could hear more about your hand. Isn't it funny that just when I'm the *most* anxious to hear from you, they seem to discontinue the mail service?

Well honey, darkness has overtaken me so I'll have to stop. You know I love you with all my heart. Very deeply and for *always*.

Yours, / Henry

Wednesday, September 6, 1944

Darling:—

The mail *finally* came through and there were ten letters from you! One from home and one from Sgt. Hinkel. Of course, I feel several hundred percent better, and so thrilled and excited I don't know if I can write or not. With no letters for so long, I was getting somewhat low. Oh, how I love you darling. Words fail to express just what you do mean to me.

I got in so late yesterday, I couldn't write. In fact, I had to get right in a window to be able to read your last letter, it was getting so late. You did a very good job in making me, as well as your Mother, believe there was nothing much wrong with your hand. Well, I'm glad it's almost well now.

The letters took up just where they stopped, from the 13th to the 23rd. The one for the 13th was just a note written by Mrs. Naveaux. (Is that a French name!) She just said she was taking you home with her for the weekend, from the hospital.

In your letter of the 14th, you were hoping I would get the letters regularly that you were writing while your hand was so bad. That's just when I *didn't* get any. I'm afraid I cried the blues quite a lot in my letters to you from the last letters to the ones yesterday.

Sgt. Hinkel said in his letter that he was fine. He wanted me to see everyone I could or do anything I could to help get him back. I don't know how much that will be, but I'll tell the old man what he said. I *hope* he does come back, for I know how I would want to get back if I should be separated from Company A. It was the first anyone had heard from him. I asked everyone about him that I thought might have seen him.

I've been laughing at the Dagwood strips. He certainly can get in some jams, but I'm still sure that *I* want to get married though.

I saw someone with a pack of Rameses cigarettes once, but I've never smoked any.

Two more fellows and I walked into a little town last evening for awhile. We tried to find some wine. All we could hear was

"Bosch" when we asked about it. The Germans had taken about everything. Finally, we saw an old man with a bottle of wine and cider. We tried to buy it, but instead of selling it, he took us home with him and we helped him drink it. I got back in time to write, but not read twelve letters and *then* write.

I haven't seen Sammie anymore. Not even a truck from his outfit lately.

Thanks for sending the picture. Libby is a beautiful girl and Nash looks all man. Give them my best. I'll send it back, since you *say* it's the only one you have.

I haven't heard any straight news for a few days, but if what I hear second-hand is on the level, everything is going O.K.

This must be all for now honey. You know I love you with all my heart and only you.

All my love, / Henry

Saturday, September 9, 1944

My only love:—

. . . Last night two more fellows and myself had dinner with a Frenchman. A rabbit dinner, French style, with mashed potatoes and good gravy. First we were served some sliced tomatoes with some kind of sauce on them, then the rabbit and potatoes and apple pie for dessert with wine to drink. I felt rather awkward at a table and I don't know enough French that I could even thank them. One fellow knows it pretty good and he said he thanked him.

That's about all that has happened, so I'll have to stop here. I love you honey, and *only* you, for always.

All my love, / Henry

Wednesday, September 13, 1944

Hello Sweetheart:—

I'm loving you darling and wishing I could be with you. Sometimes I wonder just what it's going to be like when we are able to actually touch each other and know that we are no longer dreaming of being together. I know it will be the most wonderful thing in the world.

Have you read of the point system that is to be used in releasing men after the war in Europe? If you don't have to have *too* many, I may stand a chance in getting out before so long, after the war. Everything in the *Stars & Stripes* wasn't official, but according to the text I should have about seventy points now.

This is about all for now. There still hasn't been any mail delivery so you know how that is.

I love you with all my heart and for *always*.

All my love, / Henry

The National Resources Planning Board began plans for demobilization in 1942. Other agencies and offices were consulted to produce a plan that recommended discharges, allowing a given number of points for Army service, overseas duty, combat, and parenthood. At the war's end, 85 points would give a soldier eligibility for discharge.

Friday, September 15, 1944

My darling:—

At last, some more mail came through and there were two letters. Not as many as I expected but it is really good to have them. They were postmarked August 23 & September 2, so there's eight more somewhere.

I love you honey, in every way you can think of and I'm living for the time that we will be together again.

No, I didn't think I could write as many letters as you say you have. I think I could tell you most every place I've been when they were written. We'll go over some of it at a time when I get back.

I haven't gotten the comics yet. Maybe when the mail begins coming more regularly they will soon arrive. Dagwood was a killer in the strips in these letters. Blondie thinking he was eating the glass. And her removing the ladder while Dagwood was on the roof. "And still," he says, "they marry by the millions every day."

I've already told you you could send me some handkerchiefs.

Evidently your folks had been visiting you for in your letter of the first you said they had just left. Farther on in the letter, you were telling of your trying to figure who would be what relation to whom. It does sound a little complicated, I admit.

It would be good if you could spend the Thanksgiving holiday with Irene. Maybe you will get enough time off to do so.

Oh, I wish these letters would come in the proper sequence. I don't know if Libby has written me, or if you have told me to write her. You said in this letter for me to tell her when I write her what I thought of her moving out when I got home.

This is about all for now sweetheart. I love you very desperately and think of you constantly.

Cheerio baby, and—

All my love, / Henry

11

"I hope *this damn war will soon end.*"

My only love:—

. . . Three good letters yesterday, the last ones you wrote at home and the first one after you got back to Louisville. I *would* have to get the last ones first, but they were sweet and very welcome, as they all are. From all indications, you did like your visit at home. I was hoping you would. Everyone liked you, just as I knew they would. Maybe the next time you sleep in that bed, I *will* be with you. We will go squirrel hunting too. Ever go squirrel hunting? It's lots of fun and squirrel meat is about as good as anything.

That *was* rather an unusual load for a truck. It was just like Dad to say what he did. You know it seems funny for Ray to be driving a truck. When I left he was just a kid. But it seem that everything has moved pretty fast in four years.

Of course it was alright for Mama to read one of my letters to you. Nothing wrong in that. By the way, I hear there has been another Invasion somewhere but I don't know anything about it.

So Dad got a kick out of your being afraid of hornets. They are tricky. Especially when they take a notion to sit down.

I *will* let you know just as soon as I get back to the States. I'm going to be one of the most anxious fellows in the world then.

I'm sure I don't know what could have been meant by saying "it would all come out in the wash," but whatever it may be won't amount to a damn thing.

Some kids just came by and I got a drink of cognac from them. First time I've ever tasted it. It's just like liquid lightning.

I guess this is about all for now. You won't forget for a moment how I love you. With all my heart and for always.

All my love, / Henry

On August 15, Allied forces landed on the southern coast of France. By September 5, the Allies had put more than 2,000,000 troops and 3,500,000 tons of supplies on French shores.

Monday, September 18, 1944

Hello Honey:—

It's Sunday and there are so many kids around I don't know how well I'll be able to write. One just now fell into my tent and knocked it down.

. . . When I was visiting the people in town I had forgottten my billfold and didn't have your picture with me, so early this afternoon they came here to see your picture. "She is beautiful," they said. I, of course, quite agreed with them, for I have known that for some time. I wanted to tell them how we met, but decided it was too much of an undertaking with my limited French and their English.

This is all for now Sweetheart. You know I love you—*and for keeps.* Cheerio baby.

All my love, / Henry

On September 18, the 291st headed into Belgium. On the first night, they were still in France but crossed into Belgium the next day. A short walk took them into Luxembourg.

Thursday, September 21, 1944
Somewhere in Belgium

My darling:—

Two good letters last night that I was beginning to need pretty bad. They were written the 7th & 8th. So somewhere, there is a stack of them. In the one for the 8th, it had been six days since you had had a letter and I can understand how you were feeling.

I love you my darling and when I say "I love you," I am expressing my feelings very lightly, for actually, I'm "crazy" about you and you are constantly in my thoughts. Well—one day.

You said Nash would be leaving the 11th or 12th. I'm anxious to know where he was sent. Hope it wasn't the Pacific. Too bad he and Libby have to be separated but it's good they are married and of course will have a lot of treasured memories. Give them my best when you write or see them.

Of course, what I want to do is come home when the war here is over, but if I should be given a choice, I would prefer the Army of occupation here, to the Pacific. For in the Pacific, there will also have to be an Army of occupation after the war, and it's possible that an unlucky number could be drawn then.

The suckers on growing tobacco are just part of the plant that branches from the stalk at the base of each leaf. Those Kenneth was pulling off, are called "suckering."

I too, wish I could have been with you during your folk's visit. But like your sister said, we would have to be married for sometime to be the company we should.

It was funny to read of your getting mad at listening to Dewey's speech and turning off the radio and how they found out at home, you were a Democrat.

This is all darling. You know I love you with all my heart.

Always, / Henry

Company C troops were soon operating sawmills to provide timber for replacement bridges. Company A was quickly involved in the tremendous task of building a 120-foot, 70-ton trestle bridge in Steinfort, Luxembourg.

Thomas E. Dewey, governor of New York, ran unsuccessfully for president of the United States on the Republican ticket in 1944 and 1948.

Friday, September 22, 1944

Hello my darling:—

Today, I hit the jackpot. The mail came sometime last night and was called this morning. I had 17 from you and the card that was written August 14, two letters from home and one from Irene. I've *really* gotten a lift from all the sweet letters this morning. So you see, I'm sitting on top of the world, and will *try* to answer as many as possible now, but with so many kids around, I don't know how well I'll do.

. . . I'm glad you have had the letter in the blue envelope. I'm sorry I thought some of the things I did that were wrong. After I had mailed it, those were the things I regretted writing. That is the reason I said in a later one that I didn't know whether I should have written it or not. I'm extremely sorry darling. I wouldn't do or say anything to hurt you intentionally. I love you too much for that. Anyhow—as far as I'm concerned, everything is O.K. and I love you more than ever. And one day we are going to be the happiest two people in the world.

Seems to me you could go home for Thanksgiving anyhow. Even if Irene didn't get the house. They want you to and *don't* be afraid of wearing out your welcome.

It was good that your folks could visit you since you weren't able to take your vacation as you had planned. I'm somewhat anxious to see them myself. From what you say of them, I think they are really fine people and I like them a *lot* already. And you can tell Libby if she still has the idea of moving away, if I come home first, that you and I are moving right in with her. I'll write to her when I have a little more time.

I had to laugh at your comparison of Nash and me. I'm quite sure the *four* of us *will* get along fine. Too bad if they sent him to the Pacific.

You know, (not that it means a thing) several times lately, I've dreamed of getting out of the Army and of reading my discharge. Once I had Irene fill out an order for civilian clothes and everytime, I've been going home to you. Oh, dreams are crazy anyhow.

I think, "I'll Walk Alone," is the most beautiful song you have sent me. Wish I could hear it, for just the words almost make me cry. They make me so anxious to get back to you.

I liked the picture you sent of Spring Mill State Park. Think I'll write to them and tell them we want to spend a part of our honeymoon there.

I have to stop now darling. I'll finish answering this afternoon.

All my love, for always, / Henry

Saturday, September 23, 1944

My only love:—

I was unable to write twice yesterday as I had planned, but I'm getting an early start this morning, so I can answer the eight letters I have left from yesterday.

. . . I got a kick out of the way Petie began the letter she wrote me: Dear Henry "Brother," and then "how does that sound?" And the small towel you were telling of her getting for me.

Am very glad to have Libby's letter too, but her's and Petie's letters make me very envious, in that I mean, *they* were *with you*, and wrote mostly of you and of course I liked that, for I never tire of hearing someone mention your name, and for your folks thoughtfulness and kindness towards us. I am very grateful and (just between you and me), I shall always try not to disappoint them in any way. And by the way, I am looking forward to the reunion you planned. I'm sure it will be fun.

So you're going to be tagging around after me everywhere I go when I get back. Well, *I'm* going to see that you *keep* that promise. You just *try* getting out of my sight.

You make me pretty hungry when you tell what you have for some meals, such as the supper with roast beef sliced and warmed up in the gravy with hash brown potatoes, sliced tomatoes and hot rolls. Of course, I get enough to eat, but it isn't like homecooked food. A couple of days ago one of the fellows said he should write you how I could fry potatoes. The ones I had cooked for them just happened to be pretty good.

You asked how my German was. I don't have any. I know one word, "ja" for "yes" and very, very little French.

This point system they have for demobilization may be alright but I would like to know how many points one has to have before being considered eligible for release and if priority is as outlined, one, two, three and four. And that is a good reason why we should have been married too. Well honey, maybe we will do alright once we have a chance. If we don't it won't be because we don't try. Oo-la-*la*. A little impatient.

I didn't know that Ernie Pyle had left the war. I must have missed his last article. We don't get the *Stars & Stripes* everyday. I had been wondering why his article was missing.

Yes, I too wish I could be with you some nights when it's a little cool, to "kinda cuddle up and get warm." And we will be before so long I think, and I doubt if we even notice the cold.

Mama tells me in both of her letters that she has heard from you. Irene says she is looking forward to your visit at Thanksgiving, so don't disappoint her even if she doesn't get another house and says further quote: "I love her as good as I do a sister. She's so good and kind." I guess all my folks must have fallen in love with you too. I must write to her and Mama today too.

All the kids are here today again. Yesterday when there weren't so many around we counted twenty. All wanting gum and candy and cigarettes for pop.

I think I've run out of anything to write so I'll stop here. You know I love you with all my heart and in every way.

All my love, / Henry

Ernie Pyle, a Pulitzer Prize-winning American war correspondent, was born in Dana, Indiana, August 3, 1900. He first traveled throughout the states as a roving reporter for Scripps-Howard. Early in the war years, he became one of America's most popular and respected reporters as he wrote vivid, eye-witness accounts of the combat experiences of the ordinary soldier. Writing with honesty and sensitivity, he traveled with American troops throughout Africa, Europe, and the Pacific.

Sunday, September 24, 1944

My only love:—

Once again, I love you darling and I'm desperately lonely for you today. As usual, you are in my every thought. I'll be *so* glad when I can come home to you.

For sometime, I've been trying to think of what would be just the right way to write about you having been married before, so last night I wrote Irene quite a long letter and told her. And of Libby too. I trust you will understand that it hasn't been because I was, shall we say, ashamed to tell them, or anything like that. Far from it honey, for I love you too much. And I guess I haven't presented an excuse for not doing so before now. The one thing I made plain was that regardless of how they liked it, you will always be the same to me. If they *don't* like it, and should "cold shoulder" you in the least, why have anything to do with them, for a friendship that could be as conceited as that wouldn't be worth a damn anyhow. We can do fine without them, for like a part of a song I used to hear, "I'll give up everything just to be where you are." I mean that in every sense of the word. That's the way I love you, and what you mean to me. *Everything* in the world darling and for always.

There should be some more mail before so long. Regardless of how many letters I have in one day, I'm just as anxious for more the next day.

Well honey, this must be about all I'll write again tonight. Remember I love you sweetheart, with all my heart and always.

All my love, / Henry

On October 1, 1944, the 291st was transported into northern Belgium to the deep, dark pine forests near Hockai, southeast of Liege. Company A was in Werbomont, about eleven miles west of Trois Ponts.

Tuesday, October 3, 1944

My only love:—

Today *there were three* letters, written September 11, 21 & 22. I am very glad to have these since they answer some of the questions I've been wondering about.

First, though, I love you *so* much. Everyday, that love grows, and now you are the most loved woman in the world. Darling, it *will* be a wonderful day when Germany gives up. But the *most* wonderful time will be the day I get back to you. Maybe it *won't* be long from today.

The stamps came in good time. You will get some letters I sent "free." And I sent a letter in a blue envelope.

I don't think you should worry about Nash so much as far as his ability to fly is concerned. I'm sure they must be the best before they are sent over. One thing that has burned me up is the way I've seen the heinies wait for several planes together before they fire their ack-ack. Never at one or two.

It was the coconut bars of candy I said were so good. I should get along O.K. when all my packages come through.

The six letters you had the twenty-first, I wrote while I was away from the company, and they were all mailed at one time. So that is why they were cancelled the same day. I don't like to have to do that or even miss a day writing to you, but pretty often it happens. I couldn't write you yesterday either. We will "check up" on the letters sometime and I think I can tell you what was happening at most of the times.

I too, know that there isn't a chance of either of us *ever* changing but we of course think sometimes what life would be like without the other. I always know that you are writing, even if I don't get them as regularly as I would like to.

I am glad to know that Libby is with you now, and since I'm not so good at saying things to (or for) other people in a letter, tell her hello for me and you two try not to worry too much.

This is all darling. You *know* I love you with *all* my heart. *Only you.*

All my love, / Henry

Heinies: slang for German soldiers, used first in World War 1.

Thursday, October 5, 1944
Belgium

Hello my darling:

I'm thinking of you sweetheart and loving you with all my heart and longing desperately to be with you. Maybe it won't be long now.

I've just read an article in *Yank* of the demobilization plan, but I still don't know where I stand. The article said that *any* plan would leave some fellows with unpunched T.S. cards. And of course that is right.

Some censorship rules have been changed and now I can tell you where I've been, both in England and France. The picture of the fellows and me was taken in Carentan. One day, I was in three countries—Luxembourg, France and Belgium. I was in Melun when I wrote the six letters I mailed at one time.

You know where I landed in England, and remember when I was working in town? That was Bath. That is where I first heard the record you sent me. I was near Gloucester for awhile, and Devizes. Well, if you want to know of any other places, ask me and maybe I'll know.

I guess this is about all for now baby. Remember I love you with all my heart *for always.*

All my love, / Henry

The T.S. card was the soldier's humorous expression for his tough "luck" card.

Friday, October 6, 1944

My only love:—

Today there was a good letter written September 23, and that makes the day as near perfect as possible. Of course, no day will be perfect until I get back to you. I love you honey, with all my heart and for always and so much that words won't describe it. I *hope* this damn war will soon end.

Today, I visited my old outfit. The one I left in Camp McCoy. I saw almost all the fellows I use to know and since it's hard to forget a face like mine, about all of them remembered me. Two of the fellows I went especially to see, were with me in the 19th. One is the mess Sergeant and the other, a Sergeant from Kentucky. We used to get around quite a lot and it was good to see them again. One kid who used to offer suggestions when I was writing, asked me how I was doing with my letter writing. Of course, my answer was that I only wrote to one, and was doing O.K.

I had dinner with a French family a couple of nights ago (or maybe I told you.) Anyhow, we are planning to go again tonight.

If Libby learns to play the uke, maybe we can make a trio of the piano, uke and guitar. (After some practice, of course.)

I wrote to your Mother last night. And since there is never anything to write about, I'm afraid it wasn't such a good letter. Guess this is all for now. I love you darling, and I *never* forget that you are loving me the same. Bye now and—

All my love, / Henry

Sgt. Giles was at Camp McCoy in Sparta, Wisconsin, during the fall of 1942.

———————————

Sunday, October 15, 1944

Hello Sweetheart:

Five good letters today, so it's a sure thing that I'm just about O.K.

. . . Sgt. Hinkel had several letters today, including one I wrote him while he was in the hospital. I know exactly what you mean when you say it hurts with a physical ache to be apart for so long. It's a lonely heartache that goes on and on, but of course there is also a brighter side—we know that our love is something solid, and that it will last. Some I know are not so fortunate. Others receive no letters (or write any) for weeks and sometimes, it's a month or two. And it's their wives. Seems to me there is something lacking in cases like that.

Today, a good friend of mine had a letter from someone who knows his wife and this letter told him how his wife was doing. Wow! It even makes me boil. It was signed "an innocent friend." Don't know why I told you this, but it was so disgusting to know he was being done so. In one of her letters to him, she was telling of her planning to move out to herself, when she has been living with her folks.

Yes, I was somewhat worried about the letter I wrote in the blue envelope and it was because of what I said that was wrong. I very soon decided that I was wrong. Those were the things that hurt you. Hurting you is the thing I shall never want to do. I've told you I was sorry and you have been very sweet. I know too, that we will always get along—and *good*.

Thanks for the pictures honey, but why didn't you tell me at the first of the letter that I could keep them, for all through the letter, I was sweating out that "send them back honey" phrase, but had already decided I would keep them anyhow, when I came to where you said I could keep them. Of course, I was greatly relieved. I had to trim them to fit my billfold. They were good pictures and I'll bring them back sometime.

I had to laugh at the trouble you had in sending the package. I've just read your account of it to Sgt. Hinkel and he got a kick out of it.

I'm letting my hair grow out now. Already it will almost lay sideways, but not backward. No, I would not let as small a thing as a new permanent wave bother me, for I'm not allergic to hair.

Yes, Libby and Petie both sent their letters with yours. Or did they? It seems that Petie's was in an envelope of its own. I don't know, this one track mind of mine can't remember for long. That is, except you. *You* are always with me.

It seems that someone can see the difference in a package that is a necessity and one of some other type. Such as the razor blades. Remember how fast my watch came. The funnies haven't come yet. By the way—I'll probably have enough handkerchiefs for the duration, when all of them get here.

I do get a kick out of Dagwood and everyone else does too. I don't care for Superman, Batman and characters like those so much, but Dagwood, Jiggs, Bugs Bunny, Porky and such as those, I like.

It's good that Libby is hearing from Nash as often as she is. He probably does get his orders from one jump to another.

I suppose my cousin did get a rotten deal with his girl, but he should have allowed some time. Look how long it took me to find the best and I *do* mean the *best*. Too many fellows jump at what one fellow calls "concussions" (instead of conclusions) too soon.

I too, hope you can keep on getting your letters as often as you were when you wrote these letters I had today and in the order in which they are written. I read an article in the *Stars & Stripes* that wanted all the G.I.s to use more V-mails instead of air mail. It said that some of the letters (air mail) had to be sent to the states by boat.

I don't think Libby should worry too much if Nash should have to fly missions over Germany for his chances are ninety-nine to one that he will make it every time.

It was good that you got a good break in the doctor bill on your hand. I was afraid it would be quite a lot.

This is about all honey. Imagine me writing almost ten pages, even as large as these.

Cheerio darling and don't forget that I'm loving you with all my heart and thinking of you constantly.

All my love, / Henry

Recovered from his wounds in July, Sgt. Hinkel was finally returned to Company A and again shared a tent with Henry.

12

". . . and now I'm in a hospital."

Friday, October 20, 1944

Hello Sweetheart:—

Today, I went on sick call and now I'm in a hospital. It's my ears, somewhat plugged up and at times, hurt like the dickens. But they will probably be O.K. in a few days. Didn't bring a thing with me, so as a result, I'm having to use a pencil. The battalion medical officer said I would get back today, so I didn't bring anything.

I love you darling, in every way you can think of and the one thing I'm living for is to get back to you. I probably won't get any letters as long as I'm in the hospital and that isn't going to be so good, but I'll have to sweat it out somehow. I had two letters written to you at camp. One for the 18th and 19th, but not having any envelopes, I couldn't mail them. Now they probably won't be mailed, unless Sgt. Hinkel finds them and sends them out. The 16th and 17th, I couldn't write, so this may be the only one in four days.

I hope to hell I'll be able to get back to Company A and I probably will. I hope too, that they move to a better place.

Everything is rather quiet and I feel O.K. except my ears hurt a little and I can't hear as good as I usually can. Talking in a building is only a mumble to me and it's a little embarrassing to have to ask everything to be said again.

This is all darling. Remember how I love you and that I'm thinking of you constantly.

All my love—always, / Henry

Henry was in a field hospital in Belgium.

Sunday, October 22, 1944

Hello darling:—

I don't know how penciled writing will photograph but I thought V-mail would be faster.

I'm in another hospital now. Somewhere in France. And O.K. except my ears. They are no better as yet.

I love you sweetheart and I'm thinking of you all the time and wishing I could be with you. Couldn't write you yesterday honey.

Such beds. Guess I'll have to dampen them and sleep on my boots, so I'll be able to sleep naturally. Goodnight darling.

All my love, / Henry

Monday, October 23, 1944

My only love:—

Tonight, I'm thinking of you honey and loving you with all my heart—and of course, wishing we were together.

I'm still in the hospital. I feel very well but my ears are still on the blink. Maybe they will soon clear up. I hope so anyhow.

By the time you get these letters, I'll probably be out, so don't worry. Maybe Adolf will give up by then. Well—one day I'll be back and that is going to be the most wonderful day I've ever known. When you're back in my arms to stay—always.

I saw part of a *Courier-Journal* yesterday. They took us in a Red Cross canteen and the first thing I saw was the *C-J*. But only the society pages and want ads.

Goodnight baby and remember—

I love you. / Henry

Tuesday, October 24, 1944

Hello darling:

I'm thinking of you today, as usual, and wishing it were possible to be with you. But since it isn't I guess we will have to settle with a letter. I'll be glad when I get back to Company A. This going without letters isn't so good. I don't think Sgt. Hinkel had any mail at all while he was in the hospital. I don't know what I would do if I should ever have to go that long without any. Loving you as I do, your letters are the most important thing in the world as long as we are apart. Maybe it won't be so long until we will be together again. Yes, I know we have said that many times, but one day it's bound to happen.

I've just read in the *Stars & Stripes* of a fellow dreaming of sailing into New York and the Statue of Liberty was holding a huge sign reading, "This town is off limits to all troops."

This is all for now darling and remember, I love you in every way there is to love a woman and I'm thinking of you all the time.

All my love, / Henry

P.S. I guess my ears must be doing O.K.

Friday, October 27, 1944

Hello darling:

I'm out of the hospital and in a Replacement Center waiting to be returned to Company A. I hope it won't be too long but no one can tell how long. They say maybe a week, maybe two or three— so, there's nothing sure about it.

. . . I couldn't write yesterday and I don't know how often I'll be able to write while I'm here. But you can be sure that I'm thinking of you and loving you just as much.

I didn't bring a thing with me. Even my pen and billfold, I left under my blankets. I sent a note to Sgt. Hinkel to take care of them.

I was in Paris in the hospital. Went through what they said was the center. You can write home and tell them I'm O.K. when you get this. I am short of writing material.

Be glad when I can hear from you again but it may be quite awhile. One fellow hadn't heard since August, until today.

This is all honey. Give Libby my best and say hello for me. And remember I love you—

Always, / Henry

Henry was in a replacement center in Liege, Belgium. The replacement centers remained a frustration to all servicemen. While there, the soldier was cut off from the comradeship of his outfit and his most important morale booster—the mail. It was often a long, slow, and aggravating process to get back to a company.

Wednesday, November 1, 1944

Hello darling:

For two days I haven't had a chance to write. I didn't have any material either. But I love you just as much and of course, more since I wrote you last, as my love increases with every day that passes and I am thinking of you all the time.

I'm still at the Replacement Center. By "sweating" out a line about a mile long (well, it was a long line) I got my rations and have just enjoyed a bar of Milky Way. I bought a *Collier's* magazine, since there wasn't anything better.

I'm writing in the day room and I don't know how I'm going to use even one page of this paper, the lines are so close together. It's rather quiet and several fellows are writing to someone.

Be glad when I get back to the Company. This going without letters would soon get me down. I should get a lot when I do get back.

I read in the *Stars & Stripes* today that twenty-six years ago today, the last push was started that ended the war the eleventh. Wonder when the last one will start in this one. Soon, I hope. I want more than anything else in the world, to get back to you. Well, someday, I *will* be back. Then we will really know what happiness is like.

You had better write home when you get this and tell them I'm O.K. Also, tell them why I haven't written. I'll write in a few days anyhow.

I also read of Churchill's prediction that the war would last until up in '45. His mind is just about as changeable as the weather in France.

Well, goodnight darling and keep remembering that I love you with all my heart and I'm thinking of you constantly.

All my love, Henry

German delegates signed the armistice that ended World War 1 on November 11, 1918.

Henry tried to adapt the usual large scrawl of his handwriting to the narrow lined graph paper he found to write on. Near the end of the letter, with "Well, goodnight darling . . . " he gave up and used two lines per sentence!

Saturday, November 4, 1944

My only love:—

It's Saturday night again, but for some time it hasn't been anymore than any other night and I very seldom even think of it. Of course, when I do, I just remember that it used to be the night that most everyone went out, and I also think of how you and I will go out on Saturday nights when I get back to you. *We* will have more fun than anyone ever has. Oh darling, I love you so much that I become rather impatient at times, to come back to you. Well—*one* day it will happen.

Since I'm not sure how long I'm to be here, I will send you this address and you can write two or three letters to me here but not any more than that. Think I'll write home tonight. I haven't written them since I was in the hospital.

The fellow that came with me to the writing room, writes to his wife every day too. Says he knows how it is when he doesn't have any mail for a long time and that it wouldn't be right, if he didn't write to her as often as he could.

Someone is singing "Goodbye Broadway, Hello France," on the radio. Be glad when we can reverse that.

Got my air mail envelopes today and you may get this letter before you do the others I've written here.

I've tried for ten minutes, and I can't think of another thing to write, so I'll say goodnight sweetheart, and—

All my love, / Henry

Sunday, November 5, 1944

My only love:—

Another Sunday's almost gone and I love you a *week* more than last Sunday. In fact, I love you more with every day that passes and I'm lonely without you darling. I don't know the name of the tune, but someone is going to town on a blues number, and you probably know the feelings you get when certain types of music are being played. *This* one almost makes me cry. But—if we were together, we would love it.

The fellow I mentioned being with that is from Kentucky can't read or write, so today, he asked me to write him a letter to his girl. After I finished, I read it to him. All he had told me to write, and some of the things I added that I thought he would like. He said it was the best one he had ever written. However true that may be, I don't know. Two other fellows heard me read it back to him and asked me if I would write one for them. Kidding, of course.

I *wish* I could get some letters, but as long as I'm here I don't expect to get any. When I get back, there should be plenty. And a few days ago, I read in the *Stars & Stripes* that a Liberty ship had landed in France sometime lately, loaded with Christmas packages. I don't remember how many, but an awful lot. Maybe mine were on it.

Two more days until the election. Wonder what the score will be on that. This is the second election (Presidential) there has been since I have been in the Army.

I've been wondering why two or three fellows in the last few minutes have asked how to spell "suspicion." There is a movie on tonight "Above Suspicion," and they are writing about it.

Wish I could be with you for Christmas, but I guess we will have to wait until next year before we can celebrate together. It isn't long until Thanksgiving. Next year, we'll go quail hunting together.

Darn this pencil. Be glad when I get back to my pen.

Goodnight darling, and keep remembering how I love you. In every way you ever wanted to be loved and for always.

All my love, / Henry

The following letter is addressed to Mrs. Nash Hancock. The salutation begins with "Hello" as did Henry's first letter to Janice.

Tuesday, November 7, 1944

Hello Libby:—

For some time, I've planned to write you, but for different reasons, I've kept putting it off.

Janice says you are one swell person and whatever she thinks goes double for me. When Nash and I get back we will have a lot of fun, being just one happy family. O.K.?

You shouldn't have expected me to write so much, for in the first place, there isn't anything to write about here and too, I'm not so good at writing letters. Oh, I manage to write Janice pretty often, but that's different. In fact, *we* are different from a lot of people and so much in love that some probably couldn't understand it at all.

Well, cheerio for now and—

All the best, / Henry

Thursday, November 9, 1944

My own darling:—

. . . I've just been reading the election returns in the *Stars & Stripes* and it seems that everything went satisfactory as far as I'm concerned. I also read an article under the title, "People's Choice Okayed by Joes," and in it one fellow says "I'm glad they kept the old boy in there. I'd hate to see them take out a general and put a private in to run his show." I thought that was pretty good.

Saw a fellow today from Owensboro, Kentucky. Said this was his second trip overseas. He was sent back from North Africa for something to cure that wouldn't cure there. Told him where I was from and then, that I was going to marry a girl in Louisville. Said he thought I must have gotten around pretty good, then we didn't get to talk anymore. I did get to tell him about our trip on the bus and that it led to us being engaged.

One of my ears is bothering me some but I won't go on sick call until I just have to. If it starts aching I will, but so far it's just "plugged up," it seems.

Guess I'll soon be back with the Company. From now on, I'm going to even *sleep* with my billfold in my pocket. All this time and no letters, and not even your picture to look at is not so good.

You know, it's funny to watch a bunch of fellows writing. They will be in what seems to be a deep study, then they think of something, and their face will brighten. At times, they smile broadly. Maybe I do too. Every man of course, has his own thoughts. Right now, *my* thoughts are of you darling. Most anytime, I'm thinking of you and the wonderful times we are going to have together when I get back.

Goodnight sweetheart and

All my love, / Henry

President Franklin D. Roosevelt defeated Governor Thomas E. Dewey of New York for a fourth term. Senator Harry S. Truman of Missouri was elected as vice-president.

Saturday, November 11, 1944

My own darling:

Again, I'm thinking of you and loving you with all my heart and wishing we were together, but of course, that can't be for now. Soon though, I think we will be together, before another Armistice anyhow. Someone made the remark today, that twenty-six years ago today, a lot of fellows were made happy.

We were wondering what it would be like when we are told that the war has ended and finally decided we didn't know what it would seem like. Well—we'll see. Kind of a double holiday for us, since it is our anniversary. In months, of course, but still we have been counting them, just as some do years. I don't see how it could be as long again, as it has been since we first met. It can't be.

I love you so much darling that I will always count the days it has been since we found each other and wish there was some way of counting them until we are together again.

This is all honey. (Several fellows are waiting for a place to write.) So goodnight and remember—

I love you, / Henry

Saturday, November 18, 1944

Hello darling:—

It's a little late but I'll try to beat the lights.

I love you honey and miss you more every day. Wish this war would stop, and soon. I want to get back to you sweetheart. That is what I'm living for now.

Bought five Christmas cards today and they are already in the mail box. One for you and one for Libby and I sent your Mother one and one to Mama and Irene. I don't remember Petie's address.

Goodnight baby and—

All my love, / Henry

Sunday, November 19, 1944

My only love:

It's Sunday again and I am wishing I was with you. Can't be though, so we will have to settle for a letter. Sometime, we will be able to spend our Sundays together. Some lazy ones, and we are going to like them, I'm sure.

. . . A month now since I left the Company, and going without letters for that long is pretty hard to do, but I guess things like this have to happen sometimes. I'll get a lot though when I do get back, then maybe I can do a better job writing one.

It's almost Christmas again. Since I can't get out to get any gifts, I'll tell you what I've already done. I wrote to Mama a couple of days ago and told her to send you some money for a Christmas gift from me. And it is to be just for you. I mean by that, not to get anything for "us." Get you anything, or as "many things," as you want. Of course, that is rather an impersonal way of sending you something for Christmas, but it's the best I can do. Anything over here (if I could get it) probably wouldn't be worth a damn anyhow. To tell the truth, I never gave anyone anything for Christmas in my life. (Except at home, and very little there.) I wouldn't have the slightest idea what would be the right thing to get. Well, so much for that.

I told you last night about the cards I got at the PX.

This is all for now sweetheart. I'll write again tonight.

All my love, / Henry

Monday, November 20, 1944

Hello Baby:

Started a letter last night, but the lights went out and I didn't get to finish it. So I'll write early today.

. . . I read an article in the *Reader's Digest* yesterday that was written about how men act when they get back home from the war. One part I especially liked was the same thing you have said several times. A woman said she wasn't afraid that her husband would be just the same "for in their hearts they had never been separated." He wrote, "Darling, I feel closer to you all the time." *We* have written just about those same words many times, haven't we? You have *never* seemed far away from me darling. As I write, it seems that you are right with me. Oh, I love you *so much* honey.

This is all for now. It's almost time for chow. So bye for now and—

All my love, Henry

Thursday, November 23, 1944

My own darling:—

This has been our Thanksgiving here and we had real *turkey*. Not canned or dehydrated, but the real stuff. Of course, there are plenty of things to be thankful for, but mostly, I'm thinking of you darling and of how lucky we were to have met. I love you honey, and I'm living for the day that I can get back to you.

Saw a good G.I. show today too. Good music, singing, dancing and jokes. One fellow sang, "White Christmas," and "I'll Get By." Beautiful. And I was thinking how *I'll* get by, as long as I have *you*.

I wondered if you were going home today or keeping your original plans for Thanksgiving. I don't remember if you have told me. I didn't get a pass yesterday or today. Something got screwed up both times, so I'm trying again for tomorrow.

Darling, I guess I'll have to say goodnight for now. You know I love you and in no small way.

All my love, / Henry

Monday, November 27, 1944

Hello darling:—

The lights aren't on tonight, but I'm sharing a candle with someone and will be able to write anyhow. I love you sweetheart with all my heart and for always. You are my whole world to me honey and I wouldn't have missed loving you for anything.

Went to town this afternoon and watched for someone from my Company, but no luck. And I did some window shopping. (I believe that is what you call it when you look at everything and buy nothing.) I was looking at rings but didn't see anything like we want.

This is rather short but I'll have to say goodnight, and remember—

I love you, / Henry

Thursday, November 30, 1944

My darling:—

If we ever look through the letters I've written you (as you say we will), the first one we find written after October 20, 1944, we will not look at any more written, until we find one I wrote after I had more letters. For I don't want to be reminded of these days I'm going through now without hearing from you. Of course, I shall continue writing if I don't get a letter for the duration.

I love you so much darling that I want to tell you as often as I can, that you are everything in the world to me. And I'm living for the day that I can come home to you.

Goodnight darling and—

All my love, / Henry

13

". . . *surely, by* next *Christmas, we will be together.*"

Sunday, December 3, 1944

Hello my darling:—

Couldn't write you yesterday, so tonight I'll start early. I love you sweetheart and despite this absence of letters you still seem closer to me every day. I'll be *so* glad when I can come back to you. I don't remember if I told you or not that last Christmas, Sgt. Hinkel and I decided that somehow we were going to try to be home by this Christmas. Of course, it was only a wild hope that we abandoned a long time ago and I'm not making anymore predictions. But surely, by *next* Christmas, we will be together. I'm lonely for you honey.

Read an article in the *Stars & Stripes* tonight of some fellows getting cigarettes and on the pack was written, "Hi buddy, compliments of the Arkansas Coffin Company, Ft. Smith, Arkansas." I had to laugh at that.

Saw a movie today. "Mission Tokyo." Remember, I told you about seeing it once before I left the Company. The same thing happened again. Oh, it will be a wonderful day when I can get back to you.

I'm writing to my mail clerk tonight and telling him to send me my mail if it is being held at the Company.

Goodnight my darling. I love you with all my heart.

Always, / Henry

Monday, December 4, 1944

My own darling:—

I love you sweetheart and I'm thinking of you constantly. Wish we could be together too.

One fellow got forty letters today, but some of his buddies brought them to him. I'm going to look for a truck from the Company again tomorrow.

I know it doesn't do any good to keep on writing about there being no mail, but you too, know what it's like. It's one part of war that is hell. Maybe there are better days ahead, and I hope *soon.*

Saw another movie today, but it wasn't worth a damn. "Kismet" was the name of it.

Goodnight darling and—

I love you, / Henry

Thursday, December 7, 1944

Hello Sweetheart:—

No luck today. I hitchhiked into Germany, but couldn't find the outfit. Saw a fellow that has recently been transferred out of the Company, and he told me where I can find them, so—I'm trying again in the morning.

Loving you as I do, I'm going to find a letter somehow. It may take a few days but I will eventually get to them. Oh, I love you so much honey, that words won't express it.

Well, this is three years of war we have seen. Hope it doesn't last another year. Another week will be too much.

Goodnight my darling. Maybe I'll have better luck tomorrow.

All my love—always, / Henry

Friday, December 8, 1944

My own darling:

Got started late this morning so decided not to try to find the outfit today, but I'm trying again tomorrow. I've heard that the third time's charm. Hope it is and I can get an armload of letters.

It's been longer now than ever before since I had a letter and you know how it is not to be able to get any letters. Guess I shouldn't write so much about it, but I can't help it. I love you so much that I could never get use to not hearing from you. You are everything in the world to me honey and someday I'll be back to you.

Signed a payroll last night for about ten dollars. So, soon I can get some stamps and a pen. A couple of fellows and myself are going to start shopping for a Christmas tree. We are determined to have one if we have to steal a part of a hedge. We plan on decorating it with the strips of tin you get when a C ration can is opened (for tinsel.) Each man should get a can of hash with an occasional D bar added. Should have a pretty good holiday, although we'll be short on spirits. By the way, I read in *Yank* that Louisville was pretty well stocked with Scotch. There's no way you could send me a couple of pints, is there?

Goodnight honey, guess I'll go to bed. Wish it was with you. Maybe soon. Give Libby my best.

Goodnight again sweetheart and,

All my love, / Henry

The C ration cans were opened with an attached key. The strips of tin unwound from the key could give the appearance of tinsel. The D bar, a concentrated chocolate bar wrapped in tinfoil, was included in C rations.

Saturday, December 9, 1944

Hello darling:—

I found the Company today but there was no mail. They have been sending it to some of the hospitals I was in. There was a circular from Spring Mill, the tourist camp that you sent me a card of once.

Oh darling, I love you *so* much and it is a *great* help having your pictures back. Sgt. Hinkel had kept my personal things and among them was a letter you had written October 6. Yes, I've read it several times again. By the way, there were two air mail stamps in my billfold.

I'll probably be back in the Company in a few days. They didn't even know where I was until I told them today. I had to go the opposite direction to the way I went the first time but I found them without much trouble.

I have just re-read the letter and you asked if I would like to help with the bath you were taking before going to bed. I think I would. Well—we will see how it works out sometime. Maybe I'll get some letters soon. I left my present address with the mail clerk.

Goodnight sweetheart. I love you.

All my love *always*, / Henry

———————————

Thursday, December 14, 1944

Hello darling:—

I don't remember if I told you, but when I was at the Company, Sgt. Hinkel said he didn't see my pen when he put my other things away, so I must have lost it the night before or the morning I left the Company. In the place we were, it could have easily been dropped in the mud and never seen again. So today, I bought this one for 125 francs (or about $3.00) and it isn't worth a damn.

. . . I wrote Robert a V-mail a few minutes ago. Writing so much without getting any letters is like listening to one end of a telephone conversation. This is about all honey. I just don't know of anything to write but always, I love you darling and I never tire of telling you so.

Goodnight baby, and—

All my love, / Henry

On December 16, the Germans launched a surprise counteroffensive breakthrough in the Ardennes. Not since Pearl Harbor had there been such an unexpected attack. A quarter of a million German soldiers opened devastating artillery fire on American troops. Fog, snow, and freezing temperatures complicated defense by grounding Allied planes

The 291st was ordered to Malmédy to set up and man roadblocks south and east of the city. Sgt. Giles was still in the Replacement Center in Liege. While there, he operated a .30–caliber machine gun and served in the back loading position of a bazooka for the ground defense of Liege.

Private Wiley A. Holbrook operated Company A's .50–caliber machine gun in Henry's absence. Holbrook was struck by fragments from an enemy mortar round that burst in a tree near his position and became the first casualty of the 2nd platoon.

When the weather cleared, 5,000 American aircraft moved in to support the Allies. By Christmas Day the Germans were recognizing defeat.

They had 120,000 men killed, wounded, or missing, while the Americans had 76,890 casualties. Winston Churchill described the Battle of the Bulge as "the greatest American battle of the war."

Enemy infantry greatly outnumbered the 291st but they "stubbornly resisted all enemy attempts to drive through their positions." For their heroic and magnanimous efforts, they were awarded the President Unit Citation and presented the Distinguished Unit Badge by their commanding officer, Lt. Col. David E. Pergrin.

Tuesday, December 26, 1944

Hello honey:

Christmas has come and gone, so we can say *next* Christmas, maybe we can be together. We are bound to hit it sometime. In the meantime, we will keep on loving each other. More every day. I think of you all the time darling, and will until we are together again.

Still, I haven't had any mail and probably won't until I'm back in the Company. Believe me, I need some now, as never before. Over two months now.

I'm "rooming" with a fellow by the name of Giles. A negro fellow. Probably no relation whatever.

Well cheerio for now sweetheart and you won't forget—

I love you, / Henry

Christmas Day for the 291st was spent digging out from three days of bombings on Malmédy. Many soldiers and Belgian civilians lay dead or wounded.

The men of Company A had only K rations for Christmas dinner, but they were grateful to be alive. By the morning of December 26, the enemy was finally halted.

Designed to be carried in the pockets of paratroopers, the K ration was 6 inches by 2½ inches by 1 inch thick and was intended for use in the assault phase of combat. K rations consisted of a hard biscuit, a can of meat or meat substitute, dextrose tablets, a fruit or chocolate bar, bouillon, coffee, and lemon powder, sugar tablets, and 4 cigarettes of nonpopular brands.

There were many reports regarding the dislike of the lemon powder. It was used as a cleaning agent for stoves, for hair rinse, and for scrubbing floors, but seldom as a beverage!

Friday, December 29, 1944
Belgium

Hello Honey:

I'm back with the Company now. They came for me last night and I'm darn glad to get back. Soon I should get some mail now. Probably won't take long for it to catch up with me. Lt. Hayes just told me that I had been getting about seventeen letters a day. He says they kept the packages five days then ate them. That I doubt though.

I love you darling, more than words can tell and I'm still living for the day that I can come back to you. Maybe it won't be so long now until that will be possible.

Well, this is all for now sweetheart. I'll soon be able to write more. Soon as the APO gets on the ball.

All my love, *always*, / Henry

1/Lt. Frank R. Hayes was Mess & Supply officer of Company A and also served as censor.

Company A was relieved in Malmedy on the 26th and moved to Modave, Belgium.

Friday, December 29, 1944

Hello honey:

Guess what? *Two* good letters today. Late ones. Written December 11 & 19. Of course, you know how I feel now. Believe me, I needed them. I love you *so* much darling. And in a sense, I seemed lost during the time I couldn't hear from you. Life would be empty and dull indeed without you. One day we can start our lives as we have dreamed of so long.

Glad you found something you liked as well as you liked the watch. That is a very impersonal way of giving something, but when I would try to think of something for you, I just couldn't. Think I told you, I never gave anyone anything for Christmas. Well, so much for that. Oh yes, my watch has always done fine. (Of course it stops when I don't wind it.) It has given me good service.

I know what the clusters are for in the ground forces but I

don't know if they're given for the same thing in the Air Corp. By the way, one of the fellows in the Company has been recommended for the bronze star or the silver star, one, or maybe both. I don't remember now.

Well, darling, I'll have to stop here. The lights are dim and going on and off.

Goodnight, and—

All my love, / Henry

Except for the letter Sgt. Hinkel gave to Henry on December 9 that was written October 6, the two letters arriving on December 29 were the first Henry had received since October 20.

Sunday, December 31, 1944

Hello Sweetheart:—

I'm writing early today and if there is any mail tonight, I'll write again. I love you darling and I'm still living for the day that I can come back to you. Hope it isn't far off.

The medics had me go on sick call this morning, so tomorrow I am going back to the hospital. They told me for re-classification for non-combat duty. Whatever that may mean, I don't know but I'll let you know what happens. The day they start sending me to another Replacement Depot is when I'll "blow my top." So if you have heard anything that sounds like a V-2, about the first of the year—that was me. Now I'll have to wait and wait all over again for mail that never comes through. I hope whatever they do, they will do it quick. I would like to get settled down again once more.

Haven't seen Sgt. Hinkel. He is on detached service somewhere. Most everyone else has seen him.

By the way, the socks are O.K. Real warm and comfortable.

Wish I could get lots of letters tonight, for God only knows when I'll get any more. But I'll keep on loving you darling. More every day. And I won't forget that you are loving me in the same way.

Bye for now sweetheart. I'll write you again as soon as I can.

All my love, / Henry

Sunday, December 31, 1944

My only love:—

It's late and this is going to be very brief. Just to let you know I'm the happiest man in the Company tonight, for I had 27 letters tonight. Two from Mom, one from Irene and *twenty-four* from you, and it's taken two and one half hours to read them. I love you darling with all my heart. You know that.

If it should be some time (as it was before) before you get another letter after I'm in the hospital, try not to get so upset this time. I will write as soon again as I can. It *is* my ears that bother me. The best I remember, here is how my medical chart read: "Otitis media, chronic bilat., non-supp." Don't ask *me* what that means or if it's good or bad. I don't know. And that may not be the exact words.

Well, goodnight baby and—

All my love, always, / Henry

Sgt. Giles had a chronic virile inner ear infection in both ears and returned to the hospital in Liege on January 1.

Tuesday, January 2, 1945
Belgium

My only love:

I'm thinking of you today, as usual, and wishing we were together. Maybe before so long, that will be possible. Surely the heinies can't go much longer. Whatever time we may have to wait though, we will still be loving each other more with every day that passes.

I've just written to Mom and Irene. I'll try to write them a little more often now. Robert asked if I wrote once a week.

The latest letter I had from you was the one written the day before you were going down home. Wish I could have gotten one written while you were there. But I guess I can't complain. I did do O.K. while I was there and believe me, I was needing them. I'm going to hang on to all of them until I'm settled and get some more.

By the way, I wish you would send me Nash's address. I'll write to him, although I may not get his answer (or yours with his address) until sometime next summer. When I'm settled some place, I want you to send me the sketch of Libby's life you wrote. Even if I don't think to mention it again, you'll know when to send it.

You mentioned something about the storms or hurricanes appearing almost seasonal on the coast. Why they did, and where they started. By now, you have probably seen the article and sketches of their origin in *Time* or *Newsweek*. If I remember right, they started somewhere in the Bahamas, in "still water." Don't remember much about it.

You said your mother had sent me a harmonica. You know I'll be glad to get it. I can play one some. But if it's a chromatic, I'll have a time mustering enough wind to play for long at a time.

I never smoke cigars either. Oh, sometime I will, just for the novelty of the thing but I'll try at least one of those your mother is sending. They should be good ones.

This is the third time I've started writing this letter. Took a shower when I had written the first page. (The first one in about a month.) Now, I've just finished chow.

Yes, I will have enough hankys when they finally reach me. I could never get too many though.

I must write your mother again soon. There's so little to write about, I seldom get up enough nerve to write to anyone but you. Of course, loving you as I do, I want to always be telling you about it. I know too well also what your letters mean to me. Oh darling, I love you so much that it *hurts* to have to be away from you so long.

Goodnight baby, and you won't forget that I'm thinking of you constantly and longing desperately to be home with you.

All my love—always, / Henry

1/Lt. Nash Hancock was serving as a bomber pilot with the 15th Air Corps in Taranto, Italy.

———————

Friday, January 5, 1945

My only love:—

. . . I had to laugh a little at the way you began your letter of November 20. First you said "it's been a *wonderful, wonderful* day," then "It's been raining and sleeting snow." But just below it, you said you had gotten three letters that day and I knew how you felt. Of course, I know if my situation were reversed, it would be far worse than it is when I don't get letters. I can always be reasonably sure you are O.K., where you don't know. But try not to worry too much, for I'm alright. Maybe my luck will hold. I think it will anyhow.

Hope everyone isn't as upset (or something) about me being in the hospital this time as before. Oh yes, (your letter reminded me) my ears aren't aching any today. Just popping and buzzing.

I got the *Courier-Journal* you sent me November 20 while I was in the Company. Took some over a month for it to get here. I liked it and when I left, the fellows wanted "bids" on it.

I quite agree with Nash that the greatest pain of all is being away from you. No one or nothing can ease that pain. Nothing will help until I get back to you.

Tell me, why do you call your Mother, "Lucy?" That sounds funny. I wondered if it's a nickname or just a family habit to say that once in a while. I know Irene and I used to say "Frank" sometimes when we were talking to Dad or saying something about him.

Your reading the article about a "ray" the heinies *may* have discovered and being so alarmed over it was funny. Now just *what* type of "ray" would that be? Electricity? No. A power source would have to be so large and extensive that it would not be practical *if* electricity should be the elements of the "ray." Would it be light? No. What could be "mixed" with it to have the effects you mentioned. The heinies are shrewd, but a "ray" sounds more like something in a Flash Gordon serial than reality.

Your standing in line for your bus ticket, reminds me of the one I had to "sweat out" for Christmas dinner. Think I told you it took two hours and ten minutes.

So, I am going to have a pair of homemade socks. Well, that will be fine. I'll only wear them in an emergency though. A pair of socks knitted by hand should be taken care of.

This is all for now. And is this a long letter. For me it is anyhow.

Bye darling and I love you with all my heart—

For always, / Henry

Monday, January 8, 1945

Hello darling:

Another day passing that will bring us a little closer together. Wish we had some way of knowing how much, but we've been over that one before. I love you so much honey that I'll not be contented until we are together again.

I'm leaving the hospital in a day or so. Wasn't reclassified, so after a chain of replacements, I'll be back in the Company. Maybe, I'll go through them faster this time. I heard a fellow sing some today, but he didn't know "My Shining Hour." He sang, "I'll Walk Alone," and "Day and Night," and several others. A darn good singer.

I guess this must be about all for now. I just can't think of anything more to write. You *know* I love you and in no small way, but with all my heart and for—

Always, / Henry

On January 11, Sgt. Giles was sent back to the replacement depot. Company A was in Modave.

Friday, January 12, 1945

My only love:—

A year and a half we have been loving each other, and with the days, weeks, months and years even, our love will continue to grow deeper and sweeter. Today, it means everything in the world to us. One day, we'll be together honey and we will forget these months we have been apart, and begin our lives as we have so long wanted to.

And oh yes, I'm sure I've written more letters to you than I've written to everyone else all my life. Sometime, when you have nothing better to do, count them and tell me how many there are.

Ever play "Bingo?" Last night, someone (must have been the cooks) gave a party. *I* didn't win a thing. First time I ever played it. Several pies and cakes were given as prizes and at ten o'clock, we all had coffee and donuts. By the way, I had chicken for chow tonight. It was darn good, but nothing good to go with it.

Well, goodnight baby and once again,

I love you, / Henry

This letter is the 426th in the collection.

14

". . . fate brought us together, and love has held us so."

Tuesday, January 16, 1945

My darling:—

Had a hell of a surprise a few moments ago. A Sergeant came in calling my name and when I answered, he told me I was on KP. But he was only kidding, he brought me *two* letters from you, one from Mom and a package from home. Was I ever glad to get them. I feel a thousand percent better and I love you *so much* darling that words won't express it. But someday, we will know more about it and just what we have been missing.

Remember I told you of giving "Herman" (that is what we called him) the singer, a hanky? Well, in the package today, I got three in its place. So—I guess it's O.K. to give away something sometime. I also got a box of assorted candy with some gum, shaving cream, toothpaste, and two tooth brushes.—

I stopped there and went to a movie. Saw "Seven Days Leave." A pretty good show. I may get some more mail soon, since I've been located by someone.

I had just written to Mom, so I just added to the bottom that I got the package and the letters. She sent a stamped envelope, so I'm using it to send this.

Oh darling, your letters make me *so* anxious to get back. One day, this waiting *will* end, and I'll be back. You're darn right I'll call you when I land even if I have money or not. (And I probably won't.) I'm writing like it may be any day now, but maybe it will be sometime this year anyhow.

Yes, William Giles is one of my cousins. Mama wrote me sometime ago that he had been wounded. Yes, Libby did tell me to put on my raincoat and galoshes, and at the time I went to the hospital (first), I was using the raincoat for an awning over the front of my tent, and I didn't have galoshes. Now I have.

I *do* like that much love. "Until the day after forever." I love that, and that's the way it will be, for always. I don't remember ever hearing the "Charioteers." Maybe I have. Did you ever hear the "Golden Gate Quartette?" They are good, or used to be.

I don't suppose Nash and I are related anywhere "back down the line." Maybe it's due to the fact that the two of us are from Kentucky that we say the same things, like the same qualities, etc. Could be.

I'll eat chow now—

And was I ever hungry.

I guess you noticed some of the pictures I had made at Ft. Ord were "left handed." One of the fellows developed them and some of the negatives were upside down when he made the prints. They were taken while I was in the fire department on special duty.

Don't believe I told you of the movie I saw yesterday. It was a killer. Abbott & Costello in "Lost in a Harem." A scream from the beginning.

The lights aren't so hot in here so I'll say goodnight for now and you won't forget that I love you for—

Always, / Henry

William Giles was also from Knifley, Kentucky.

Saturday, January 20, 1945

Hello darling:

I love you and I *wish* it were possible to get back to you, and *soon*. But, we'll have to wait some more it seems. One day though, this damn war will have to end, and I'll be coming back to you.

I'm still in the Replacement, but soon I should be back in the Company, or so they tell me here. We have the best in food at this place. So far, I haven't seen any C rations. We have had beef roast, steak, turkey and the things that should go with them since we've been here.

I would like to know where Nash finally was located. When I get some more mail I'll probably know more. In some of the letters, you have said he was in North Africa.

I'll stop here sweetheart. You know I love you in every way there is and for—

Always, / Henry

Wednesday, January 31, 1945

Hello darling:

Came back to the Company today and I got *six* letters in today's mail, so you know I'm feeling fine now. I've already read the letters twice. Can't get enough of them. The sweetest letters anyone could hope to get. You *were* a little anxious to get some word from me, and maybe by now you have. Oh darling, I love you *so much*, that the three words, "I love you," fall very short in expressing what you mean to me. Well—one day.

By the way, the news is still good, but as I have said before, I refuse to become "hepped up" again, until there *is* something happening. The Reds are still doing O.K. apparently.

Sgt. Hinkel is in the Company now. I've been with him some since I came in.

It was good that your mother spent Christmas with you, for I'm sure it helped make your Christmas a better one. I believe I sent her a card Christmas. I too, hope she had good luck in going home on the bus.

You know honey, I'm *sure* you will be the "best wife a man ever had." We're too much in love for it to ever be otherwise and *I* will always do *everything* I know to keep you happy. And why do you ask "if I mind" that you bought the desk. You know I said it was for you, for anything you wanted.

What was wrong with Nash's ears? Maybe you have told me before in another letter. You told me once of how you and Libby thought we were alike in some respects. I wondered if we both had to have the same ailments too. What he said about me gives me a feeling that I or you or anyone can't explain. Just a good feeling that everyone is pulling for you.

And you know what? We can always be thankful that we have the Air Force we do and the men with the nerve and brains to operate it. If it hadn't been for the Air Force, we would have been pushed west of the Mississippi by now. I've thought of that I guess more than anyone else. Of course, every phase of war has its hazards, but with two of the sweetest little women in the world pulling for two guys like us, we *have* to come back.

I had to laugh at Irene saying Mama always loved me more than any of the rest. I never noticed any difference, but if it's true, I can see where I have failed her many times.

Oh yes, the sketch you sent of your desk looks rather neat. Must be O.K. Hope you had good luck removing the varnish and re-finishing it with your "Red Devil" scraper.

Well, honey, I'll stop here. It's almost time to go to bed. Good-night and

All my love, / Henry

Company A was near St. Vith, rebuilding the destroyed Bailey and fixed bridges over the same rivers and streams they had bridged before through Trois Ponts, Malmédy, and Hockai.

Thursday, February 1, 1945

Hello darling:—

Two more good letters today. The first one written as you were waiting for the bus to go to Louisville. The first letter I've had where you told of being home.

. . . It's really something the way you and the folks like each other and the way you enjoy yourselves when together. That I like, but it wouldn't have made any difference to me as far as you are concerned. I guess my folks are pretty good judges of quality and beauty, too.

Yes, I long ago (even before I met you) decided that I wouldn't live around home when I got out of the Army. I know what it's like. Don't think I'll ever get "homesick" for the Army when I get home, but a bunch of fellows such as I know in Company A, a fellow could never forget. I've been in several outfits and known a lot of fellows, but none have I ever liked more than the boys here. Officers & enlisted men alike. Coming back was just like going home, with everyone saying, "Glad to see you back." Shaking hands, etc.

So Nash is in Italy. The last letters in which you mentioned his location, he was in North Africa. In this one you said he was in Italy. Guess he will be home before me at that. But I'll be there. A man flying missions over enemy territory deserves *all* the breaks he can get.

Did a little laundry today. A suit of underwear, some socks and a jacket. And I also boiled my white handkerchiefs in something (as usual) that faded and turned them green in spots. Guess it was the socks.

Guess I'll say so long for now sweetheart. You *know* I love you with all my heart and for always.

All my love, / Henry

———————————

Sunday, February 4, 1945

Hello honey:—

It's rather late and I'm pretty tired so I'll just write a V-mail tonight. I can tell you I love you even on this and that is the most important thing of all. You are everything in the world to me darling.

Tonight, I have seven letters, your picture with the Valentine and Libby's letter, which I will try to answer tomorrow. Couldn't write you yesterday at all. Thanks for the picture honey. It's good, and only a few days ago, I was wishing for a new one. The Valentine is really cute. About the best I've ever seen.

Had two letters from home tonight too, and one of them leaves me very much depressed. Mom says Dallas Badger, my best pal I had around home (including a number of cousins), has been killed in the Philippines. Such is war.

Goodnight my darling and you know I love you, more every day.

All my love & kisses, / Henry

Dallas Badger was killed on December 7, 1944.

———————————

Monday, February 5, 1945

My only love:—

I'll begin to answer your very sweet letters I received last night, and hope I'm not interrupted.

. . . By the way, I'm sending you a picture. Well, a group picture that I was in. It's no good and if you don't want it (or the other one) you can send them home.

I guess it won't take so long for the two of us to be convinced that our being together is real. Oh, we are going to have a *lot* of fun honey.

I'll be glad when some of my packages get back around to me. Reading where you sent me a jar of boned chicken makes me hungry.

I was just about where you hoped I was when the breakthrough started. Things are a lot brighter now than they were then. Maybe the war will end someday. I hope *soon*. And no, we didn't get to have a Christmas tree. I will have Christmas though when my packages arrive.

You can tell Libby how glad I am to get her letter and that I'll answer in a few days. She really wrote a good letter. Said *you* could cook too.

I think we both have the same ideas about souvenirs. If it isn't against regulations, I want to take a German rifle home with me. Not for a souvenir but just to have a good gun. They're really accurate and light. I fired one once, four or five times and they would be O.K.

By now you know I've lost my pen, but if you haven't already, don't send me one. It would take so long for it to get here and I can get one sometime soon.

Your letters written on the twelfth are always aces. For it is then we remember that on *one* twelfth of the month, we started what has amounted to the most wonderful love in the world, with more yet to come. We will always thank our lucky stars that fate brought us together, and love has held us so. A lot of sweet memories we have of those few hours we were together.

Everything you write is always good. Even if you only tell me of going to a movie, or having a lunch, and things like that.

You should see my electric candle. I took two flashlight batteries, about a foot of tape, six inches of copper wire and a bulb, and rigged them up and it's a pretty good light. Hope this information doesn't get into enemy hands. Lt. Hayes called it the "Giles secret weapon." I'm really proud of it.

Mama said William Giles was back in New York. He must have been wounded or shocked pretty bad. I would like to get back, but not like that. Did I ever hate to hear of Dallas Badger being killed. He was one of the finest fellows you ever saw and the best buddy in the world. Guess I was one of the last fellows around home to see him too. In Paso Robles, California, we were together for the last time.

So long for now baby. I've written all I can think of. You know I love you for—

Always, / Henry

Friday, February 9, 1945

Hello Baby:

Had three good letters tonight. So, everything is just as near right as could be, with so many miles between us. I love you honey, and in no small way.

Say, I'll bet it will soon be Captain Nash, since he is Squadron Leader. I don't know so much about Air Corp promotions, but it seems that there would be a lot more responsibility. Well, everyone knows that those fellows deserve everything.

I know now, pretty well, what part of Louisville Hepburn is in. Once I was hitchhiking from Indiana to home. I used a city map and walked all the way through Louisville to be sure I didn't get lost riding buses. I remember the big bend in Bardstown Road that you show in the sketch.

Oh yes, I'm *sure* I'll like being married to "my half" of the "Moore gals." Yes, you can say *that again*. I'm sure that Nash and I will be the best of—shall we say "buddies." I've seen a few people I didn't like but none I couldn't get along with.

Maybe I haven't said so in just those words, but I *do* like for you to visit my folks and it's really something the way you and they "clicked." Of course, I didn't know of any reason why you shouldn't, even before you went the first time. And since *I* can't be with you, some of my folks just as well be.

Of course, the people around my home (my aunts & uncles & etc.) made it their business to just "accidentally" happen to see you, to, as you say, see if you were "stuck up" or anything. Of course, I don't mind them knowing that I'm marrying a woman that is "crazy" about me. In fact, I like it.

I've heard the song you mentioned, but I think it will be pretty easy for *me* to forget my "Good Old Rambling Days." By the way, you can inform Libby that when I yodel it's strictly for my *own* entertainment.

Think I've told you that "Herman" didn't have the music and didn't know the words, so I still haven't heard "My Shining Hour."

Honey, I guess my chances for a furlough are about as slim as a snowball in Hades, but if I *could* get one, I'd take it.

I didn't write yesterday. Couldn't. And if I did the day before, it was a V-mail. That reminds me, I heard the Germans were about to launch another V-weapon. V-quit.

Goodnight darling and—

All my love, / Henry

On February 7, 1945, the entire 291st Engineer Combat Battalion moved towards the Huertgen Forest in Germany. After locating, Company A was busied building an airstrip while all three companies continued to repair bridges and roads. Wet snow, mud, and terrible weather increased the frustrations of the tasks.

Monday, February 12, 1945

My only love:—

It's our "anniversary" again and after nineteen months of knowing you darling, I love you so much that words don't begin to express what you mean to me. In some ways (a day at a time) it seems an awful long time, but on the whole, it seems to have passed quick enough. It doesn't matter how long we may have to wait, we will still be loving each other more with every day that passes. One day, we *will* be together again.

I've heard the song, "Don't Let Your Sweet Love Die," but I don't know it. In fact, I've almost forgotten all songs I ever knew. Robert sent me a song but I've never heard it. "Mother's Prayers Guide Me." Beautiful words, but I can't match them with the music.

Did I ever tell you of reading Bob Hope's book, *I Never Left Home*? You should read it, if you like his programs. There's a lot of laughs all the way through it. That reminds me that my comics still haven't come through. Probably still following me through the Replacement Depots. The letters I've had so far are direct from the states.

Yes, I remember the letter I wrote Christmas day and I did express my feelings a little too freely. I try not to sound too gloomy when I write, but sometimes I guess it *will* show up. But Christmas *was* an exceptionally blue day.

Oh yes, I thought you remembered the bet I made when we left Nashville. I bet you I would kiss you before we were in Memphis. When you called it so quick like, I figured I had made a bad bet, so I immediately called it off. Remember it now?

I had to laugh at your learning to sleep with the covers tucked in just for me. That *is* real love. But you shouldn't bother yourself on such a small a thing as that. Guess we'll both be kicking them off some. I'll stop here sweetheart, by telling you again I love you and I'm living for the day I can come home to you.

All my love always, / Henry

Tuesday, February 13, 1945

My only love:—

I'll now attempt to answer the three letters I was too sleepy to last night. First though, I love you my darling, with all my heart and for always. You are everything in the world to me honey and I'm thinking of you all the time. I agree with you that it doesn't look like we will have our April wedding, but we'll have one someday and I *hope* it won't be much longer.

What you said you thought you would have engraved on your watch sounds O.K. And of course, it *was* given with all my love.

You know, the other night, we were having a card game (poker) when someone brought my letters in and I started reading them while still playing. Someone would yell at me when I was high, or when it was my turn to open. I would skip the deal while I was reading them, and when I finished reading, I had won almost every pot for that time. The onlookers said I should have your letters to read everytime I played, while the players said no more letters should be given me until after a game. Of course, all I won wouldn't buy a whiskey sour. Just small stakes.

Did I ever tell you that a lot of fellows (most everyone) call me "Uncle Henry?" I don't know why unless it's because my name is a good one to attach "Uncle" to. There used to be a hillbilly band on WHAS that was called "Uncle Henry and his Kentucky Mountaineers." They used to come to Knifley once in a while. Kelsey (Casey) Jones from Knifley, was in this band for awhile.

Guess I'll say bye for now darling, by once more sending you—

All my love, / Henry

Saturday, February 17, 1945

My only love:—

I'll now try to answer the letters I had last night, by first saying I love you. . . . I also had a letter from Mom last night. She told me another one of my cousins was killed over here. I knew the Goode boy you said was wounded. He didn't live so far from home.

Yes, we have really learned what it's like to go without letters. Hope Nash and Libby are never so unfortunate. You can tell Nash that ordinary G.I. soap will stop a pup tent from leaking if it's just a seep. It might work on a larger one too. Just rub it on the outside. Nothing I know of is more disgusting than a leaky tent. Further on, you say it was holes burned in the tent, so that wouldn't work.

Yes, I guess Mama did hope I would stay back in the Replacement Depot but if she knew the situation as I do, she wouldn't like it. I really did some sweating while I was in them.

You really did spend a "lazy" Sunday, January 14. Of course, it wasn't a lazy one, you just needed rest. If I had been with you, we probably *wouldn't* have slept as much. Darling, I want you with me all the time, when I get back.

I too, wonder what has happened to the comics you sent me. Maybe they will be along sometime. You know, it happens everytime I can get stamps, it isn't more than two or three days until I get some from you. But I like to have a lot. Sometimes one of the fellows may not have any and need one. So now, I have quite a supply.

This last letter (February 7) did O.K. in reaching me in nine days. If only mine would do as well in getting to you.

Bye for now honey and you won't forget—

I love you, / Henry

The United States Postal Service did an incredible job handling the staggering volume of mail sent overseas. 571 million pieces in 1943 increased to 3.5 billion in 1945. The speed of delivery was phenomenal considering the endless mobility of millions of military men and women in service during the war.

Henry's cousin Edward Bottoms, also from Knifley, Kentucky, was killed on Christmas Day, 1944, in Belgium.

15

"War is hell."

Sunday, February 18, 1945

Hello darling:—

. . . I *wish* this damn war would stop. One day it will, and then I'll be coming home darling.

Had a good shower today with a complete change of clothes that left me feeling like a million. I took it with my watch on. Didn't know if it would hurt it or not and I don't think it has. First time I've ever done it, but I forgot to put it in my pocket when I took my jacket off.

Been reading the *Stars & Stripes* tonight, but there's no outstanding news in it.

Goodnight my love and you won't forget that I'm thinking of you constantly and loving you with all my heart.

All my love, / Henry

Sunday, February 25, 1945

Hiya Baby:—

Gotta letter tonight, so I'm doing O.K. . . . The news is good tonight. Maybe the war *will* end someday. Who knows? (That doesn't sound so good, does it?)

Irene wrote quite a long letter tonight but nothing in the way of news. Just ordinary chatter, I guess it could be called, but a good letter. Oh yes, in *your* letter last night, you said in the next war, you wanted me to be in the Navy (if anything). Well, I won't. My idea of the Navy isn't like everyone else's.

None of us had heard of the Russians being in eight miles of Berlin. Reminds me of what Gen. Eisenhower says in tonight's *Stars*

& Stripes. Said he wasn't as frightened during the breakthrough as he was when he read of it in the papers from the states.

This is all for now darling. Goodnight and—

All my love, / Henry

Thursday, March 1, 1945

Hello Baby:—

Ever get about five dozen letters at once? Guess not. Well I did last night. *Forty-eight* from you! That is including V-mails, Christmas cards, etc. Twelve from Irene and Mama together and something from the Church of God in Anderson, Indiana. I still lack twelve of yours being through reading them. Just haven't had time yet, and I wanted to write tonight too. I couldn't yesterday.

Oh darling, they are such *wonderful* letters! So full of love and everything that goes to make you the most *wonderful* person in the world. I love you honey, oh *so* much. I consider myself *very* fortunate in finding you, the sweetest little girl in the world. You're going to be *so* nice to come home to.

I'll not try to answer any of them tonight, except a few of the things I can remember. About the biggest surprise was Rollin Dixon being the one that married Fay. He is a fine kid, but it seems odd that those two are old enough to marry.

Had *chicken* tonight for chow! I got a breast with a wing attached. (That is a sudden change of subjects, but I belched.)

Honey, it's late, I'm on guard *and* sleepy, so excuse me for now, and I'll grab a few winks.

You *know* I love you and in no small way. Goodnight baby and—

All my love, / Henry

Friday, March 2, 1945

Hello my darling:—

I've just finished reading *all* your letters and everyone has been thoroughly enjoyed. Although the last few were written during the breakthrough and you were uneasy. If the situation should have been reversed, I would have been *frantic*.

I didn't tell you of the letter I had from Mary (Petie to you, but I'm calling her Mary, O.K.?) with your picture in it, a good one too. At the bottom, she had written, "This is the package we would like to have placed by your Christmas tree," and would *I* have liked having you for a Christmas package. I'm darn glad to get the picture too. I wish you could read the letter. Beautiful, I guess is the word for it. Six *big* pages, and I'm going to write some of what she says.

She was telling of the fall beauty she had seen of the trees, etc., and she writes, "The serenity of my life made me delve the depths of my being to hold to that beauty, and try in some way to transfer some of it in letters to you—everything beautiful I see, I see it for all of you. Everytime I laugh, even the meals I eat—and when my husband holds me in his arms, I hold tight in memory of the aching arms of countless thousands who would give anything on earth to have the joy of holding their loved ones." *Isn't* that beautiful. I could cry a little I guess. When she told me to get comfortable while she tried to acquaint me with the Sullivans, she says, "It happens I am inclined to a brand of wit bordering on the 'idiotic.' " I think that's good. In fact, the entire letter is good.

Think I'll send the photo of Nash and Libby back. I don't have room to carry it and if I did, I'd have to cut it down and it's too good a picture to trim. It *is* a *very* good one.

You should hear some of the fellows cry that didn't get any mail the night I got mine. But I reminded them, once I went for more than two months without any mail. In one of the letters there were stamps. Maybe now, I'll have enough to last for the duration. I hope so. Wish I knew where I could trade this fellow's pen for a good goose quill.

I've got a good German rifle now. If I can get hold of something to mail it in, I'll send it home. Maybe we'll go deer hunting with it sometime.

Guess I'll stop here sweetheart. You *know* I love you, so—

All my love, / Henry

Friday, March 2, 1945

Hello Honey:—

I'm terribly sleepy so don't expect a very long letter. I've already written you once today. Rather a long one for me. I've just written home about the letters I had the night before last. By the way, I got two *Courier-Journals* too.

. . . Tonight, I got an official army envelope and what do you suppose was in it? A letter I wrote you November 6 and only put my return address on it. So I'm using the envelope. No point in sending you the letter.

Oh yes, you know darn well I didn't mind you using five dollars of what I sent you to help buy Libby a gift for us. That is what you should have done.

You can expect a birthday present sometime this month by cable. I *hope* it reaches you before your birthday. In case you're wondering, it's sixty dollars. I had already told Mama to get you something for me for your birthday, so if she doesn't get the letter I wrote her tonight, you'll get something else.

Well, goodnight baby. Maybe I'll see you in my dreams.

All my love, / Henry

Saturday, March 3, 1945

Hello honey:—

Guess I'll begin answering the letters I got the other night, although a lot of the things in them have already been answered or I know about them. I'll have to answer Mary's letter pretty soon too. Hope I can write a letter as interesting as her's is, but that, I doubt.

Don't expect me to "stick to the point," in this letter, for in answering so many letters, this will be more like a school kid's written grammar lesson. Just sentences. But all through it, I'll be telling you, I love you. And we both like that.

One thing I'm wondering about is *where* my packages are. Maybe the Krauts *did* get them. I hope not anyhow.

I guess Nash will get home before me, but I believe I've said before that those fellows *deserve* the breaks. Not so long ago, I saw some of our planes in action and believe me, they went through something. But they kept going, and returning again and again.

Of *course*, I "realize" that your Mother (and the rest) will be out to see us. They had *better*, if they want to stay in my good graces. And we'll go visit them when we can, and first too, if you like.

I get a kick out of the way you say you and Libby want to be talking of your own man. Well—someday you'll be able to talk *to* me. Hope it isn't long.

Your telling me of Nash's house they built reminded me to tell you of the "burn out" I nearly had this morning. The other fellows were asleep and I started a good fire, and part of the blackout material we had packed around the stovepipe caught on fire. I yanked it out, inside the building (a tarpaulin truck top) but couldn't put out the fire on the tarp from inside so I ran outside and with a handful of snow and mud, put out the fire. *Then* I remembered the burning sandbag I had left inside and raced back in, in time to prevent it from spreading. After I finished chasing myself, all the damage that was done was my cap that I had left on top of the stove when it first started. It's ruined.

In your answer to the letter in which I asked you to send me some cigarettes, you said there must be a racket of some sort going on. But wonder where those are that have been sent to me.

Guess this is enough for this time, so bye for now and—

I love you, / Henry

Monday, March 5, 1945

Hello my darling:—

. . . Was unable to write to you yesterday, so don't expect one. There were more stamps in one of these letters, so now, I *surely* have enough to last for the duration.

A cigarette lighter *will* be just the thing for my birthday. *Don't* pay too much for it for I had just as soon lose a ten cent one as a five dollar one. And I'll probably lose it too. We get lighter fluid with our rations. Sometime you could send some extra flints. Back in France, we could use Calvados for fluid, and we did. Calvados has the kick of a bay mule. A few drinks and you're on top of the world. A few more and you fall off.

Had a V-mail from Mom last night, and she says Edward Bottoms, my cousin was killed in Belgium, Christmas Day. Believe me, war *is* hell.

No packages have come through *yet.* I'm going to soon give them up for lost. (War is hell.)

I've written Robert this afternoon and sent home some German money we found here.

Well, so long for now baby, and you won't forget that I love you and think of you constantly.

Always yours, / Henry

Tuesday, March 6, 1945

My darling:

Two letters last night, postmarked October 23 and November 6. Just a bit late, but sweet ones and I like reading this "ancient history." (You said that.)

. . . There's nothing in these letters that needs answering, so I'll just tell you of my housecleaning today. I started by throwing some glass and cans out a window and the owners heard me, so three of them (Krauts) came up and cleaned up everything. Carried out some little old stands and everything we didn't need.

Someone gave me a pack of German cigarettes. It's like smoking weeds. No taste at all. Guess there's no place in the world where things are as good as in the U.S. Even our "rollings" are better than anything I've tasted on this side of the pond.

I'll answer some of the 48 letters. In the one you wrote November 2, you say you will be glad when we can do our loving at closer range. You can say that again! For that is exactly what I want more than anything in the world. Just to be where you are. I agree with you in that I don't see how a "long distance" love could be more perfect than ours. Well, we're in love, and we understand and trust each other.

You know, *I* wonder just where Irene lives now. It must be one of the houses just up the road from home.

Will tell you in this letter, in case it reaches you before the other one, I sent you $60 for your birthday. It will come by cable. I hope you get it in time.

A fellow found a mandolin today and gave it to me. I'm going to send it home if I can. Guess it's a pretty good one, but I've forgotten what key the strings are, so *I* can't tune it.

Well I'll close now honey, you won't forget that I love you in all ways—

Always, / Henry

Wednesday, March 7, 1945

My only love,

Another good letter last night to make the day end as near perfect as is possible to do so over here.

You were somewhat hopeful of an early end of the war when you wrote this letter, weren't you? Well, maybe it will end some-day, at that, but I'm afraid that a lot more of Germany will have to be conquered and occupied than already is. How long that may be is anyone's guess. Frankly, I think it will be *months* yet.

Send me a fountain pen. A good one if you can find one. If you haven't already.

No honey, our love will not be any older in twenty years than it is now. Just more of it. We'll still be just as crazy about each other. I hope I won't have to stay over here so long that we'll have to adopt our family if we want one. (I read that in the *Stars & Stripes.*)

This letter was written February 22, on the "sunshine" sta-tionary. You were listening to Bing Crosby's program and one song you mentioned is "When the Blue of the Night Meets the Gold of the Day." While I was on the Gulf Coast in Texas, we had several dances and that was on the electric victrola and I believe it was played as much as all the other records. I would think of you then, although we didn't know so much about each other then. It's beautiful, and if I remember, with Hawaiian music. The others you heard, I've never heard of.

Guess by now, you've heard about the re-classification I didn't get or want. I would rather be up here than back in rear echelons. If you (or Mama) knew it as I do, *you* wouldn't want me re-classified either. Oh, if you could be sent back to England it would be O.K., I guess.

By the way, we've gotten some kind of a French citation. Don't know just exactly what, but something.

Guess I'll stop here. I almost have an envelope full written, so bye for now and,—

All my love, / Henry

On March 7, 1945, American troops were successful in crossing the Luden-dorff Bridge over the treacherous waters of the Rhine at Remagen. Within 24 hours, more than 8,000 troops, with tanks and artillery, had crossed for what

General Eisenhower would declare as "one of my happy moments of war." The Allies "pierced the defensive barrier to the heart of Germany." Hitler later admitted that the invasion of France and the mass movement of troops across the Ludendorff Bridge at Remagen sealed the fate of Germany.

The 291st Engineer Combat Battalion was assigned with the 998th and 988th Treadway Bridge Companies to build a treadway bridge across the Rhine near the north side of the Ludendorff Bridge. The men labored intensely under constant shelling and bombings from German artillery. Company A was designated to construct and connect treadway rafts and suffered their second casualty, Pvt. Merion A. Priester. Five men from Company A were wounded during the shelling that killed Priester with shrapnel.

On March 10, 1945, the 291st successfully breached the Rhine in what was cited as "the most important and dangerous bridge assignment in the history of the Corps of Engineers." Confirmed to be 1,032 feet in length and completed in thirty hours, the bridge constructed by the 291st at Remagen remains "the longest tactical bridge of its type ever built under enemy fire."

Col. Pergrin received the following note from General Dwight D. Eisenhower: "The whole Allied force is delighted to cheer the U.S. First Army whose speed and boldness have won the race to establish our first bridgehead over the Rhine. Please tell all ranks how proud I am."

The 291st received the French citation, a streamer in the colors of the French Croix de Guerre with a Silver Star embroidered MALMEDY.

16

". . . one happy day, this waiting will be over . . . ."

Monday, March 12, 1945

Hello my darling:

This is our "anniversary" again, and I love you more than I can ever tell you. Twenty months ago we were together. Wonder how long it will be until we are together again? Well, if it should be as long again, we would still be waiting as we have been this long and our love growing with each day that passes. Every day darling, you are dearer and sweeter to me than before. Every day I'm more anxious to get home to you. Couldn't write yesterday, so now I'll answer some of the letters I had night before last. (No mail last night.)

You were hoping I would soon get a letter with air mail stamps in it and by now you know that I have plenty of them. Maybe too, you are getting my letters more regularly by now. By the way, I got one of the newspapers too, with the letters. Had one letter from Robert and one from Mama.

You are still debating with yourself if you should get the shoes you saw and wanted. If you haven't already, why don't you get them for your birthday. (Hope you get the money I sent before your birthday.) Or are you supposed to give something like that for presents? Whatever you get for yourself will be O.K. with me.

This is a German pen I'm using. The kind you have to dip in the ink, but it writes pretty good. Guess what we have for a mascot? A *canary* and it is singing now. Don't know how long we'll be able to keep it though.

You know, another good reason I wish I had met you sooner, is that I would have a little more money. Once I asked Mama how much I had and the answer came in the letter written November 14. Then I had $400 clear, in less than a year. But, without you, there didn't seem any good reason to keep any.

Possibilities of a furlough or being home before the war is over have been so small, that I've just never mentioned to you what we would do. We definitely *would* be married. And you would be with me as much as possible in that case, you could work *if* you wanted to.

Bye for now honey. I'll write tonight if I can.

All my love, / Henry

Monday, March 12, 1945

Hello Sweetheart:—

This will be twice I've written today but guess it isn't too much. It being our anniversary anyhow. I love you so, I could never tell you, even if I wrote a dozen times each day. But I always want to tell you those three little words everytime I can. You are my entire world darling, and twenty months ago it started.

Read the article you sent me from *Time* magazine and it is a good one. Everyone seems to be about the same everywhere. Just waiting. Hope this waiting doesn't last so much longer.

I too, hope we (here's Jeff with a bottle of Cognac) won't have to spend so much time unmarried and I don't see why we should have to but at least a few hours, and that would be if I got home during the night.

I've just been telling a fellow that twenty months ago was when I met you. Most everyone knows how we first met. One fellow still teases me about getting the money from you in Dallas. By the way, I really *meant* to pay it back.

It was just like Dad to tell you to be sure to vote. And no, I didn't vote. In fact, I wasn't even registered until just a while before I joined the Army.

Here you say Nash had fresh eggs. That reminds me, I had *two* eggs this p.m. Found them while they were still warm. Also, I fried some bacon with them. *They* were *good.*

Here's the first letter I've gotten that you wrote while you were down home. There's nothing much to write about it, except that I'm glad you enjoyed it as you did. Only a few days ago I had a letter telling just where Irene moved to. Did she tell you about when we were kids and lived down in the woods from there? Gosh! That seems like centuries ago. Guess Cora Mae wouldn't look like the kid she used to, since you say she is larger than Mom or Irene. So you read the letter I wrote Irene, eh? Well Honey, I'm not the *least bit* afraid that I'll ever regret marrying you.

Wrote to Robert this afternoon on a typewriter. Someone picked it up, so I used it.

Jeff gave me a harmonica he found. A German make, key of A, but they're not so good unless accompanied with another instrument. Wow!—this Cognac is really powerful.

Goodnight baby, and you won't forget that I love you and think of you constantly.

All my love always, / Henry

Wednesday, March 14, 1945

My own darling:—

All your letters are always wonderful but one's especially like the latest ones I have here are *tops*, for you had gotten quite a bit of mail from me and you seemed to be sitting on top of the world. I like that. I *love* you darling with ever breath I draw. I *wish* I could get home to you—but I guess that is still a few months in the future.

Got three *Courier-Journals* last night too. Don't remember what the dates were, but they were sent sometime about election time. I've given up getting my Christmas packages. What a shame for everything to be wasted like that. Makes me sick.

I started this late in the afternoon and was interrupted. After the interruption, know what I did? I killed a chicken and fried it. It was pretty good, but I don't know if the trouble was worth the chicken—or vice versa.

I agree that this is going to be the most exciting time we ever had. But just wait until I come on home. Wow! I'll be looking for the sketch of Libby's life. So, if you haven't already, send it along honey.

Someone found a funny looking musical instrument and gave it to me. It has a head (guess it's called a head) like a mandolin. The neck is about six inches long with only five frets and it has *seven* strings! Guess there had been a key to tune it with, but we used a pair of pliers. Finally got four strings tuned Hawaiian style, but the strings were too close to the neck for that. Do *you* know what the name of it may be?

We have just been given our ribbon for the Presidential Citation and the campaign ribbon with three stars. I'll look like a hero with all these on and of course, I'll have the good conduct and pre-Pearl Harbor one too. I think the French citation gives us a braid to wrap around the shoulder some way.

No letters tonight, except a V-mail from Mom—no news.

So—in twenty months I've averaged 23 letters a month. That is a *lot* for me. But I've loved it.

Guess I'll close for now Baby. Think I'll worry the boys some with my mandolin now. Goodnight my darling and—

All my love, / Henry

Monday, March 19, 1945

Hello honey:—

Another day passing that we won't have to sweat out again. I'm one day nearer home and love you one day more. Maybe it won't be so much longer until we see the end of the war, and have some idea when we can be together.

Yesterday, my watch went haywire and I sent it to you. Have it repaired, but you don't have to be in a hurry. I don't know why it stopped so suddenly but I believe it was the balance wheel. Lt. Hayes said he would send it First Class.

I've done a little laundry this afternoon. A fatigue blouse and pants, a wool shirt and three pairs of socks. Found an old washboard and it wasn't so hard washing them.

Maybe I'll have some mail tonight, since it's been two or three nights since I've had any. If there should be, I'll write again tonight.

For now I guess I'll say so long Baby and

All my love, / Henry

Monday, March 19, 1945

My only love:—

I've written once today, but I had, let me see—*nine* good letters tonight and I'm really "overflowing" with my love for you tonight. Darling, *how* I wish we were together tonight. Well—we'll just have to be as patient as we can until that day.

It's a little cool in here. I'm in a cellar and there's no heat, so it's just a little cool for comfort. The first night we were going to sleep, a mouse ran across my forehead. It wouldn't have bothered me so much if his feet hadn't been so cold. Just like ice.

About the letters—four of them were written in March, the others in the latter part of October and in November. I read the latest ones first. Not that there is ever any difference *in* the quality but I just wanted to know how everything has been lately. I had one from Mom and Robert. Mail service isn't so bad now.

I think it's a little cool to be comfortable enough to write, so I'll wait until tomorrow to answer. I could go upstairs to the fire but I'm sleepy too.

Goodnight my darling and—

All my love, / Henry

Tuesday, March 20, 1945

Hello my darling:—

Now, I'll attempt to answer some of the letters I had last night. In your letter written October 17, you were telling how you always went to sleep on your right side pretending I'm there with you. I laughed at it, but I wouldn't say you are "silly." (You said for me not to think that.) Guess I will sleep on your right side, (the right side of you) if you think it's best. Then you'll be sure not to miss me.

This "drawing" you sent of Kenneth's. I didn't know what it was supposed to be until in the letter you say it's a tree and house. Maybe he could do better now. It says here, Irene was about to move to Roley! Must have been ten letters from you last night. That's what I have here now.

This is certainly some sad looking writing. Almost lying down and using my knees for a desk. *Maybe* you can read it.

By the way, I have a good cigarette lighter now. One came in the rations a few days ago and I was lucky enough to get it. Just like a blow torch.

I like it when you are doing so well in getting letters from me. No, I don't mind if you think you are the luckiest woman in the world. *I'm* the luckiest man in the world too! Had you ever thought of that? One day, we're going to be the *happiest* two people in the world! Hope it isn't long.

In the history you were reading of Kentucky where there was a bill of sale to a John Giles, I used to hear my Grandfather talk of an Uncle John, of being around Casey Creek. Guess that was him. If you don't know, my grandfather's name was James Washington and my grandmother was Mary E. Campbell before they married. I remember they used to mention a "Grandpap Printle," but I don't know which side he was on.

You say here you have already bought a pair of shoes. Wish you could have gotten the ones you wanted, but I guess you couldn't get another stamp for them could you? (I don't know much about this ration business. There wasn't any when I left.)

I've read some in the *Stars & Stripes* of the flood you were having. I figured you would be O.K. (according to a sketch you sent once of Louisville). You were talking of having to switch cigarettes so often lately. I still prefer Luckies.

So you *do* like crossword puzzles. One of the fellows gets the *New York Daily News* and when we can, we do a few of them together. Usually our combined efforts work all of it.

Darling, I guess I'll have to stop here. You know I love you in every way for—

Always, / Henry

Wednesday, March 21, 1945

Hello my darling:

. . . Bet you didn't know I could type did you? This one evidently needs cleaning, or something, and not knowing how that is done, I'll have to hope you'll be able to read it. I wrote to Mary yesterday on one. It's interesting to peck around on one anyhow. (You can see how I forget to space my words sometimes.)

I've just read why the letter I got last night was so late. It says that the ship that sailed with letters from December 4–14 had to be repaired three times before it finally reached the continent. It's probably just as good for me that it was delayed for it should have been following me around all this time anyhow, and if it hadn't been for it, I wouldn't have gotten one last night. Maybe I'll have some more tonight too.

I've been looking at your pictures. (I do that often.) Of course, it makes me more anxious everytime to get back to you. Well, one happy day this waiting will be over and our dreams will begin to come true. Oh darling, I love you *so* much. Why doesn't this mess end?

Jeff has been trying to find me a guitar. Said he saw a fellow with one yesterday, but he couldn't get it from him in any way. He brought the rest of the bottle of gin around last night and had me trying to play the mandolin for him. I can't do so well with it yet though.

Here's hoping you truly appreciate this letter. It's taking a lot of concentrating and patience with my hunt and peck system. Guess (in fact I'm sure) you will like it even if it doesn't have the "personal touch." We are always eager for just any letter aren't we?

It's almost chow time, so I will say so long for now. Bye darling and all my love.

Yours, / Henry

Tuesday, March 27, 1945

My only love:

I did have *two* letters today. *Very* sweet ones indeed, but all of your letters are that way. I never expected a "sour note" in one and for a good reason, for they have always been full of love. Your love darling, is what makes life over here easier to endure. It's wonderful loving you, and knowing you love me in just the same way. There'll come a day when our dreams will come true and our fondest hopes realized. Oh, I love you *so* much darling.

The news seems pretty good now. Think Patton is blowing his top again. It looks like this should end soon.

Guess what! The funnies you sent me August 1, have just been handed to me. There are five of them and it looked as if they had been re-wrapped. I'll read some of them after I've finished this.

I know it was wonderful for Nash to see his best friend. I know how it was when I saw Sammie and also the fellows in the 44th. It's really a good feeling.

If you remember, once I wrote you that I had been thinking of what I would like to do most when I'm out of the Army. I've thought that for a long time. Almost exactly what you wrote in this letter. Except I hadn't thought of the government loan. Never before being interested in it, I don't know a darn thing about it. What the requirements are before you can get it or anything. But I think if there isn't too much red tape attached, it will be O.K. What you say you were thinking would be our best set up, is the very thing I've been thinking of—a long time. It should be O.K. and work.

I had thought of a small truck farm along with your garden and the chickens, but I (and I'll swear this is the truth) had dealt the cow out because I can't milk one and I wouldn't want you to. The two most important things, it would assure us is being together and being our own boss. Those two things respectively, I want more than anything else, once I'm out of the Army. Glad you told me what you would like, and like about most everything else, we have the same general idea. I guess we can figure on just about something like that, but I doubt if we can start as big as I would like to. Not knowing how prices are going to be, you don't know how high to try to shoot.

Well, goodnight baby. I'll write some more about our plans, (well ideas anyhow) later. Maybe we can soon actually start planning.

All my love always, / Henry

Thursday, March 29, 1945

My only love:—

. . . You should see my "house" for tonight, the Kraut version of a pup tent. About six feet square, tapered to the center and in four sections of camouflage material. A good tent, which was evidently meant for four but I have this one to myself. Last night, I didn't pitch a tent, just lay down in my blankets with my shelter half laced around them. (Had my mandolin wrapped in my sleeping bag.) Sometime during the night, I woke up and it was sprinkling rain, but I just turned over and decided I was going to *have* to start getting wet before I moved. Luckily it didn't rain though.

Found a sweet little .22-caliber rifle today. The stock was broken, but I repaired it and I think I'll actually send it home. It's a "mauser," clip fed (about five shots) and bolt operated, with slight graduations up to two hundred yards. Well, I guess it's yards, I don't know what else it could be. Accurate too.

Thanks for the picture of Nash and his crew. Seems like he looks different in every picture. But I guess it's just that I think he does.

Honey, I'm pretty sleepy tonight so I'm stopping here and I'll answer the letters tomorrow. O.K.? Goodnight darling and—

All my love, / Henry

17

"Yes, you are my entire world . . . ."

Friday, March 30, 1945

Hello Baby:—

Another day is almost gone and I'm thinking of you, loving you with all my heart and wishing desperately we could be together. Once again, I'm going to say that maybe it won't be so long now until we can be together.

Outside some of the fellows are having a songfest. Singing everything from classics to cowboy songs. One fellow has my mandolin. We had quite a bit of music this p.m. with it, a guitar and some harmonicas.

I too, am looking forward to when I get that piece of paper saying Honorable Discharge, so "we" can be my own boss! And of course, many more things too. You've probably had letters from me by now. In your last one, they had been slowed up for some reason.

You asked if a hen "sits" or "sets." Your Dad, I think, was right. You set them; they sit.

I think as you do that the Germans will never surrender formally, but will just keep backing up until the last one. Today, one came in all decked out with his pack, clean clothes and shave, and carrying his little white flag. They said he was a warrant officer. I've seen some happy Russians, Frenchmen and others. The Russians get a kick out of Jeff's calling them all Stalin. We've been wondering when *we* are going to be liberated.

Goodnight my darling. You know I love you with all my heart and

Always, / Henry

———————————

Sunday, April 1, 1945

My only love:

. . . So far, the mail hasn't come in tonight, but it should now anytime. I will probably have some. Should anyhow, since it's Easter. Here it is now—No luck except for two letters from Mom.

In one, she says Charlie is home. Some are just lucky and some of the fellows from home have gone back the hard way, and a few won't be going back at all. Maybe *I'm* lucky after all. One day, I'll being going home too.

I sent the .22-caliber rifle home yesterday. Think it was the first time I ever wrote a letter to Dad. Told him how to put it together if it ever got there.

This isn't such a hot letter, but it is the best I can do now. Goodnight darling—and,

All my love, / Henry

Friday, April 6, 1945

Hello there Babe:—

Had *five* of the sweetest letters tonight that anyone could ever hope to get, so I'm "Sitting on Top of the World."

I've had some pretty good fish to eat today. (As far as fish goes.) Some of the fellows have a very unique way of catching them. A block or so of TNT thrown in the water and after the explosion, the fish drift to shallow water and are picked up with a net. They started pretty good, but I couldn't fry them very brown without them tearing up.

You know, I can't imagine how you could think so much of the snapshot I sent. I've had one taken alone (without a hat). I'll send it to you when I get it.—

The way you and Libby compare (or something) Nash and me, I'd like to listen in on you two sometime when you are in one of those sessions. I imagine your chatter would sound like two girls after their first date. (And I don't even know how that sounds.)

Maybe by now, you are pretty sure that I wasn't on the Remagen Bridge when it fell. Sometime I may get to send you a picture of the first bridge across the Rhine.

I too am glad that Charlie got a chance to go home. Wish *I* had a ship to be repaired.

I thought I knew why Mama was somewhat sick most of the time. But she always writes like everything is just "hunky-dory."

Say, I'll be glad when the story of Libby gets here. Here I've been looking for it and you say in this letter you have been typing some more on it. Let's "get on the ball" sweetheart.

If you remember, it was the last of February I got my back pay, and had it not been for that, I would have had to use some other way to remember you on your birthday. I hope it reached you in time.

I got the *Louisville Times* last night. There wasn't any crossword puzzle in it. Otherwise, it's O.K.

I'm a little sleepy, so I'll answer the other two letters tomorrow.

Goodnight my darling, and you *know* I love you—

Always, / Henry

Saturday, April 7, 1945

My only love:—

Guess now I'll answer the two letters I didn't get to last night and I'll write tonight if there is anymore. Otherwise, there won't be anymore to write for today.

Been listening to the radio some today. Have heard some good songs and the news is still good. Someday, the war may end. I heard on the radio that we now have nine more bridges across the Rhine than the Germans ever had. You say here, by the time I get this letter *I* would probably be across and I think I was across when you wrote it.

I heard a song today that was good. Some girl was singing "Sam, release that man for active duty tonight." Ever hear it? It's somewhat comical, but has a lot of good ideas at that. Now *that* type of active duty would be a bit alright. We got a kick out of the song.

Well, this is all for now honey and you won't forget that I'm thinking of you constantly and—

Loving you, / Henry

The American engineers, 75,000 strong, built sixty-two bridges across the Rhine.

Sunday, April 8, 1945

Hello Honey:—

It's Sunday and if I were there with you, it would still be a few hours before we would even think of getting up.

. . . You know, I keep thinking of our plans (or maybe it would be called an idea now) for our farm when I get out of the Army. The more I think of it, the better it seems. With the proper location, good soil, etc., I don't see how we could miss. Of course, the most of our income will be in the summer. It seems that an early crop of all different kinds of vegetables should bring pretty good money. We will have to have something saleable during all the summer months. I've thought too, of what the cost will be to start, but I still like the idea. The greatest pleasure will be that we can be together all the time and our own boss.

Bye now darling and—all my love,

Henry

Monday, April 9, 1945

Hello Honey:—

Whaddaya know, I got one of my boxes for Christmas today! It was the fruitcake you sent, and it was *good!* The best I've tasted yet. It was in good condition, too, but the caramels were melted and stuck together. Thanks a million sweetheart. With every day that passes, you are dearer and dearer to me. Someday, I'm coming home darling.

You asked what my speed of typing is. Instead of words per minute, it's about a sentence per hour. My hands are slow at typing.

I possibly could have gotten a pass back in Belgium, or France, but now it's so far back, I don't want any. There's no one missing *me* back there either.

By the way, I've heard we were to get two more campaign stars, although I don't know if it's true or not. Today, I saw my first Purple Heart. One of the fellows in this platoon received it. Two were awarded the Bronze Star.

Found a pretty good guitar today and we have played a little tonight, but we didn't seem to get off so well. No Cognac maybe was the reason.

I also had a letter from Mom and Robert last night and tonight too. Think I'm going to be too sleepy to write tonight though.

You asked who Jeff is. He's just an ordinary cider shocked G.I., loony as can be, but a darn good hillbilly from New York. His name is Jeff Elliott.

Listen Honey, I don't want you to think I'm actually a drinker. True, I do drink some, but I'm always sure that it won't affect my getting around, or hinder anyone concerned. When I get back, *you* will always be present if I should take a drink, and we probably will occasionally.

Mama said in her letter today that Charlie had gone back. That reminds me that I should write Irene soon.

Goodnight Baby. I'm getting sleepy, so I'll get a little shut-eye.

All my love, / Henry

T/4 Jeff Elliott was in Company A's 2nd platoon motor pool. One humorous account of his driving skills involved giving Col. Pergrin his first ride in a MK-5 German tank. Elliott drove the Panther straight into a bomb crater and sank about 4 feet of the gun barrel into the bank of the crater. The tank was stuck, so the colonel got out. The next day, Elliott was able to get the tank out, only to have it confiscated by an ordnance unit.

Wednesday, April 11, 1945

Hello darling:—

. . . Twenty-one months ago, it started. Of course, the twelfth is officially our "anniversary," but today it has actually been twenty-one months. *Surely* it won't be this long again until we are together. I like to remember our short time together as something kind of sacred. Our "chicken" dinner in Nashville. How I so abruptly backed out when you took me up on the bet that I would kiss you before reaching Memphis. (And how you wouldn't stop in Memphis).

If I should ever forget any of the trip, it won't be the "special" scene of the moon shining in your face while you were sleeping, as we went through Arkansas. I was just wondering about you, and unknowingly wishing I knew you as I do now and thinking of how I would like to have someone like you to love and someone to love me as much.

Guess I dismissed the idea, thinking my standards were too rigid, and that I was born about a century too late to ever expect anything like that. I was wrong in that, for in you darling, I have found *everything*. The love I've always wanted and in these twenty-one months, I've learned to love you in such a way that words won't express it.

Goodnight darling, and—

I love you, / Henry

———————————

Thursday, April 12, 1945

Hello darling:—

. . . You know, it's just short of two years since this started. The time has passed fast, it seems, and in some ways it has been a long time. Guess loving you so much and knowing you as I do, makes it easier and as a whole not so long. Wanting to come home to you so much, makes individual nights and days seem like years. Oh, I love you *so* much honey.

Jeff and "Hooks" killed a deer last night and today I've been cooking some of it. The first venison I have ever eaten and it's good.

A few days ago, when I got several letters at once, a fellow asked, "Giles, does your woman still write you every day?" When I told him you did, he said, "Wow! If I had a woman like *that* I would *really* marry her." I asked him what he thought *I* was going to do. I know of some fellows who write every day and their wives write them too. Every day.

Twenty-one months ago tonight we were together. Wish we had known *then* what we do now. We would at least have more memories than we have. But at that, we have a lot anyhow. Loving you has been the most wonderful thing I've ever known.

This is all for now Sweetheart. So—goodnight and

All my love, / Henry

———————————

Sunday, April 15, 1945
Germany

My only love:

I had another good letter last night and started to answer then, but got too sleepy to make sense, so went to bed and now I have the time to answer with this. I like to mess with a typewriter, so if you would rather for me to write all the time and not use this, just tell me.

. . . You should hear our three piece band. One fellow plays the clarinet, another the guitar, and I play the mandolin. "In the Mood" and "Deep in the Heart of Texas" are two of our favorites. We can do alright on a few more.

It is a lot better since I got back with the Company and your letters and can know something of what is going on and get the latest news, etc.

It's alright about what you said about canaries. This one we have is really something though. Everytime he hears music of any kind, he sure sounds off. A good singer too.

I read an account of the President's death in the *Stars & Stripes* today. Guess the greatest man in history passed then. In my opinion, one of the best anyhow.

Guess I'll stop here Honey. I'm sleepy, tired and—

I love you, / Henry

While sitting for a watercolor portrait being painted by Madame Elizabeth Shoumatoff, loved and respected President Franklin D. Roosevelt suffered a cerebral embolism at 1:15 p.m., Thursday, April 12 and collapsed. The first American president to be elected to a third term followed by a fourth, Roosevelt died at 3:30 the same afternoon at the Little White House in Warm Springs, Georgia.

The sudden and unexpected death of the sixty-three year old president shocked and saddened the nation he had kept informed throughout the long term of the war. Exhausted from the Yalta Conference with Winston Churchill and Joseph Stalin beginning February 4, he had arrived at Warm Springs on March 30 for a much needed rest. Americans mourned that his death preceded the peace he had sought and came so near the conflict's end. He was buried April 15 in the formal garden of the family home at Hyde Park, New York.

Wednesday, April 18, 1945

Hello Sweetheart:—

No mail tonight, so didn't get any letters. None last night either. Maybe next time there will be some. Hope so anyhow.

I love you my darling. More with every day that passes. *When will* this mess end? And when can I come home to you? That is a question that only time can answer.

I just wonder if the rifle I sent home will ever get there. One fellow I know of sent one and it got through.

I've just been listening to Bob Hope, but there was static or something wrong with the radio, anyhow the reception wasn't so good and I couldn't hear it so well. I like his programs.

Keep thinking of our plans (or ideas) of our truck farm. I still think it is a good idea even if it shouldn't work. Guess we'll try anyhow.

Mama said in her last letter that William Giles had married since he went home and I've been trying to think who he may have married. Probably someone I don't even know though.

I've just been looking at your pictures again and I can't see why Libby thinks she looks the largest. (Not that it matters.)

Goodnight honey and—

I love you, / Henry

Friday, April 20, 1945
Germany

My darling:

Still no mail has come in, but soon it should and then I'm almost sure to have some.

I've heard that Ernie Pyle was killed in the Philippines. Guess his luck ran out as he had said it would sometime. I had always rather read his articles than any other war correspondent. But— that's some more of war.

Jeff found a new set of guitar strings and our box sounds a lot better.

Guess this is all for now darling, so in saying once more that I love you, I'll stop here. Goodnight darling and—

All my love, / Henry

Ernie Pyle was killed on April 18, 1945, by a Japanese machine gun bullet on the island of le Shima, during the battle for Okinawa. In the last paragraph of *Here Is Your War,* Pyle wrote: "That is our war, and we will carry it with us as we go on from one battleground to another until it is all over, leaving some of us behind on every beach, in every field. . . . They died and others lived and nobody knows why it is so. They died and thereby the rest of us can go on and on. When we leave here for the next shore, there is nothing we can do for the ones beneath the wooden crosses, except to pause and murmur, 'Thanks pal.' "

Friday, April 27, 1945

Darling:—

If there was ever a time when I didn't know where or how to begin a letter, it is now. The mail came through and I had one letter and the story of Libby's life. I've already read it and there's no words that will express the pleasure I had in doing so. I've never read anything that held my attention as much, or anything as interesting and full of life. For some reason, I feel closer to you and if possible, love you more. You already know that I love you more than words can tell.

Wish I could be with you for your vacation. Sometimes I have the crazy idea that I may be there for the last part of it, although I won't or can't exactly count on it.

Had a lot of good laughs at some of the things about Libby. Such as where you are giving her a lesson in mathematics and to make it easier to divide the apples, she would get a bowl full and let her friends help themselves. That was good. The Mr. Smith episode and the swim in the reservoir and others. The more serious incidents were there too, but all told, it is wonderful. Or maybe the word "Beautiful" would be the word to describe it best. Thanks a million for sending it. I'll read it again as soon as I can.

Guess Nash will soon be going home. No doubt he has been busy lately with things happening as they are.

Bye for now Sweetheart and—

All my love, / Henry

The eighty-eight page manuscript "Elizabeth-Libby" by Janice Moore, dated December 14, 1943, Louisville, Kentucky, is in the Giles manuscript collection of Library Special Collections, Western Kentucky University, Bowling

Green, Kentucky. There is also a revised and longer version, "My Darling Daughter," which includes the war years.

The second manuscript, with the title changed to "Sugar 'N Spice," was submitted to Houghton Mifflin in 1953. It was rejected for publication with a letter from Anne N. Barrett, editor, stating, "It is a remarkable picture of a wise and understanding mother but it is very personal and very special in its appeal. I should think it might go better in a magazine than as a book." It was not submitted to a magazine.

In the original copy sent to Henry, Janice wrote:

Mr. Smith came to live with us one day, very unexpectedly. Quite literally he dropped in out of the blue, for he was a figment of Elizabeth's imagination. I met him at breakfast.

"Give Mr. Smith some oatmeal, too, mother," Elizabeth said as I placed her bowl of cereal before her.

I glanced around to see what toy had been thus christened for the time being, but there was a conspicuous absence of toys.

"Are you sure Mr. Smith likes oatmeal Elizabeth?" I asked, sparring for time until I could take this in.

"Mother," she said reprovingly, "Mr. Smith must eat his oatmeal even if he doesn't like it. It is very good for him. It will make him strong and healthy." Stopped by my own argument, I set another bowl of oatmeal before her.

. . . Mr. Smith lived with us nearly a month. During that time we learned to be very careful where we walked and to be very careful where we sat. Mr. Smith might be underfoot anywhere in the house, or he might be taking his rest in the exact chair in which we wished to sit. An anguished wail from Elizabeth was our warning that we were going to step on Mr. Smith, or sit on Mr. Smith. Once I even made up a bed where Mr. Smith was taking his nap. Elizabeth reproached me bitterly.

"Mother, I just don't believe you can *see* very good."

Elizabeth, I couldn't see Mr. Smith except with your eyes. But I *could* see a lonely little girl—lonely in spite of the fact that she was so surrounded with love that she breathed it in as naturally as she did the very air itself. You wanted someone who thought with your thoughts. You wanted someone who was your height emotionally and spiritually. We had used up the years of our childhood, and even with all our love we could not quite enter into your world. So in your own way you supplied the need you felt.

How long Mr. Smith might have remained with us, I don't know. But four-year-old Bobby and his parents moved next door.

And eventually the day came when I said to Elizabeth, "I haven't seen Mr. Smith for some time. Has he gone on a visit, or is he ill?"

Elizabeth looked at me blankly.

"What Mr. Smith?" she said.

Saturday, April 28, 1945

My only darling:—

Tonight I have *nine* letters to answer. Two came yesterday after I got one with Libby's life story and *seven* tonight. Not bad, eh?

. . . I guess we were just meant for each other and I agree with you that our plans or ideas of what we want for the future are just more proof that we were. When I'm thinking of it, I really get anxious to start. I know too that it is going to take a few weeks to even get started on it, after I'm out of the Army. We'll have an open fireplace for you too. And the kitchen you want. As soon as we can. The whole idea sounds very practical and sensible to me too.

Heard on the radio tonight that Himmler wanted to surrender unconditionally to the U.S. and Britain, but that wouldn't be worth a damn. I *sure* wouldn't want to fight the Russians.

Honey, I'm sleepy, so goodnight with—

All my love, / Henry

Second in power to Adolf Hitler, Heinrich Himmler was the most notorious leader of the Third Reich. He was head of the Gestapo, the German concentration camps, and was one of the most vicious exterminators of the Jews. Without consulting Hitler, Himmler began surrender negotiations, which were rejected, with the Western Allies.

Wednesday, May 2, 1945

Hello Baby:—

I was arranging my bed and the fellows asked me what I was doing and if I wasn't writing you tonight. I asked them if they thought I should and they said I had better. Five of us in Headquarters squad always are in the same room and we know all about each other. Of course, I was going to write anyhow without them reminding me, so here I am once more trying to tell you I love you. Yes, you are my entire world and I think of you constantly and dream of the time we will be together again.

The news is good tonight, with the squareheads in Italy surrendering to Clark unconditionally. Don't think the war will last but a few days longer now. At this time, there's a good reason for thinking so. In fact, I'm thinking it will be over before you get this letter.

The mail hasn't come in tonight but it should be here anytime now. Today, we entered the outskirts of a town and six Krauts came marching across a field with a white flag, and a civilian for an interpreter, and surrendered to us. Advanced troops had by-passed them.

They say the mail will be here tomorrow, so in that case, there isn't anything more to write, so—Goodnight honey and—

I love you, / Henry

P.S. This pen is really a good one.

German headquarters in Italy agreed to an unconditional surrender on May 1, 1945, to General Mark Wayne Clark, commander of the U.S. Fifth Army in Italy.

Friday, May 4, 1945

Hello honey:—

You know things are looking a bit O.K. along about now. Just a few minutes ago it was announced that German troops in northern Germany had given up. Tonight, we got the *Stars & Stripes* announcing Adolf's death. Guess that will help too.

Maybe before long, we will be together. I think so anyhow and I'm loving you darling with all my heart and for always.

No mail again tonight. Maybe tomorrow. Hope so anyhow.

Goodnight darling and once again—

I love you, / Henry

On May 2, Associated Press headlines read: HITLER DIED IN BERLIN BATTLE. In reality, the German dictator, responsible for more destruction than any other man in history, took his own life on April 30, 1945.

Sunday, May 6, 1945

Hello Baby:—

The news continues to be good and anytime now I'm expecting an interruption for the announcement of the final collapse of the German Army. Of course it may not come until tomorrow. There have been a lot of thrills listening to what has been going on lately.

I love you sweetheart. In every way you can think of and it goes without saying that I'm somewhat more restless and anxious to get home to you. I still think I'll be there in three or four months.

I think we must be in the home of some very religious Catholics. We can hear them going through some kind of chanting ceremony and then they will come out crossing their heart. I've just heard a good rumor, but I'll not tell it.

Well so long for now darling and—

All my love, / Henry

18

"The war is over! *Thank God.*"

Monday, May 7, 1945

Darling:—

The war is over! Thank God. Tomorrow is officially V-E Day and for some reason, it seems strange that it has actually ended. Of course, I don't know anything yet about our part from here on, but everything has a brighter outlook, at any rate.

Had a letter tonight, written April 19 and that helps a lot. I love you so much it hurts darling. It probably won't be so long now until we are actually together! Confidentially, I think it will be to stay. Wonder what this point system will amount to anyhow? We'll see.

Guess by next spring we can try our hands as farmers. Sounds good doesn't it? And *I* believe it will work too.

Tonight for the first time, I heard "My Shining Hour." The best time in the world to hear it too. I think it *is* beautiful.

Guess I'll find room to wear my decorations after I get back. The one thing I hope is that I don't have to stay away so long that it will take two blouses to hold the overseas stripes.

The reason I haven't said so much about Sgt. Hinkel lately is that I'm not with him but little, since he isn't the platoon Sergeant anymore. Shot the breeze with him a while tonight. Well Honey, this is all for now. You know I love you, so good night and—

All my love, / Henry

My Shining Hour

This moment, this minute and each second in it,

Will leave a glow upon the sky, And as time goes by,
It will never die.

Refrain:

This will be MY SHINING HOUR,
Calm and happy and bright,
In my dreams, your face will flower,
Through the darkness of the night.
Like the lights of home before me,
Or an angel watching o'er me,
This will be MY SHINING HOUR,
Till I'm with you again.

Tuesday, May 8, 1945

My only love:—

No doubt you have just finished listening to the President's of-ficial announcement of the end of the war in Europe, as we have of Mr. Churchill's.

It's a great day for all of us, but it's still a little hard to realize it is over, here. It has ended somewhat more sudden than I thought it would. Maybe soon we can start on some plans of our own.

I love you my darling. More than I can ever tell you and now it looks like our fondest hopes and dreams will soon begin to ma-terialize into realities. Oh isn't it *wonderful* honey!

A big celebration is going on in England and some of it, we are hearing on the radio.

Guess Nash will soon be home, but I don't think he will be but a few months ahead of me. I'm anxious for the release of the demobilization plans. With everything as it is, I don't see how I can miss.

Sweetheart, I just can't think of anything more to write, so for now bye and—

All my love, / Henry

V-E Day
Tuesday, May 8, 1945

Hello there honey:—

It's V-day in Europe and not a drink in the house, or the country either, it seems. Did get a good letter tonight though and they are always more stimulating than any wine or anything and sweeter than nectar. I love you darling. More than any words will ever express. Soon I think, I'll be coming home to you.

This letter (and one from Irene) was postmarked April 27. You mentioned sending the article that some men would be released by mid-year (those with four and five years service) and I've already written you about it and what I think my chances are. That and the demobilization plan, I'm pretty sure, will get me out. In fact, *I'm* counting on it (mid-year is July 1), although you say you *mustn't* count on it.

If you want a new wedding dress, it seems that now would be alright to at least start thinking about it.

About the money I sent. All I could do is ask Lt. Hayes about it. Didn't even get a receipt when I sent it. I think it will eventually get there.

I've already written this afternoon, but after this good letter, I couldn't resist writing again.

Goodnight now my darling and you *know* I love you—

Always, / Henry

———————————————

Friday, May 11, 1945

Hello my darling:—

Although tomorrow is our "official" anniversary date, today it has been twenty-two months since first all this started and it's been the most wonderful thing in the world. Wouldn't have missed it for the entire world. And today, I love you more than I had ever thought possible to love a woman, with all my heart and for *always.*

On the 9th, I got seven letters and wrote one in answer. Yesterday, I was on the truck with my jacket hanging on the side (upside down) and the first thing I knew, there were letters flying everywhere behind the truck. So—I lost the seven from you, the one I had written in answer and two from home. So you won't get one for yesterday and probably not the one I lost for the day before.

I remember some of the things in them though. One thing was, Libby getting frightened at the turkey. I laughed at that, but confidentially, *I* don't like for a goose to lower his head and run at me hissing.

Another thing was that Nash was on his way home. That's *wonderful*. I'm still almost certain that I'll be home in a couple or three months. You have by now read of the point system in de-mobilization. It calls for a minimum of 85 points before you are eligible for discharge and I have *90*. Wonder when they will start the ball to rolling?

Our plans for our farm seem just around the corner now, don't they? I get more anxious for it all the time.

Here's a couple more pictures. I still haven't gotten the one I had made that I wrote you about. That's my platoon Sergeant with me.

I'm running out of space, so I'll say bye for now sweetheart and—

All my love, / Henry

1/Lt. Nash Hancock returned home the 12th of May, 1945.

Saturday, May 12, 1945
Germany

Hello Sweetheart:—

It's our anniversary once more and today I love you more than words can ever express or tell. Don't think it will be much longer until we can begin our life as we have so long dreamed of and hoped for. Oh honey, I'll be the happiest person in the world when the time comes to start home to you, and thrilled speech-less when I finally arrive in Louisville.

The mail hasn't come in today yet and if it does I'll write again.

Wonder if by next spring we will be on our own farm? It seems that there's no reason why we shouldn't be. I still think I'll be out of the Army in three months. Four at the *most*.

Did you ever see the dress uniform of the Engineers? I think you would agree that even the dress blues of the marines aren't any flashier. Well, they are blue also. Maybe about the same thing. The braid of the Engineers is all over it. Of course, they were only worn in peacetime and very few fellows had one.

Say, I'm anxious to get the letters you wrote around V-E day. I know they are going to be something. Of course, all of them are tops but you know what I mean.

It's hot as the dickens here now, (I love it) and I have my tent up so it makes a good shade and will hold more junk, etc., and today it has been used by almost everyone listening to the guitar and mandolin and dodging the sun. (There's been some Schnapps mixed with it too.)

We are to start getting A rations soon. *That* will be a bit alright.

It's chow time now, so bye for now, and—

All my love, / Henry

P.S. The mail just came and I got a Christmas package. The candy with the jar of chicken in it and the Dagwood comics. If this is the candy you made, it is certainly good. Tell me if it is. It wasn't hard or soft. *Just* right. That is all the mail I had. I'll try the chicken later.

Field ration A contained 70 percent fresh foods. It most closely approximated the garrison ration and diet of soldiers stationed in the United States.

Tuesday, May 15, 1945

Hello there honey:—

Well, another day has passed and I'm feeling a bit alright, for I got two good letters from you, one from Mary and one from Mom. I got a *Courier-Journal* too. And I love you some more.

The letter for the 22nd was a little blue and in one place, you almost tore it up. Good thing you didn't, for after all, it is a good one. Full of love as all of them are. You were just a little blue.

Just a little about the last package. It must have been the candy you made. Looked like homemade wrappers. I ate all of the chicken and believe me, it was something good. The candy was as fresh as if it were packed the night before and I'm *not* saying that because I'm writing about something you sent me. You say in one of these letters that I may have said the fruitcake was O.K. just because you sent it. They have been just as I've told you.

I haven't seen any of the Nazi "slave labor" camps, but I always read about them. Tonight's *Stars & Stripes* says that Himmler has been turned over to the Allies. Sometime when I can, I'll tell you of some of the places I've been in Germany.

I have never had the idea that you thought I was a drinker. I usually tell you when we have had a "spree" or something a little rare to drink.

If you should see a ring you want, by all means, have it put away.

I'll answer Mary's letter in a short time. That reminds me that since *I* call her Mary, you have never called her "Petie" any more. Gee, you *are* flexible. Mary, to me, sounds best, but it's your business what or how you want to mention her. She can really write a letter. In this one, she asks if I'm practicing "I do." Says you don't have to practice the knee shaking. It comes natural.

Goodnight Sweetheart, and you won't forget—

I love you, / Henry

Heinrich Himmler was captured by the British. As soon as his identity was discovered, he committed suicide by biting into a small vial containing poison.

———————————

Wednesday, May 16, 1945

Hello Darling:—

I have just signed my card with my points for demobilization on it so I thought I would write you about it. I have ninety points and as you know, eighty-five is the minimum, so I think I have a fair chance of being released before so long. I'm counting on it anyhow and the *Stars & Stripes* favored me last night too.

Hope I can get out by the time I finish five years, although that isn't likely. Maybe possible. Today makes fifty-eight months.

I've already written a V-mail today, so I think I'll use an Air Mail stamp for this one. You probably couldn't read it, if it was photographed.

Don't think I told you that I have my hair clipped to the scalp again. It's so much easier to keep clean this way and it's warm too, now, so I had it clipped.

I love you sweetheart, and from the way you feel, you can tell how anxious and restless I am now, since there is a possibility of coming home to you before so much longer. It's going to be the most wonderful thing in the world to get home to you.

We have pretty good living conditions now, since it isn't raining and we are by a river where there's plenty of water (*cold*) to wash clothes with and take a bath. We are also getting class A rations, so everything is about as good as could be under the circumstances. Bye now, and—

All my love, / Henry

Sunday, May 20, 1945

Hello my darling:—

. . . Read in the *Stars & Stripes* where fifteen thousand men were to leave for the states by the first of June. It also said the quota would be increased for June. Somehow I feel like I'll be lucky enough to get in on the June shipment. Hope I do. I wonder what it would seem like, to actually be starting home. Guess I won't know what to do or say. I'll think of something when I get there anyhow, after I have a chance to get my breath.

It's kind of funny the way you are envious of everyone having or going to have their babies. Well—we'll have our chance before so long.

Heard Bob Hope in "G.I. Journal" last night. Seems like he gets better everytime. Have you ever listened to programs like his with someone around that would never crack a smile or laugh at anything that was said? I have, and it seems funny that things I get a big kick out of, to them it's just so much noise. Of course, some jokes I don't get, but most of them I do.

Didn't get any mail last night. No letters for anyone. This will have to be all for now, so bye and—

All my love, / Henry

Wednesday, May 23, 1945

Hello Honey:—

A month from today is my birthday and I was just thinking that it would be wonderful if I could spend it as I did my last one—but going the other way. Maybe I will.

Got a good letter today, written the eleventh and you were expecting Nash to call at anytime. Guess he is there by now.

. . . The censorship has been lifted to the extent that we can seal our own letters. Of course, we were told what we couldn't write.

As I think you know, I wasn't in any actual combat, but several times under artillery fire and for me, that was enough. The first was at Carentan where the Krauts were trying to knock out a bridge we were maintaining. We have laughed at how scared we were there. I'll never forget the last barrage we were under. We could hear the report of the guns, and was there ever sweating until they would come screaming in and explode. Wow!

Once, we were working on a road and a gas alarm got started. Rifles were being fired into the air, men yelling "gas," and of all things *I* didn't have my gas mask with me that night. It was some phosphorous shells that someone had smelled and I think it had turned a gas detector red too. While everyone (but me) was still wearing their gas mask, we started in and drove right into an area that was being shelled and for some reason *stopped*. But luckily, the last shell landed just as we stopped. You can bet *I* aged some that night.

About the worse thing there is to sweat out is a buzz bomb after the motor stops. The last time I was in the hospital in Liege, in ten days there must have been a million sent over. I'm strictly allergic to those things. I'll tell you more about them some other time. A few times, the Krauts bombed pretty close. You could hear the bombs falling, and that isn't anything pleasant to listen to. Some good fireworks to see are tracers being fired at night at a plane. The first plane I fired at was at Carentan, then no more until Remagen. That's where I mashed my finger reloading a .50-caliber. They used those jet propelled jobs trying to knock out the bridge and are they fast. Just like lightning.

Well, this is all for now. So—goodnight honey and—

All my love, / Henry

On Henry's last birthday, June 23, 1944, Company A was en route from Carentan to Omaha Beach.

Wednesday, May 30, 1945

My only love:

Had two good letters tonight, and of course you know what a difference that makes in a day. I don't understand why you hadn't heard from me for two weeks. It could be because we changed armies along about then that caused a delay but I don't see why. Maybe long before now, you have had some.

. . . I'm glad to know my watch finally got there. I was beginning to think it wouldn't. Now where could the money be? Wonder if you will get it by your next birthday. By the way, I would like the "stretchy" band for my watch. With no heavier work than I do, it will be just what I want. Don't send it back here though. If it *could* talk, it could tell you of a few air raids we sweated out together, when everything would get so quiet (and me so scared) I could hear it ticking at arms length. Ordinarily, I had to hold it over my ear to hear it.

You say Mama (and you) were hoping I would get home by the time you went down again. I think I have told you before that I'm counting on it, or maybe before.

You were counting my points right. I have 90 now and if the other two campaign stars come through, I'll have a hundred.

This is all for now darling, so goodnight and—

All my love, / Henry

Friday, June 1, 1945

Hello Baby:

We're in rather a nice place now. Bivouacked under a long hedge of trees, with plenty of room for ballgames etc. A clean place and lots of sunshine.

The other day when Colonel Pergrin was around the area, one of the fellows (an 85 pointer+) asked him when he thought the men with enough points would get to go home and his answer was that we *may* have to wait until around the first of July for transportation. Today was the first time I had heard of him saying anything, and I *hope* he had some idea of what he was talking about.

You're not the only one who gets anxious and restless when you hear something like that. My own motor races too! Oh, I love you so darling that it is impossible to tell you what you do mean to me and one day soon, I'll be coming home to you.

All my love, / Henry

Tuesday, June 5, 1945

My only love:—

A year ago now, we were sweating out the invasion. Today, it's going home we are waiting for. Always, there is something "coming off." I'm hoping that before many more days, I can be on my way home to you. I love you sweetheart, and I think you know that by now, but I still like to tell you that you are everything in the world to me.

Didn't write yesterday. Worked pretty hard all afternoon until nearly sundown, then laid down to rest and went to sleep again and slept until after dark. Built me a rather roomy house, with a good floor in it. Got my last clothes all dirty, so today, I've washed two suits of O. D.'s two suits of underwear, some socks, hankies and a pair of shoes.

No mail last night, but today I got your letter written May 25. I don't know why you said, "forgive me" because you were writing mostly of Nash and Libby. You should know by now that I'm just as anxious to hear about them as you are inclined (as you put it once) to write about them. I'm not being sarcastic honey. Your letter telling about spending your first evening with them was just what I wanted to hear. *I* don't understand why Nash says it's difficult for him to feel like he had done much of anything. There's nothing more thrilling than knowing and seeing bombers that are tearing at the heart of the enemy. I wonder what a man finds to think about when he is going through flak so thick you could walk on it! It takes guts to keep doing that.

This is all for now darling so goodnight and—

All my love, / Henry

19

"The quickest way home to you is too slow."

Monday, June 11, 1945

My only darling:

I love you and I'm longing desperately to get home to you. I still haven't heard anymore than I've already written you about. Wish someone, somewhere, would *do* something. The quickest way home to you is too slow. Well—soon I hope.

I know exactly what you are talking about when you say you are more impatient than you have ever been before. *I am too.*

So brown is supposed to be unlucky to be married in. Why wouldn't blue *and* white be O.K.? If it is, I would like that. But let's not worry too much about colors. Pink and white I guess would be lovely too.

Maybe I *will* be there to help you take your last week of vacation.

You know I've thought that when we get married we will stay two nights in Louisville and then go home for a few days. As soon as you want to, we will go see your folks. How does all of that sound to you? We'll also go to Spring Mill or whatever place we can find, when you want to. What were your ideas? I mean in terms of days between the places we want to go.

Goodnight now baby and

All my love, Henry

Tuesday, June 12, 1945

Hello Sweetie:

Wish I could have gotten some mail today, but none came.

This is our monthly anniversary and in one more month, it will be two years since first we started loving each other, with a love that grows more deeper with each passing day. Wish I could be home by the time it has been two years. Now, I don't know about it, but I'll be there sometime.

We are in a town now that has really taken a beating. Without seeing it, it's hard to imagine it in rubble. Only the walls standing, with the top and inside parts piled inside. No doubt Nash has helped do this, and believe me, the town has really been saturated. Now we are having prisoners clean it up.

According to the *Stars & Stripes*, the third and seventh Armies are for occupation over here. I think the units with the most time overseas are the ones in them. Soon the point minimum should be announced.

Bye for now darling and—

I love you, / Henry

Company A was in Munich, Germany.

Saturday, June 23, 1945

Hello Honey:—

Still haven't had anymore mail but there isn't so much coming for anyone.

I love you my darling and I think of you constantly. *Wish* I could come home to you and soon. Haven't heard anything more about it though.

Today is my birthday. Twenty-nine! If someone doesn't do something to get me out of the Army soon, I'll be so old that if I want a family, I'll have to adopt it. (I read that in a *Stars & Stripes* once.)

Someone brought a book into the room and the name of it is *Happiness in Marriage.* I've looked over some of it and there are a lot of good things in it, I believe.

I've just washed a suit of O.D.s in gasoline, so if this letter smells funny, it's gas.

Bye for now honey with—

All my love, / Henry

Sunday, July 1, 1945

My darling:—

Got three good letters tonight, to make the day end as near perfect as it possibly could.

. . . You were telling me in one that I sent one of your letters to Robert! Wonder how I ever did a thing like that? Guess you will get one of Robert's addressed to you. Good thing I don't write to anyone else or I might sometimes get my wires crossed. *That* would be something.

So your Mother has given us her wedding ring. It has, no doubt, stood for a lot of love for a long time and we shall keep it that way for another long time. You were wondering if I would like the idea of having your Mother's ring for our wedding ring. I think it's perfect. I have always guessed it would be hard to find a solid gold wedding ring.

The first Sgt. told me yesterday that the Colonel still says we will be home by September. It's my guess that the ones with enough points will go home and then be discharged. I haven't heard that. Just guessing.

Goodnight honey, and—

All my love, / Henry

Monday, July 2, 1945

Hello Baby:

I always like to tell you first, that I love you. You are everything in the world to me sweetheart and I consider one day, about two years ago, a *very* lucky day. Maybe before so much longer, we can begin our lives as we have wanted to for so long. I *hope* so anyhow.

I'm going to be one restless fellow once I get started home; until I get there. All the way across and until I finally arrive in Louisville. Don't think I'll be able to sleep much.

There *was* some difference in the picture I sent of the Remagen bridge and the way it looked when I first saw it. They were still shelling the town, and some vehicles were still burning or smoking. I'll soon have a picture of the first bridge across the Rhine.

Think I told you before that we are now in a large hotel. I'm on the third floor. Another fellow and I are in one room. We have hot and cold running water and occasionally the lights go on. The two of us sleep in the same bed. I can sleep, either in a bed or on the ground. And I don't think it will be such a problem getting used to sleeping with you.

You know, I can't remember the name of a single town we have been in since Remagen. We were supporting the 99th at the Ruhr pocket and in a small town. In fact, all of them have been small. We have passed through Nurnberg a couple of times and once, south of there, we somehow or other got ahead of the infantry and some divisional Colonel said we were credited with taking two small towns. We were the first troops in them, but there wasn't any firing. This town of Munich is rather large—*and* rather flat.

I don't remember why I started to write Liepzig. Maybe someone was talking about it. Don't think we have been there. *No*, the 291st isn't a part of the First Army. I was in the Third in Texas part of the time.

Having your Mother's ring is going to make our wedding faster. You know, I really appreciate that. I'll write her soon and thank her for it.

Bye for now baby, and—

I love you, / Henry

Thursday, July 5, 1945

My own Darling:

Your letter of the 22nd of June came today and you had visited the bus station in Dallas where we said goodbye. You wished I was there. I too, wish I could have been with you. In fact, I would like to be with you any place. Maybe it won't be so much longer, for according to rumors, something is to happen within the next two or three days. Just what, I don't know, but I will let you know as soon as I find out.

I love you my darling and things can't happen too fast to suit me, if it means coming home to you. Hope the processing isn't too slow.

No, I don't believe we did talk much while we were at the station in Dallas. All I can remember are two sentences. You said, "I could get awful fond of you," and I answered, "Just like me." Of course, we said more than that, but I recall that the clearest. There was something about money, for it was there I "borrowed" the three bucks. Remember? All of our time together was *wonderful* and I still wish we hadn't been so "leery" of our feelings (or something.) We would have been married for two years now. Almost.

I'm tired sweetheart, so I guess it is goodnight for now, and—

ALL MY LOVE, / Henry

Monday, July 9, 1945

My only love:

I hit the jackpot today with seven letters from you and one from home. Today, the first of the fellows left for another outfit and several men came to Company A that have more than 85 points. So—someday, they may start us home. Who knows?

Yes, I am glad that I'm not in the 2nd division and have to go back to Camp Swift. Although, that, in comparison with over here, would be good. I agree with you that waiting is a hard thing to do. In the Army, it's "hurry up and wait." Guess we will just try to have patience though.

Your idea of us having our honeymoon right at home sounds alright to me. So, I guess we will do just that. Anywhere we could be alone is what we want, and I'm sure that at home will be just the place. Don't know why I hadn't thought of it before. I think when I get home it will be on discharge. We will get around to seeing our folks before so long.

It doesn't matter to me if a minister marries us or not. The idea is to get married. But quick. No one will marry us who must judge if you were justified in getting a divorce. I'm afraid questions to that effect would result in someone having the chance to "turn the other cheek."

The fellow who owns the typewriter is leaving and has to pack it, so I'll finish with a pen. You were wondering how I found time to write as much as I did during the war. Guess I just took advantage of the time I did have.

Maybe we can get one of those roomettes when we go to see your folks. They sound O.K. to me. I've just thought that I don't have your Mother's address. I remember North 39th Street, but that's all. Sometimes I get disgusted with myself at things like that.

I'm getting out of uniforms just as soon as it is possible. I'm afraid *you* will have to tell me what to wear and help me get my first civilian clothes, O.K.?

I don't remember where I got the box I sent my watch home in. Just picked it up I guess. I'm glad the $60 finally reached you. I had never mentioned it to Lt. Hayes. Others had, and he always assured them that everything was under control. Guess it was, in a slow way. By the way, I got the *Courier-Journal* you sent the 2nd of July. Pretty fast.

I got a letter from Mom and she was telling me that my rifle had finally arrived home.

I *will* get myself home as soon as possible. I'll wire you when I land.

They haven't started any classes as yet, and if they should, I'm definitely *not* interested in anything they have to offer. I know what a farce Army schools turn out to be.

Bye for now honey. I think I've done pretty well answering the letters.

All my love always, / Henry

———————

Thursday, July 12, 1945

Hello my darling:—

Remember two years ago now? I do. It was a beginning of the most perfect love in the world. I will always be thankful for the rain that day, and for every other little thing that happened that caused us to meet. In these two years darling, you have been my entire world. And from here on, more. For we have reason to believe that soon we will start our lives *together*. I love you sweetheart.

I guess the war in the Pacific is going alright. In the *Stars & Stripes*, a number of battleships were identified by name and our fighter planes have been challenging the Japs, daring them to come out and fight. It will no doubt go on for sometime yet though.

I still don't know when I'll get started home. I went to H & S Company this morning for awhile and they have *ten* first Sergeants in the Company to be sent home. It doesn't seem that they would keep them here for so long, paying them what they do. But you can never tell.

This is all for now baby, so goodnight and—

All my love, Henry

_____

Monday, July 16, 1945

Hello my darling:

Got two good letters today. I love you honey and I *want* to come home to you. Some of us decided today that there probably hasn't been *one* man discharged since the war ended over here, and that the point system is just a farce to keep us hoping. Guess we are just anxious to start home.

You probably know by now that I'm in Munich. Today I was at the Red Cross and was looking at a *Life* magazine with pictures of Hitler's beer garden entrances. Someone was painting the insignia of the 45th division on a post.

Another fellow and I were also in a cafe. At around 7:00 o'clock, all civilians had to leave. We drank two glasses of beer and listened to their three piece band for a while. This soon after fraternization has been allowed all the German people seem to want to be friendly. I don't know if it's going to work toward any good or not, but maybe it won't be any worse than before it was allowed.

Weighed myself today and if I know the difference in kilos and pounds, I weighed 150.7 pounds (coat and all).

So—if you "marry in blue, your love will be true." Let's see, maybe *I* can get a blue pair of socks or how about a blue handkerchief. Not that *I'm* superstitious, but you never can tell. I'm only kidding honey.

I didn't talk anymore to Sgt. Hinkel and he is gone now. Hated to see him leave. In fact, I hated to see all of the fellows go, but that's the army, and war. This was the first time any of the fellows have been separated from their buddies and they really cried the blues.

Think I'll write Robert tonight and tell him to order a couple of song books from the Vaughn Publishing Company and maybe from Stamps Baxter. Just got to thinking of singing (or trying).

Goodnight my love and I hope that soon I can come home and help you look at the stars, etc.

Yours always, / Henry

Friday, July 27, 1945

Darling:

Yesterday, I guessed that my mail was pretty well caught up but was I slightly off. Today, I got *five!*

. . . You know of course, that what I've written concerning dates of when we may come home have been strictly rumor. Nothing official. From here on, I won't mention any I may hear. With but few exceptions, all of the fellows in the 291st have more than 85 points or, are in class D from a physical exam. Unfit for combat. Sgt. Hinkel and Jeff are both gone.

Your plans of our wedding suit me to a "T." Couldn't be better in my estimation. Be glad when we can "proceed according to plans." You must write your Mother telling her how much we appreciate her thoughtfulness in giving us her wedding ring, or words to that effect anyhow.

I too, like the form you sent for our wedding announcement. As to who they can be sent to, I don't know. You have Mama tell you. I don't know who would give a damn if I was or wasn't married.

How did you guess I played 2nd in ball? Oh well, you say here how you arrived at the conclusion. At second, there is just about the right amount of activity. I like shortstop and in softball, one position is known as "roaming short," but I don't like that so well. You have to play every place too much. Haven't played any lately. No place.

Well, I think this is just about all for now. I've pretty well answered the letters and there's nothing extra to write. So bye for now and—

All my love, / Henry

Monday, July 30, 1945

My darling:

This is pretty good. I got two letters in the afternoon and I've lost them somewhere.

I remember in one of them you told me you had written our wedding ceremony and that I say, "I will," instead of "I do."

I must have lost them as I was taking the prisoners back to the cage on the train.

I love you sweetheart and I can't tell you how anxious I am to get home to you. *Then* you will know more about my loving you.

Goodnight baby, I'm *so* sleepy.

All my love always, / Henry

Sunday, August 12, 1945

My only love:—

I wonder how many more anniversaries we are going to have to make up before we are together. To date, we have seen two yearly ones pass and 25 months.

. . . You are my entire world honey and I consider myself very lucky in finding you. Our time for being together will come eventually. That is going to be the most wonderful thing in the world. Just to be where you are.

Several of the fellows who left the outfit are to start to the staging area next week. To the Pacific direct. That is a rotten break. I hope the war there will end by the time they are ready to go.

Goodnight darling and—

I love you, / Henry

Tuesday, August 14, 1945

My darling:

Two good letters today and I'm feeling one hundred percent better. Of course, you know what a difference a letter makes in ending the day right.

. . . I think the war in the Pacific is almost over now. It seems that everyone is just waiting for an official announcement. Hope it is as near over as I think it is.

In the older type army shirt, I did wear a 14½ x 33. The shirt I have on now is a 15 x 34 and is just about right. I guess in a pre-shrunk material a 14½ x 33 is just about right, but you needn't bother getting any until I get there.

I suppose the $300 mustering out pay is for buying clothes. I don't guess it's any too much. I think I have some money coming from what we used to be allowed for clothes. Sgt. Love once told me we had around sixty or seventy dollars coming. It used to be that when you didn't use all your allowance, you got it upon re-enlisting.

It *is* O.K. for you to make arrangements with the minister you have in mind, when you know I'm starting home. It wouldn't matter to me if he were Buddhist.

You gave Dorothy the right answer when you told her she didn't know what the word "anxious" meant. Guess there are others just as anxious but none could be anymore than we are. Oh well—maybe soon.

Bye for now darling and,

I love you, / Henry

Wednesday, August 15, 1945

Hello Honey:—

I think the war is over and as I'm waiting in the Red Cross for the *Stars & Stripes* to come in, I decided I'd just as well write a letter. If the war is over, we may get home sooner. No, I guess they will just decide to keep us in over here. That's a hell of a way to talk, isn't it— I've just heard on the radio that the war *is* over!

I've gone far enough without telling you I love you. I do honey, and more with every day that passes.

Got another letter this morning that came yesterday that was sent or taken to the wrong room. It was written the first night you were down home. It is a good letter as usual and you were wishing for me. *Surely* it won't be so much longer until we can go together.

Bye now darling and—

I love you, / Henry

Thursday, August 16, 1945

Hello Baby:

Didn't get any mail today but I think they are very well caught up though. I love you darling and I *hope* it won't be *too* long until I can start home to you.

Another rumor. Quote: We are to start home soon. Not later than September 10. Un-quote. That one was supposed to have come from our executive officer. My informant said he heard the Major say it.????

Saw in the *Stars & Stripes* where *seven million* members of the armed forces are to be released in a year. I'm afraid someone will have to get on the ball, but quick.

Does it seem to you that the war in the Pacific should be over? It's harder to realize that than it was when it stopped here. Everyone has said so much that the Japs could just go on and on fighting. In my opinion, it was the atomic bomb that brought about the end so soon, even more than Russia's entry into it. Do you think so?

All my life, I've read of different ones who wanted or tried to split an atom and I still don't know what an atom is composed of or where they are found or anything.

I've already seen posters up telling the Germans of Japan's surrender. You can hear remarks that Japan is kaput.

Bye for now darling and you won't forget—

I love you, / Henry

On August 6, 1945, the first atomic bomb used in warfare was dropped on Hiroshima. On Sunday, September 2, 1945, three years, eight months, and 22 days after the bombing of Pearl Harbor, the Allies and Japan signed the surrender agreement. World War II, the most devastating war of all time, fought by the greatest number of men gathered from five continents, had ended.

Millions had lost their lives in the mightiest struggle mankind had ever seen. Miraculously, of the 600+ men in the 291st Engineer Combat Battalion, only eight men were killed and ninety-three wounded.

Friday, August 17, 1945

Hello my darling:—

Got three more of the letters you wrote while you were down home today and of course my day is ending about right.—

And I love you one day more. Guess it won't be so many more days until we can be together. Tomorrow we are to turn in all the machine guns. Things like that make you think going home is closer anyhow. Now there are only two companies. We have three first Sergeants. B Company's first Sgt. is from Kentucky, somewhere around Harlan. We have been in the same outfits all the time, were sworn in the same day. He says he is going to re-enlist after a furlough home. Not me.

Your account of the meeting at Spout Springs was good. Seems like I was there myself. Just like I still remember them. Guess Welby Allen wasn't there. You didn't mention him. He, Charlie, Ruell and I always sang together when we were all at the same place.

You blistering your legs and then scratching them up on briars!

Kenneth's letter isn't so "newsy" but I guess he meant well. You know what I've thought of a lot? I have thought that if it were at all possible *I* personally was going to see that he gets an education. I mean high school and college. Before I die, I would like to see just *one* Giles amount to something. So far, not *one* of my generation has been worth a damn. For several years, I've had that in mind. I could have gone to high school anyhow, but *no*.

Guess this is about all for now baby, so bye, and

I love you, / Henry

Henry completed requirements for a high school diploma under the G.I. Bill in 1947.

Wednesday, August 22, 1945

Hello Sweetheart:

I'll probably be at home or pretty near anyhow when you get this. *I'm starting Sunday!*

I love you my darling and it seems very unreal to think I'm soon going to be with you. Then we'll begin the process of "catching up." Still think you will like it?

Got two letters today, written the 14th and 15th.

Don't believe there's so much to answer, except we were both very happy that the war ended so soon, and to both of us, it seemed like a dream. Hard to think that it is all over.—And it has caused me to start home sooner.

Goodnight baby and *I'll see you soon!*

All my love, / Henry

Thursday, August 30, 1945

Hello Honey:

I'm in Thionsville, France, and on my way home. We are to leave here the 3rd of September for Marseilles and fly from there. You know being so anxious to get home to you, makes every day seem like a week.

I love you darling and it seems unreal that soon we will actually begin the life we have wanted for over two years. You can go ahead with anything that will make our wedding faster when I get there.

Hope we don't take the long way home when we do start. I want to get there *quick!*

Bye now sweetheart and—

All my love, / Henry

Friday, August 31, 1945

Hello my darling:

Hope you get these letters I'm writing here by the time I get there so you will know about what time to expect me home.

We leave here (Thionsville, France) on the fourth instead of the third of September and are to come by air from Marseilles and go by way of Africa and through South America and to Florida.

I love you sweetheart and that doesn't make the days so short either. Thinking of you and what it's going to be like to be with you soon, I'm *restless!* Guess you are too.

Saw a good USO show this afternoon. Some Negroes from Chicago. Three women and three men. Good music and crazy songs and a lot of nonsense.

Saw Sgt. Keenan last night. He's on his way home too. First thing he asked me was, "How is Janice?" He left the Company the first of January and didn't come back. Was wounded afterwards.

Bye now and—

All my love, / Henry

Sgt. Ellis W. Keenan was transferred from Company A to be assistant construction supervisor of Headquarters and Supply Company.

Monday, September 3, 1945

Hello Honey:—

Tomorrow night, I leave here for Marseilles, France, and from there I don't know how long it will take to reach Florida. I love you sweetheart and believe me, these have been long days of waiting. Especially since I've known I'm on my way home.

I'm going to a movie now. Abbott and Costello in—something. Will call you as soon as I can after arriving in the U.S.

Bye now, and—

I love you, / Henry

For the first time Henry used Knifley, Kentucky, as his return address.

Tuesday, September 4, 1945

Hello Honey:

In a few hours I'll be on my way home to you. By train to Marseilles and then by plane.

This waiting really gets you down. Hope we don't waste any time after we start flying.

I love you my darling. More than I can say and soon I'll be able to actually tell you so, and if you remember, we are to do a little "showing" too. Better not say or think much more along that line as there are several miles between us yet.

Bye now, and I'll see you soon.

All my love, / Henry

Monday, September 10, 1945

My only love:—

Been thinking of you a lot today and of course, loving you so much it hurts. This delay is getting me down.

We still don't know when we get started home. Planes to the states have been discontinued and no one seems to know just when we may get a boat. Wish I could get home before this letter does, but that is very doubtful. Even if it is sent free. I gave all my air mail envelopes away before I left the Company.

This is a hell of a place. Just barren wasteland and even the Red Cross isn't any good. The chow is lousy; enough, but it isn't cooked so you can eat it. After all the propaganda I had read, I had supposed it would be fairly decent in a staging area, but *this* is a hell hole.

Sgt. Keenan left this morning by plane. We sat for nearly two hours last night waiting to see a movie (outdoors) and when it finally started, it began pouring down rain.

Guess this is all for now baby. Wow! Just think, we can soon be married and begin our lives together! *That* will really be something! *You be ready* and maybe soon I'll be there.

All my love, / Henry

Epilogue

"Do we honestly hate war?" wrote Janice in the unpublished manuscript "My Darling Daughter."

Theoretically I am certain we do. But actually, I don't know. Isn't it, I have asked, a time both nationally and individually when we come alive, join hands and purposes, strengthen our spines. . . .

Why have the men of the Second World War never stopped telling their stories? Because, whether they are aware of it or not, there is a still, small voice that keeps telling them those were the best years of their lives. . . .

I have examined my own emotions during those years. Mine and Libby's. We were afraid, certainly. We were horrified, certainly. We grieved, certainly. But we also stood on the streets and watched the men march by, rank on rank, clean, tall, stalwart men, and were stirred by our pride in them, by our great love for them, by our strong sense of glory in them. . . . We never saw a parade, nor heard a band, that we did not see Henry and Nash among those men. And we saw them with pride. Libby never went without Nash's wings pinned over her heart. I never went out without Henry's small Engineer's insignia pinned on my lapel. . . .

It may have been that during those years I was at the peak of physical health and vitality. It may have been, too, that the whole world was tinted by the fact that I was in love. But I am certain, also, that war had something to do with the fact that I was vividly, thrillingly, tinglingly alive every second of the time! Wasn't it President Roosevelt who said, "What a glorious time to live!"

Now the war was over; the soldier was on his way home. Henry Giles sailed on September 15, 1945, from Marseilles, France, aboard an old *Liberty* ship that was three weeks in reaching New York Harbor. He received his discharge from the army at Camp Atterbury, Indiana, on October 10, and arrived in Louisville at 2:00 A.M. on Thursday, October 11. Janice Holt Moore and Henry Earl Giles were married in the small living room of the 1437 Hepburn Avenue apartment at 9:00 P.M. the same day.

The wedding was performed by Rev. James M. Gilbert, Jr., in the presence of Dorothy and Lloyd Naveaux. Immediately following the ceremony, Janice telephoned her daughter in Santa Fe. The newlyweds did not go to the Spring Mill resort they had written about, but soon after the wedding traveled to the ridge to visit Henry's family and then to the West to visit Janice's.

In unpublished manuscript pages of *The G.I. Journal of Sergeant Giles*, Janice wrote:

Few men getting out of the army could have had a more difficult time of adjustment than Henry Giles. After five and a half years in the army, the last two of them overseas with a very closeknit outfit, it was hard for him to become a civilian. I have vivid memories of his discomfort with civilian clothing. It didn't fit. It was too loose. The trousers flapped around the ankles; the shirts were baggy. And I recall his lost feeling that he didn't understand civilians, the way they thought and lived, their aspirations, or even their conversations. "I have nothing in common with anybody," he used to say. "Nobody talks my language."

A country boy, he had also to live in the city, which he loathed. A bachelor for a good many years, he had to learn to be a husband. And he added a final difficulty in returning to school and having to learn to study again. Twice in the first year he was on the verge of re-enlisting in the army, feeling almost desperately that he was so conditioned to "soldiering" he would never be happy doing anything else. To this day I am not sure it was wise of me to counsel patience. Perhaps a career soldier was precisely what Henry Giles was best cut out to be. Certainly as farmers, when we finally achieved our farm, we didn't amount to much.

But fortunately we didn't have to. We discovered that both of us could write.

After their marriage, Janice continued to work for Dr. Lewis J. Sherrill at the Presbyterian Seminary. With her encouragement, Henry returned to school under the G.I. Bill during the first year of their marriage and earned his high school diploma. He also began working as a machinist for International Harvester.

The confinement during that first winter in an apartment in Louisville drove the country boy in Henry in search of land ownership and the peacefulness of a pastoral setting. In the spring of 1946, Henry and Janice found and purchased an old cabin on, as Henry described it, "a few square yards of land" near Bullitt's Lick in Shepherdsville, seventeen miles from Louisville. They spent their spare time restoring the structure for a weekend retreat in the country.

That following winter, in routine third-class mail, an announcement from Westminster Press, a Presbyterian publishing house, appeared on Janice Holt Giles's desk. The press was opening a fiction department and offering an award of $8,000 and publication for the best manuscript submitted that year. The announcement inspired Janice to respond. She began writing a novel at night, after an eight-hour work day, on a typewriter borrowed from the seminary.

The story was developed from a plot suggested by Henry and closely paralleled his own life, including the bus trip meeting of Janice Moore. Every remembered particular, Henry's army serial number included, was used in the story of Hod and Mary Pierce.

Although *The Enduring Hills* did not win the award, editor Olga Edmonds wrote that she considered it publishable if it could be rewritten adequately. Diligently, Janice Holt Giles worked on the revision and resubmitted the manuscript to Westminster Press in 1949. *The Enduring Hills* was accepted for publication and appeared in April 1950. Four years from its beginning, the book was selected by Doubleday for their Dollar Book Club and had a sale of over 140,000 in its first printing. By the time it was published, much work had been done on a second manuscript, *Miss Willie*.

On the strength of the contract for *The Enduring Hills*, and with *Miss Willie* almost completed, Henry and Janice bought a house and forty-acre farm for $1,100 in Knifley, Kentucky, and moved there on May 30, 1949. Her book *40 Acres and No Mule*, published in 1952, vividly describes that adventure. The only farming they did on this hilly tract of land consisted of raising a garden and a small tobacco crop.

In 1953, the Gileses purchased a 106-acre farm just up the ridge from the forty-acre place. The "big farm" allowed Henry the opportunity to realize his dreams of becoming a full-time farmer and being his "own boss." He planted forty acres of corn, tended beef cows and calves, pigs and chickens, and learned to milk a few dairy cows. Hard work, droughts, and freezing temperatures persuaded him that three years of farming were enough. The Gileses moved to an apartment in Campbellsville, where Henry began working as a printer, linotype operator, and pressman for the *Campbellsville News-Journal.* Janice continued to write.

The first stories and novels written by her found their beginnings in the early childhood and young adulthood happenings of Henry Giles. His name appears as author on the first edition of *Harbin's Ridge*, published in 1951. The preface to the second edition reveals the true authorship:

> It was not intended as a hoax when *Harbin's Ridge* was originally published in Henry Giles' name alone. The book was actually written largely by me, Janice Holt Giles. But my husband had helped me so much with *The Enduring Hills* and would not allow me to use his name on that book, so I was determined when *Harbin's Ridge* was written he should have the credit; for as with *The Enduring Hills* he had furnished me with the idea. We are sorry to have deceived the public, but both my agent and publisher recognized my style of writing and knew the truth. So I don't feel too badly about it!

In a letter dated November 28, 1951, to literary agent Oliver G. Swan, Janice wrote, "I don't know how unethical I was in writing *Harbin's Ridge* and submitting it under [Henry's] name. I didn't think of it as being unethical at all. It may seem very odd to you, but I felt as if I were Henry writing it. It came out of a man, rather than out of myself."

In 1957, Janice and Henry purchased several old log houses for the timbers to use in constructing their own large home on the seventy-six acres they owned in Spout Springs Hollow. That experience became *A Little Better than Plumb*. They moved into the log house in August 1958, only to have to relocate the house later up the creek and across the field because of a flood control dam being built on the Upper Green River.

In the thirty-four years of their marriage, Henry and Janice Holt Giles farmed and wrote books, short stories, and newspaper columns. Janice wrote a book review and personal experience column for the *Campbellsville News-Journal*, first entitled "The Bookshelf" and later called "Around Our House." The column, which began in 1954, continued for several years and became her own source material for the book *Around Our House*, published in 1971.

Following the experience of newspaper work in Campbellsville and during construction of the log house in 1957, Henry became a feature writer for the *Adair County News*. He wrote "Spout Springs Splashes," an informative and humorous column revealing his intense enjoyment of life on the ridge. Much of the Gileses' daily life was shared through the small-town weekly newspaper until he retired the column in 1970. Henry's stories were quite diverse, as illustrated by such titles as "Writer's gardening hasn't turned out so well," "Squirrel season should be good this year—if there are any squirrels," and "Master of Spout Springs wishes to be a poet." The writing of the column produced limited earnings but immense enjoyment for Henry and his readers. Viewing the writing as a labor of love, the feature articles also allowed him his own creative outlet.

Although Henry had stated in a letter, "I could never see a wife of mine working," Janice's writings provided the major source of their income. With the success of her writing came the necessity for Henry to remain home from the newspaper office to protect critically needed privacy for her work. "With a writer an interruption causes hiatus in the rhythm of work, in broken concentration, which cannot be picked up or quickly abridged," Janice wrote, then added, "People began to find the road to us." With a steady stream of cars now turning into the narrow gravelled lane to Spout Springs, Henry saw his job as one designed to "head'em off at the pass," at Janice's request.

Four books show joint authorship of Henry and Janice Holt Giles: the second edition of *Harbin's Ridge, A Little Better Than Plumb, The G.I. Journal of Sergeant Giles* and *Around Our House*. In *Around Our House* Janice wrote of Henry: "I take for granted his love, for in a good marriage love is something so basic and unseparable that it is hardly necessary to speak of it. It speaks for itself and like food and sleep and breath, it is always there. But it is a happy boon that my husband should have so grand a sense of humor. That his everyday speech should be so pungent with it and his wit that it is a constant delight to me, that we should often laugh together. It makes him a very special companion."

In an unpublished manuscript, "Rode Hard and Put Up Wet: Autobiography of an Appalachian," written by Henry in 1966, he expressed his appreciation for Janice:

It wasn't easy at first—for a long time at first—for Janice to leave the city and try to make a go of it down here in Adair County with an Appalachian husband. And I know now that she went through a lot more in adjusting to me and the country life than she ever told me. Once when she was ailing— physically—a doctor told her that what she needed to do was get the hell out of the country. Go back to the city life where people are decent and civilized, the doctor recommended. We tried it, and Janice was the first to decide that that was exactly what she *shouldn't* have done. But why does one go to a doctor?

On other occasions we have tried to live elsewhere. Because Libby and Nash lived in Santa Fe, it seemed that we should be able to make a go of [it] there. Living there near Libby and Nash and three fine young grandsons to watch over and be with should be the life for us, we said. So, we went to Santa Fe, and even rented an apartment near the kids. I believe that was our first trip away to stay *indefinitely*. We lasted for about six weeks, then headed back to Kentucky.

We moved from Columbia back to the woods—Spout Springs—in 1956. Twice since then we have been to Fort Smith, Arkansas to live indefinitely; maybe the rest of our lives, we told people. We could live with Janice's mother for as long as we wanted to do so.

The first indefinite stay lasted three months; we came back with the springtime. And the second time we went to Fort Smith to live, that was it. We would probably live there forever, we said. And we had a good friend, Joe Spires, and his family move into our house. We're gone for good, this time.

That time we did stay gone for nearly six months—while Janice was writing a novel with an Oklahoma setting that was near Fort Smith. Then she finished her work, and a night or two later it came. (Although I was always ready at any time to return, I usually waited for Janice to make the decision to go home.) We talked and talked that night, then all at once Janice got to the point. Write Joe a card and tell him they will have to move. I've got to go home.

That's the way it was for a while. Indefinitely between us

doesn't mean much. And today Janice is as much an Appalachian as I am.

A historical marker stands monument at the beginning of the lane leading to Spout Springs Hollow. Among other attributes, the marker records that the books written by Janice Holt Giles "reflect her adopted home, the Green River area where she lived with her husband Henry."

Henry Giles could not have known that his fateful meeting with Janice Holt Moore, their eventual marriage, and the life they shared together would endear him to the hearts of many people who read the books his encouragement inspired her to write.

The courtship, romance, and literary legacy that began on a bus ended on Friday, June 1, 1979, when Janice Holt Giles died at dawn of congestive heart failure in nearby Campbellsville at the Taylor County Hospital. At her death, flags were lowered to half mast in Adair County and remained there until her burial on June 4. Henry Giles's death came early in the morning on the first day of October 1986 at the Westlake Cumberland Hospital, Columbia. The last battle of his seventy years was fought with leukemia.

In his letters, Henry repeatedly wrote, "When I'm back Honey, I don't want you to *ever* leave my side." She has not. They are buried side by side at the Caldwell Chapel Separate Baptist Church cemetery in Knifley, Kentucky.

Janice Holt Giles: March 28, 1905–June 1, 1979

Henry Earl Giles: June 23, 1916–October 1, 1986

Letters by Date

1943

July **19, 21**

August **1, 7, 15, 22, 30**

September **1, 6, 9, 10, 19, 19, 19, 20, 21, 22, 23, 26, 27, 28**

October **1, 5, 6, 20,** 22, **23, 23,** 24, 25, **26, 29,** 30, 31

November 1, 2, 4, **7, 8, 11,** 13, **14,** 15, **17,** 19, 21, 22, **23,** 24, **25,** 26, 27, **28,** 29, 30

December **1, 2,** 3, **4,** 5, **6, 7,** 9, 10, 11, 12, 13, 14, 15, **16,** 17, **18,** 19, 20, **21,** 22, 23, **25,** 26, 27, **28, 29, 30.**

1944

January 2, 4, **5, 5,** 6, 7, 8, 9, **10, 11,** 12, 13, 14, **15, 16,** 17, 18, 19, 19, **21,** 22, 23, 24, 25, **26,** 27, 28, 29, **30, 31**

February 1, 2, 4, 5, 6, **7,** 8, 9, 10, **11,** 12, 13, 14, **15,** 16, **17,** 18, **19,** 20, **21,** 22, 23, 24, 25, **26, 27,** 28, 29

March **2,** 3, **4,** 5, 6, **7,** 8, 9, 10, **10,** [no date], 11, **12,** 13, **14, 15,** 16, **17,** 18, 19, 20, 23, 24, 25, 26, 27, 28, 29, 30, 31

April 1, **2, 3, 4,** 5, **6,** 7, 8, **9,** 10, **11, 12, 14, 15,** 15, **16,** 17, 18, 19, **20, 21, 22,** 23, **24, 25, 26,** 27, 28, 29, 30

May 1, 3, 4, 4, **5,** 6, 7, **7, 8,** 9, 10, **11, 12,** 13, **14,** 15, 16, **17,** 18, 19, 20, 21, **22,** 23, 24, **25,** 26, 27, **28,** 29, 30, 31

June 1, 2, 2, 3, 4, 5, **6, 7, 8,** 9, **10,** 11, 11, 12, 13, **15, 16,** 20, **25,** 26, 27, 29, **30**

Boldface numbers indicate letters included in this book.

July **1**, **3**, **4**, 5, 6, 7, 9, **10**, **11**, **12**, 13, **16**, **17**, 19, 20, **22**, **24**, 25, 26, **27**, 28, **31**

August 1, **2**, **3**, 4, **5**, **7**, 8, 9, 9, 10, 12, **13**, **15**, **18**, **19**, **21**, **22**, 23, **24**, **26**, 28, 29, 30

September 1, 2, 3, 4, **6**, 7, 8, **9**, 10, 11, 12, **13**, **15**, 16, **16**, **18**, 18, 20, **21**, **22**, **23**, **24**, 24, 25, 26, 26, 27, 28, 28, 30

October 1, **3**, 4, **5**, **6**, 7, 8, 9, 10, 11, 11, 12, 13, 14, **15**, 15, **20**, **22**, **23**, **24**, 25, **27**, 28, 29

November **1**, 2, 3, **4**, **5**, 6, **7**, 8, **9**, 10, **11**, 12, 16, 17, **18**, **19**, **20**, 20, 21, 21, 22, **23**, 24, 25, 25, **27**, 28, 29, **30**

December 1, **3**, **4**, 5, 6, **7**, **8**, **9**, 10, 11, 12, 13, **14**, 15, 17, 19, 20, 25, **26**, 27, 28, **29**, **29**, 30, **31**, **31**.

1945

January 1, **2**, 3, 4, 4, **5**, 6, 6, 7, 7, **8**, 8, 9, 9, 11, **12**, 13, 14, 15, **16**, 19, **20**, 21, 22, 23, 24, 25, 26, 27, 28, 29, **31**

February **1**, 2, **4**, **5**, 7, **9**, 10, 11, **12**, 12, **13**, 14, 15, 16, **17**, 17, **18**, 19, 20, 20, 21, 22, 23, 24, 25, **25**, 26, 27

March **1**, **2**, **2**, **3**, **5**, **6**, **7**, 8, 9, 10, **12**, **12**, 13, **14**, 14, 15, 15, 18, **19**, **19**, **20**, 21, **21**, 21, 22, 23, 24, 26, **27**, **29**, **30**, 31

April **1**, 2, 3, 5, **6**, **7**, **8**, 8, **9**, 10, **11**, **12**, 13, **15**, 15, 17, **18**, **20**, 21, 22, 23, 24, 25, 26, **27**, **28**, 29, 30

May 1, **2**, 3, **4**, **6**, **7**, **8**, **8**, **11**, **12**, 14, **15**, 16, 16, **16**, 17, 18, 19, **20**, 21, 22, **23**, 23, 25, 26, 27, 29, **30**, 31

June **1**, 2, 3, **5**, 6, 7, 8, 9, **11**, **12**, 13, 14, 15, 16, 18, 20, **23**, 24, 25, 26, 27, 28, 29, 30

July **1**, **2**, 3, 4, **5**, 7, 8, **9**, 10, 11, **12**, 14, 15, **16**, 17, 18, 19, 20, 21, 22, 25, 26, **27**, 29, **30**, 31

August 1, 3, 5, 6, 7, 7, 8, 9, 11, 12, **12**, 13, **14**, **15**, **16**, **17**, 21, **22**, 28, **30**, **31**

September 1, **3**, **4**, **10**

Index

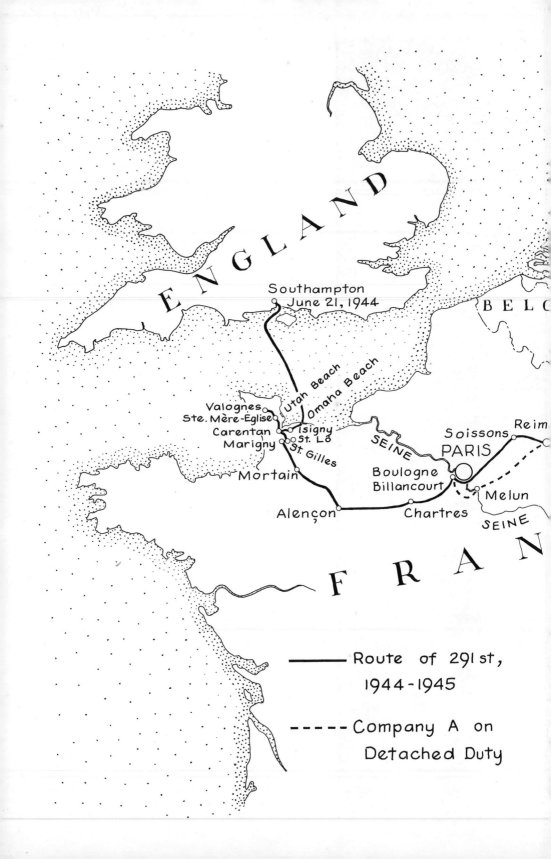

ENGLAND

Southampton
June 21, 1944

BELG

Utah Beach
Omaha Beach

Valognes
Ste. Mère-Eglise
Carentan
Marigny

Isigny
St. Lô
St. Gilles

SEINE

Soissons
Reim

PARIS

Mortain

Boulogne
Billancourt

Alençon

Chartres

Melun

SEINE

FRAN

——— Route of 291st,
1944-1945

----- Company A on
Detached Duty